Praise for
Leading Across New Borders: How to Succeed as the Center Shifts

"Understanding context and building self-awareness are two of the cornerstones of successful leadership in our inter-connected world, where executives increasingly have to work outside their home cultures. *Leading Across New Borders* provides compelling anecdotes, frameworks, and practical tools for better understanding context and building self-awareness for the global leaders of tomorrow."
—Rajiv Ball, Partner, THNK School of
Creative Leadership

"Leapfrogging technology, innovation, and boundary blurring are dramatically changing leadership. Workers must collaborate and compete across continents to be relevant. *Leading Across New Borders* positions you to succeed in a world where the former infrastructure requirements dissolve and in their place is a mandate to leverage multiple centers of influence from deep inside individuals with varied experiences."
—Erin S. Gore, Executive Vice President, Wells Fargo

"This book helps you to reflect on situations you face every day. Not just concepts but practical insights!"
—Shrimathi Shivashankar, Associate Vice President,
Diversity and Sustainability, HCL Technologies

"This reading gave me a renewed appreciation for the impact of global forces shifting between fast- and slow-growing economies on leadership values. It is a great reminder of how nuanced global leaders must be to succeed, leveraging cross-cultural astuteness and critical thinking at the same time. Out with binary thinking and on with ever-evolving algorithms!"
—Caroline Visconti, Vice President-Talent
Development, L'Oreal

"*Leading Across New Borders* goes well beyond identifying global leadership competencies to help practitioners and scholars understand what global leaders actually do. The fascinating stories about global leaders in action, drawn from the authors' extensive consulting work, are complemented with useful research findings. This is a must-read book for global leaders, full of insights and practical tips."
—Joyce Osland, Ph.D., Lucas Endowed Professor of Global
Leadership, Executive Director, Global Leadership
Advancement Center, School of Global
Innovation & Leadership, Lucas College
and Graduate School of Business, San Jose State
University, and co-author,
Advances in Global Leadership

"If you are weary of endless empty references to the global village and wish someone would provide useful, practical insights, you will find that this powerful guide to our future fills that gap. Based on a thorough analysis of world commerce and culture, the seasoned authors and consultants provide us with a fresh view on leadership in times of global transition. They bring an incisive focus to the specific tasks that capable leaders must master to thrive among the rapidly emerging economies and to lead their organizations to cross-border success."

—Janet Bennet, Executive Director,
Intercultural Communication Institute,
and author, *Intercultural Competence:*
Vital Perspectives for Diversity and Inclusion

"This book presents a fascinating and invaluable integration of rapidly changing global business trends and the evolving leadership competencies needed to make sense of them. *Leading Across New Borders* provides a culturally competent look at new world effectiveness."

—Ray Leki, Adjunct Professor, American University,
School of International Service; former U.S. Peace
Corps Acting Country Director, Pakistan; author,
Travel Wise: How to Be Safe, Savvy and
Secure Abroad

"This book articulates what the shifting global economy means for each of us and how we can respond, whether you're part of the private sector or non-profit. I would encourage this to be required reading for those operating in any global environment."

—Susan Ridge, Vice President,
Marketing and Communications,
Save the Children USA

"*Leading Across Borders* articulates the critical vectors of the 'new normal' in leading and operating globally. Excellent input for awareness and action beyond conventional thinking."

—Eva Boesze, Head of Global Human Resources,
KraussMaffei Group

LEADING ACROSS NEW BORDERS

How to Succeed as the Center Shifts

ERNEST GUNDLING
CHRISTIE CALDWELL
KAREN CVITKOVICH

WILEY

Dedication from Ernest Gundling
With love to my wonderful wife Kacey
for her encouragement and inspiration,
and to my warmhearted and good-humored family,
especially Anne, Chris, Katherine,
Theo, Gabe, and Emma!

Dedication from Karen Cvitkovich
To my children, Matt and Sorine—I am thrilled
that you share my love of global
adventure!—and to David and the
rest of my family, who support me in
so many ways. You help me to cross
borders every day.

Dedication from Christie Caldwell
To Johnny Xiong, whose conversations,
stories, insights, humor, and perspective
inspired this author and many aspects of this book.

CONTENTS

The Shifting Center: Emerging Markets Have Emerged

What Is Changing and Why This Matters

THE FUTURE ARRIVES

The world's economic center is shifting with breathtaking rapidity. The trends are clear, both in the numbers and in the new realities on the ground; the general direction is from west to east and from north to south. This shift in power and influence is not only economic but also demographic, political, and cultural.

China and India

China recently passed the United States to become the world's largest economy defined in terms of gross domestic product (GDP) purchasing power parity. Although this news created only a small blip in the Western business press, it represented a historic milestone that is likely to be followed soon by other landmark events. Calculations based on market exchange rates—a more common yardstick of

GDP—indicate that China will surpass the United States to become the world's undisputed economic leader by 2030.

India is also expanding rapidly; current estimates indicate that by 2050, China, the United States, and India will be the top three economies in the world.[1] While China and India still have many rural and comparatively unaltered areas within their borders, their growing industrial and technological prowess as well as their higher ranking among the world's economies signify that they have officially graduated from "emerging" to "emerged."

Europe's relative economic position is changing simultaneously. Membership in the Group of Seven (G7), an economic forum originally founded in the 1970s by the world's most industrialized countries, provides a symbolic example. Original G7 members from Europe included France, West Germany, Italy, and the United Kingdom. If the same organization were to be recreated in 2050, it would probably include no European member nations. According to current projections, *there will not be a single European country whose economy is among the world's top seven* by that time.[2] In order to offer Europe G7 entry, it would be necessary to combine two or three countries, or perhaps all of Europe.

Humanity has witnessed these kinds of changes before. China and India previously dominated the global economy for centuries. China, for example, created revolutionary innovations such as gunpowder and printing that were later exported to Europe while supplying the Silk Road and far-reaching maritime trade routes with precious goods. Each country has approximately four times the population of the United States and more than double the number of people in Europe as a whole. Nonetheless, the ongoing recasting of global positions represents a tectonic shift in the modern economic order and is in part a transition back to the future (see Sidebar 1.1).

Personal Consequences

The world's shifting economic center has vast implications for almost everyone, particularly those who have been at the top and at the bottom of the global economic order. During the past century, U.S. and European leadership and business models largely dominated multinational corporate cultures. The economic shift toward markets such as China and India means that these countries and *their leaders* will increasingly shape the way business is conducted.

New leaders from Asia and elsewhere will need to consider their own core values and vision for the future and how they can inspire their global colleagues. Beyond material success, what will make their careers fulfilling and worthwhile? If current or aspiring leaders from Europe and North America go on with business as usual—assuming

SIDEBAR 1.1 THE SHIFTING WORLD CENTER: CHINA AND INDIA

The Shifting World Center: China	The Shifting World Center: India
• China's current population of 1.4 billion exceeds the entire U.S. population of approximately 320 million by well over 1 billion, and comprises almost 20 percent of the people on earth.	• India's population will eventually exceed China's due to its higher birth rate, reaching an estimated total of 1.6 billion within 30 years.[10]
• There are over 160 cities in China with a population over 1 million people. In the United States, there are just nine cities that exceed 1 million.[3]	• If the Indian state of Uttar Pradesh were to declare independence, it would be the fifth most populous country in the world, with over 200 million people.[11]
• China's steel industry production is now more than 8 times larger than that of the United States; the production of its state-owned mills equals the combined production of the rest of the world.[4]	• India will soon have one-fifth of the world's working-age population and the number of people in the country who are working age will rise by more than 200 million over the next 20 years while China's working-age population declines.[12]
• China reportedly used more cement in a recent three-year period than the United States used during the entire twentieth century.[5]	• India, which is still more rural than China, is now in the midst of what is likely to be the largest rural-urban migration of the twenty-first century, with some 10 million people moving to towns and cities each year.[13]
• The volume of trade between China and Africa has increased by more than 20 times since the year 2000[6]; more than 1 million Chinese are currently living and working in Africa.[7]	• India is already the fourth-largest consumer and net importer of crude oil and petroleum products in the world after the United States, China, and Japan.[14]
• China consumed 155 million cases of red wine last year, more than France's 150 million and Italy's 141 million.[8]	• India's GDP, too, is projected to overtake that of the United States and become the world's second largest economy by 2050 in terms of purchasing power parity, though not using GDP at market exchange rates.[15]
• China is by far the world's largest producer and consumer of coal, accounting for 46 percent of global coal production and 49 percent of global coal consumption—almost as much as the rest of the world combined.[9]	

that their privileged position will last forever—they risk looking like human ostriches, heads buried in the sand to avoid the speeding freight train of globalization. Rather, they must embrace the planet's inexorable tilt toward rising economies and learn how to succeed together with employees from around the world who want to be treated as full partners. Sometimes the consequences are very personal, and one's career can take an unexpected turn.

Promotion Postponed

Ingrid speaks in quick spurts over the phone from her office in London, where she has just returned after three years in India. She is Swedish, but started her career with a company in New York and then moved to London, so her accent is hard to place. Ingrid is in her mid-30s, works for one of the world's most famous banks, and saw the opportunity to move to Bangalore and gain international experience as critical for her career.

Ingrid comments, "I had just completed my first year in Bangalore and had a perfect performance rating. I was on the list to get VP, but then, three days before the promotion lists were finalized, I was pulled off the list and no one could tell me why.

"This really impacted my engagement. There were so many times when I just wanted to leave, especially during my third year in Bangalore. To be honest, I called my contacts in London and said that they needed to find me a position back in the U.K. or I was going to look at other opportunities.

"I realize now that there were a lot of things going on under the surface that no one talked about. The plan when we originally went into India was to outsource business processes to cut costs, and it was cheaper initially. Then we started to move India from an outsourcing center into a more strategic role, with business and revenue driven out of the Bangalore office. It is now its own entity, and the bank just celebrated 10 years in India. The goal of this more strategic positioning was to gain better access to India's talent pool. While the initial objective was to employ cheap talent, people are actually paid very well now—even by the bank's London standards.

"Part of the reason I was passed up for promotion was about wanting to build a local leadership model in India, as a retention strategy and as part of a broader global strategy generally. Because my contract in India was three years, the company had at least another year to convince me to stay. I think that they took the risk to give my promotion to someone in India because they were getting a lot of pushback regarding all the expats in Bangalore. Local nationals were saying, 'Why do we need all these expats coming in to oversee everything?' It was better to sacrifice my promotion to address this and then try to reengage and offer me a promotion during the last year of my contract.

"But now I have a bit of a different view of all the expats in Bangalore. These people go back with a broader perspective, so their time in India might also educate them about the country. They can bring that new perspective with them wherever they go next in the world. Having returned here to London, I am asking why people are not involving their Indian team members more. I work to give these newer members of the team a voice because I know how capable they are. The further west you move, from London to New York, it seems the less understanding there is about how serious we are about the Asia-Pacific region."

Ingrid's experience is likely to become increasingly common as companies seek to expand their leadership talent pool. Her career prospects are still bright, even though her promotion was delayed by a year or two. She is now distinguishing herself through a different kind of role. Based on her knowledge of both India and London, as well as her strong personal network, she is able to draw out the full strengths of her team members to accomplish joint projects, a skill that is very important to her employer. People who join a global organization today and aspire to a leadership position should consider how they can best contribute as the center shifts (see Sidebar 1.2).

SIDEBAR 1.2   WHAT ABOUT ME?

Many individuals are concerned about the impact of cross-border commerce and migration on their careers and personal lives. Regardless of where they are currently living, they face many common—and sometimes deeply personal—challenges, asking themselves questions like:

- What can I do to advance my own career prospects and to make a more secure and prosperous life for myself and my family?
- Will I be able to compete with other employees or people in rival firms who may have more education or better skills, or who are hungry enough to work even longer hours than I do already?
- Does my employer appear to favor some individuals based on their personal background or nationality, and how can I best respond to this?
- Will I be able to understand and to work well with colleagues who were raised in a different culture, speak other languages, and perhaps belong to a different religion?
- How can I comprehend the needs of faraway customers and create products they will buy?
- How can I afford to educate my children well and prepare them for an increasingly competitive world?
- What will happen to my personal life if communication across time zones requires additional hours from my early mornings and late evenings or if I have to travel more and work harder? Can I still be present with my children while they are young, take care of aging parents, and keep my marriage intact?

The best approach to most of these questions is to clearly grasp the changes that are on the way and to cultivate the skills that you and your family will need to survive and prosper. The purpose of this book is to help people from any country succeed in this changing environment.

More Countries on the Way

Change is occurring in other places that could affect the careers of Ingrid and her colleagues. Although China and India are the biggest players in the shifting global economy, a number of locations in Asia, the Middle East, South America, and Africa continue to grow rapidly. Countries like Turkey, Malaysia, and Poland are already or soon will be among the ranks of the emerged nations.

Trend lines seldom remain constant over time, and unpredictable events occur: natural disasters, civil unrest, war, disease, economic crises. The BRIC (Brazil, Russia, India, China) countries were once touted as the growth economies of the future, but Brazil and Russia have both since experienced economic turmoil and stagnation. Even China's once torrid double-digit growth has slowed to single digits and what its government is calling the "new normal," although this is still double or triple the growth rates in the United States and Europe. And, as many companies that invested in Russia have discovered, geopolitics can scuttle once-promising trends. Investing in Russia seemed like a fine idea based on its size and market potential when the BRIC acronym was coined, but the country has turned out to be a far riskier place for investors than many predicted.[16] Corrupt governments, poor infrastructure, and limited educational opportunities also hold back development in many locations.

Such caveats notwithstanding, the general trajectory from west to east and north to south has been in place for decades. Projected global population growth of at least two billion more people, almost all outside of the developed world, suggests that this trend will continue. One calculation places the global economy's center of gravity in 2050 between India and China, or more than 5,000 miles east of where it was in 1980.[17] Carlos Ghosn, renowned CEO of automaker Renault-Nissan, remarks, "Growth is going to come from new markets—we all know China, India, the Middle East, South America —but also from the countries of the future, which are going to be the next wave coming."[18] In particular, projections based on population and/or natural resources often point to countries such as Mexico, Indonesia, Nigeria, Turkey, Vietnam, Iran, Egypt, Colombia, and the Philippines. Acronym lovers undeterred by the mixed performance of the BRIC nations now refer to the first four of these as the MINT countries.[19] Their continued growth will require further investments in infrastructure along with ongoing social and political reform, and some will be more successful at harnessing their potential than others.

While the future will undoubtedly bring surprises as well as further developments based on existing trends, Ingrid and others are beginning to experience a new world with many centers and a fracturing of previous lines of power, investment, technology transfer, and political authority. Dozens of regional economic hubs are bursting with activity and rapid development. The largest cities on the planet now include Beijing, Mumbai, Lagos, Chongqing, Jakarta, São Paulo, Karachi, and Mexico City, with more on the way. Two-thirds of global economic growth is being driven by cities in the developing world; there will be approximately 370 new cities of over half a million people by 2030.[20] Asian consumers are also increasingly shaping demand, and within 15 years will account for a significant majority of both the global middle class population and of worldwide consumption.[21]

Cutting-edge technological advances are as likely to be visible in newly emerged locations as in renowned centers of innovation. Infrastructure in many Chinese cities, for example, is often more advanced than in Silicon Valley—skyscrapers, bullet trains, subways, and cell phone connections are all more modern and efficient. It has become common in many locations, including parts of Africa, to leapfrog whole generations of technology, for example, by skipping the installation of landlines for telephones and the build-out of a

---

SIDEBAR 1.3   MAJOR INDUSTRIES: LEADING GLOBAL ENTERPRISES

- *Steel:* ArcelorMittal (India), BaoSteel (China)
- *Mining:* Vale S.A. (Brazil)
- *Shipbuilding:* Hyundai (South Korea)
- *Oil Production:* Saudi Aramco (Saudi Arabia)
- *Automobiles:* Toyota (Japan), Hyundai (South Korea)
- *Personal Computers:* Lenovo (China)
- *Cell Phones:* Samsung (South Korea)
- *Food Processing:* JBS S.A. (Brazil)

---

nationwide retail banking infrastructure, and instead moving straight to e-commerce via cell phone. Top talent, too, can come from previously untapped sources, as Ingrid's bank is learning. Workers in an ever greater number of professions must both collaborate and compete with colleagues from other continents.

Under New Ownership

Western firms have been scrambling to augment their presence in global markets, where they are anticipating further growth. They encounter rival enterprises that were once primarily local, but which have now expanded beyond their home markets to compete with fellow multinationals worldwide. Huawei competes fiercely with Cisco, Lenovo with Hewlett-Packard, Hyundai with Ford, Emirates with British Airways, SABIC (Saudi Arabian Basic Industries) with Germany's chemical giant BASF, and Tata Consultancy Services with Accenture.

This trend is gathering momentum: McKinsey estimates that whereas 95 percent of the Fortune Global 500 was headquartered in the developed world in the year 2000, by 2025 almost *half* of the world's companies with a billion dollars or more in revenue will be headquartered in other markets.[22] Due to rapid growth, along with mergers and acquisitions, leading global enterprises in economic sectors once integral to Western technological prowess now have owners based in Asia, the Middle East, and South America (see Sidebar 1.3).

IMPLICATIONS FOR LEADERSHIP

The global economy's ongoing transformation is a mixed blessing, bringing thrilling opportunities for some and headaches or deferred dreams for others, regardless of their location. The upshot for almost everyone is likely to be a career with more contacts and competition from all over the world—as well as a vast number of new leaders from emerged countries.

Fast-Growth versus Slow-Growth

Instead of the outdated contrast between developed versus emerging economies, it is now more relevant to compare markets growing at different rates. Leaders and organizations that aren't aware of rapidly shifting customer tastes and preferences in fast-growth markets such as India will be left behind as other firms grow more quickly. On the other hand, those who fail to make careful strategic choices in slow-growth markets such as Italy or France are likely to wither in the face of high costs and fierce competition. Global organizations must make decisions and develop strategies for different regions, and encourage meaningful participation by people from those locations who possess the deepest market knowledge. Some common differences between the two types of markets are listed in Table 1.1.

Successfully navigating today's global business environment requires that companies straddle the inherently competing demands of both fast- and slow-growth markets. Here is an example of the cross-border business challenges this global contrast can produce.

TABLE 1.1 Fast-Growth versus Slow-Growth Markets

	Fast-Growth Markets	Slow-Growth Markets
Society	Younger population, internal migration to cities, widespread corruption, variety of evolving administrative forms	Aging population, immigration pressures, democratic governance, rule of law
Economy	Dynamic marketplace with many opportunities, fast-moving competition, newer brands and companies starting to globalize, government intervention a wild card, unforeseen risks	Efficiency and cost-cutting, targeted investments, process and quality focus, established multinationals and paths for entrepreneurs
Career	Rapid promotions and compensation increases, on-the-job learning, expatriation for learning and development, ample domestic opportunities, company challenges for retention and development	Specialized professional education, careers developed over decades, expatriation for opportunities abroad, company challenges with expensive workforce and need to shift costs elsewhere

Air Filters for Shanghai

Alan, an expatriate based in China, comments, "Global headquarters just keeps slowing us down here; they don't understand how China works. We need more flexibility on the ground and more decision-making power. For instance, at the end of Q3, we had an overstock of aging air purifiers in the warehouse just outside Shanghai that we needed to move quickly. My local team came up with the solution to initiate a promotion to sell them."

Alan suddenly becomes animated by frustration and begins to raise his voice and speak more slowly for emphasis. "It takes three weeks just to get the discount application for this promotion signed by the global team. Then, halfway through this approval process, the entire southeast region of China got hit with extremely serious air pollution—and suddenly everyone needed air purifiers. Within the span of one week, we sold all of our inventory and the warehouses were completely out of stock.

"This is what I mean by needing more flexibility. When we tried to reverse the discount application and replenish the stock of air purifiers, we got a message back from the global supply team asking for a three-month lead time in order to fit into the global supply planning process!

"How am I supposed to do business here in this market with processes that take three months? I am competing against local companies who don't have to wait, and who wouldn't dream of implementing such a rigid process. They would just call up their suppliers over the weekend and work night and day with them to make 20,000 new filters in two weeks. The market here is constantly changing; we can't survive if we aren't flexible. But the global team just does not understand this, and they always push back that we are not following procedure or providing enough lead time. They don't realize that these procedures make my life impossible here."

Alan's struggles illustrate that a one-size-fits-all process or mindset could be fatal for organizations seeking to succeed globally. Individuals and corporations that have grown up in one kind of environment or another must now adapt to multiple worlds, thinking and acting with both slow-growth and fast-growth parts of their brains.

Global Agility

The shifting global economy has several other implications for people in almost any country. Many companies are expecting more than half of their growth to occur outside of their familiar strongholds in the coming years, which underlines the constant requirement to be agile. Present or future leaders will likely need to traverse new borders in several ways: crossing unfamiliar geographical boundaries, adapting to a changing home environment, and challenging artificial boundaries imposed by outdated mental models.

- **Crossing unfamiliar boundaries.** Many people will be asked to go to places they have never visited or perhaps never even heard about previously. Europeans can expect to do business in China, Chinese in India, Indians in Africa, and Africans in Europe. And beyond the usual capital locations, leaders may find themselves drawn to expanding second-tier cities such as Surabaya in Indonesia's province of East Java, Chongqing in southwestern China, or Belo Horizante in Minas Gerais, the Brazilian state north of São Paulo.

- **Adapting to a globalized home.** Once-familiar places are also changing rapidly. Urbanization, migration from abroad or within the same country, economic growth, and other forces are all altering what is "known"—whether that is in Los Angeles, London, Beijing, or Kolkata. Old physical boundaries that once provided clearer demarcations between different national cultures have grown more porous and flexible. Meanwhile, new kinds of borders—socioeconomic, religious, ethnic, linguistic—have arisen in places we thought we knew. As China's economy has grown and previous restrictions on individual movement have been relaxed, Tier 1 such as Beijing and Shanghai each have attracted millions of poor migrant workers from other parts of the country; these internal immigrants speak different dialects and have set up their own community networks for mutual support. Europe's Islamic population is already 6 percent and increasing quickly relative to other groups; there are 9 million immigrants or children of immigrants from Turkey alone. Demographers also predict that white citizens of the United States will no longer be the majority by 2050, while the country's Hispanic population will comprise almost 30 percent of the total.[23]

  This massive flow of people across former boundaries within and between countries has numerous practical consequences. For example, immigration has markedly impacted the domestic health care industry in the United States, which some might think would be slow to transform:

  - Some 27 percent of U.S. physicians are foreign-born.
  - Up to 15 percent of U.S. nurses are foreign-born.
  - Between one-fifth and one-quarter of U.S. direct care workers (nursing aides and home health aides) are foreign-born.[24]

- **Challenging mental models.** Experienced leaders may still be relying on mental models that no longer reflect reality, and which create artificial boundaries among past, present, and future. If one's mental map of the world still highlighted the biggest cities of 100 years ago, it would be seriously flawed today. Countries and their markets change, which alters our map of the world's economy. For instance, Japan's star has fallen rapidly as its once-booming economy has stalled and other countries have grown.

South Korea followed Japan's ascent, becoming one of the next wave of Asian tigers; however, the achievements of this relatively small country now seem to pale next to those of its Chinese neighbors. And while the Chinese economy is still growing at breakneck speed by current Western standards, it is starting to cool off as its population ages, with some industries experiencing more severe slowdowns or boom and bust cycles. Regional disparities in the level of development and economic growth between China's east coast and interior make the real picture quite complex.

We must also reexamine models for how to lead and to best cultivate new leaders as global markets shift. In addition to boundaries between or even within nations, there are new borders to be crossed at the edge of every outmoded concept, and these may be as important as lines on a map that are enforced with guard posts and customs officials. Global talent may object to *outsourcing*; global mindset means more than *culture* there are global teams that cannot be rescued by *facilitation*; there is more to *diversity* than race and gender acquisitions can fail in spite of proper *diligence*; successful innovations require more than great *products*; and global ethics means going beyond the immediate interests of shareholders to create a broader definition of *integrity*.

Global leaders need to approach familiar tasks in novel ways and lead across geographical, cultural, and mental borders. Current leadership development methods might not be adequate to address the fast-growth/slow-growth dichotomy or to meet the urgent need for a vastly larger talent pool of people who can take an agile approach to global business opportunities.

The Failed Assignment

Huang Shiguang leans back and takes a drag of his cigarette, shifting his gaze to look out through the sliding glass doors of the office building café. He uses this moment to gauge how he should respond to the question about his assignment to Germany, from which he has just returned. By all accounts, the assignment was not a success. His former boss and close ally, an American with over 20 years of experience in China, described in detail how painful it was. "They basically threw him into Germany in the midst of an integration process between two companies and he foundered. You need someone who is very aggressive, vocal, and strong in that environment. Huang is not afraid to say what he feels, but he's not German. So there he was in Germany trying to deal with a group of senior leaders who don't have any experience working internationally, and he really struggled to make the connections he needed to make. They just thought that he was this Chinese kid sent to Germany to get some training, and they ignored him.

(Continued)

(Continued)

"Some of the Germans told me that he couldn't be effective; that he is a finance guy who is good with data and numbers but, in this case, he needed to actually work with people. The German plant manager told me, 'This guy needs to go out and push people and fight his way through. He didn't do that, so we couldn't respect him.'"

Huang leans forward finally and comments that he learned a lot. He says he learned how critical it is to understand how other countries work, and what is important to them. "I thought that I had a lot of global experience because I ran projects out of China and dealt with colleagues in Europe and the United States. But I didn't really know how other people think. You need to know that." Huang's sentences get shorter and begin to seem disjointed as he goes on. He is unsure how much to divulge, wary of painting the situation with a negative brush. The years working for an American firm show up in his reticence to complain, his determination to show professionalism. But the experience in Germany clearly shook his confidence, and he has not yet found a way to articulate what went wrong.

Huang is relatively young, just entering his late 30s, and has grown up professionally in this American organization. The manufacturing firm was his first job out of university and he has stuck with it for 15 years, taking on challenges and developing quickly. This assignment to Germany was supposed to be a reward, a stretch role allowing him access into leadership at the organizational level, not just responsibility within China.

Huang leans forward, stubs out his cigarette and picks up his cappuccino, shifting his attention back to the conversation. "To be honest, my opportunities lie in China. There is a limit to how far I can go with this organization. At some point, I need to look at using my skills to build something here, maybe with a local company. This is where the opportunities are for people like me if we really want to lead. Or I could just stay with the company and run things out of China. I need to do what I am good at. I know China. I know how to do business here."

Huang's knowledge of China is mission-critical to his current company. The organization has invested close to 1 billion U.S. dollars there and has promised shareholders to hit a growth trajectory almost entirely dependent on performance in China. To meet that business plan, the company needs at least a hundred local nationals at the director level (Huang is one level below and was a prime candidate for promotion before his assignment to Germany). They have nothing like these numbers, and the slots are currently filled almost exclusively by expatriates on two- to three-year rotations.

In many industries, the rate of growth in China is still so high that the volume of work outgrows the number of qualified people available to perform it. In three years, the company has gone from a 100-million-dollar business to a 1-billion-dollar business in China. But they cannot seem to grow local leaders fast enough to handle the complexity of this progression. For that matter, there is no global leader who has experienced a similar situation anywhere else in the world. This makes it all the more crucial to have local leaders in positions where they can influence organizational strategies for their unique market.

Huang's 15 years of experience and the company's ability to retain him for that long are very rare in China. He is a source of knowledge about China's market and how the industry works that many organizations would pay large sums of money to recruit. The interview turns to growth projections and the company's big bet on China to determine its fortune. "How did the organization

(Continued)

(Continued)

leverage your knowledge about China when you were in Germany? There is a strong hub of global business unit leadership there and a lot of collaboration with China. How did you contribute to strategy decisions and cross-pollination while they had you so close?"

Huang disengages, shifting back in his seat again to look out the window. He is quiet for a length of time and then refocuses and answers very slowly, "They never invited me to any meetings. They never asked me one question."

COMMON LEADERSHIP TASKS

Ingrid (promotion postponed), Alan (air filters), and Huang (failed assignment), are each high-potential future leaders who have held important roles in vital markets. Their performance is critical to their multinational employers, but they are struggling. What could each of them do to have a better chance of success? And what could their organizations do to make success more likely?

Leaders in organizations everywhere must find ways to grow their businesses, to make them more efficient, and to develop employee capabilities. They need to leverage the best talent, bridge differences, run teams, engage diverse employees, integrate mergers and acquisitions, innovate to create new hit products or services for customers, and make difficult ethical choices on behalf of the organization.

Given the differences in culture, languages, time zones, and institutions inherent in global business settings, these common leadership tasks become significantly more complex and demanding. Leaders at all levels must work within matrix organizations that seek to balance the interests of business lines, functions, and geographical regions. They are also likely to have less direct authority, less accurate information, broader responsibilities, and significantly more stakeholders.[25]

Most writings on leadership focus on competencies—that is, individual skills or characteristics that allegedly produce better results. *Leading Across New Borders* focuses primarily on specific *tasks* that leaders like Ingrid, Alan, and Huang must accomplish. It answers the question: What does each of them need to do in order to succeed in cross-border contexts, with many stakeholders and little or no "command and control" authority?

Global leaders have to carry out their tasks within several contexts: self and other, team, and organization. Subsequent chapters will examine standard best practices for each task, point to the limitations of current leadership models as the world changes, and offer new ideas and approaches. Each leadership task—displayed in Table 1.2 —must

TABLE 1.2 Global Leadership Tasks

Global Leadership Tasks: A Roadmap	
Context	**Task**
Self and Other	Leveraging Talent
	Bridging Differences
Team	Running a Matrix Team
	Leading Inclusively
Organization	Integrating a Merger or Acquisition
	Innovating Across Borders
	Making Ethical Choices

be handled with an awareness of how we can alter pre-existing paradigms to reflect new realities.

ABOUT THIS BOOK

Close examination of these key tasks provides a useful road map for learning to lead in a global context. Although there is still value in learning about protocol or general paradigms for cultural awareness, this book goes beyond these familiar nostrums. Recommendations provided in each of the chapters to follow are based on contemporary examples and wisdom gleaned from practical, hard-working people in real companies. We will introduce leaders from many industries and locations, the work of scholars from various countries, and fresh data from our own proprietary tools.

Aperian Global, the authors' firm, delivers consulting services and learning programs every year to in excess of 15,000 people in more than 15 languages and 60 countries. We have served corporate audiences in many of the world's largest companies (including one-third of the Fortune 100) and in all major industries for over 25 years. This has provided us with deep knowledge and experience in addressing global business issues pragmatically, without getting mired or lost in complexity. Readers will have temporary access to the GlobeSmart Profile[SM], a personal inventory backed by strong research that will allow them to quickly assess their own cultural patterns based on five dimensions of culture and to compare themselves with others. We will introduce aggregate data gathered from recent users of this profile, a part of the GlobeSmart® web tool that has had over 800,000 registered users to date. In later chapters, we will also provide revealing new data gleaned from analyzing thousands of responses to two other proprietary surveys, the GlobeSmart Teaming Assessment[SM], and the GlobeSmart Innovation Assessment[SM].

AN INVITATION

Successful global leaders take on their jobs with eyes wide open to the rich variety of markets and employees that exist around the world, blending their hard-won prior experience with fresh insights and a willingness to experiment with new approaches. They are constantly alert to ways in which the world is changing, as their daily choices have crucial strategic and bottom-line implications.

Along their respective paths, people in leadership roles are also compelled to make tough ethical choices that push them to widen their frame of reference and to consider others' (often fervently held) ethical perspectives. They may even begin to include previously invisible participants in their considerations, such as the migrant farm workers who spray pesticides on crops in the field and drink water from the pump nearby, or the animals that live there as well. As Mother Teresa once stated, "The problem with the world is that we draw the circle of our family too small."

Leading Across New Borders is an invitation to take a journey shared by people in an ever-increasing number of professions from all parts of the globe. The path is different for everyone; yet there are common dilemmas that leaders face as the center shifts and their personal circles widen. Some may be just embarking on this journey, while others are likely to be well on their way. Readers at every level of experience will find this book to be a game-changing guide to the rugged terrain ahead.

Global Talent: Beyond Outsourcing

Who "Global Talent" Is, What People Want, and What They Need to Learn

RETHINKING TALENT

Many organizations have realized that if they still hope to be relevant in the near future, they need to radically adjust their thinking about where they are located, how they do business, what they produce, and who will lead them. While the need for change is glaringly apparent, the path to success in this new global playing field is often elusive. The transformation to a global talent management model is a high-stakes endeavor fraught with difficulties and well-intentioned strategies gone awry. As the world shifts, some approaches to talent will produce far greater success than others.

Allergic to Outsourcing

Sohail is a mid-level manager for a global pharmaceutical conglomerate that has invested millions in its sprawling Hyderabad campus and has aggressive hiring plans to fill the site with Indian talent. The break room where we meet resembles a Moroccan riad, an open courtyard in the center of the white building with light pouring in from a glass roof. Well-spoken, whip-smart, and sharply dressed, Sohail leans forward with his elbows on his knees and uses his hands to talk.

"I'm actually part of a new team in Hyderabad. We used to be in a BPO [business process outsourcing] relationship with the company, but now we are part of an integrated global business services [GBS] center. The organization takes major decisions based on our input."

Sohail bristles when asked to further explain the company's former BPO setup. He seems allergic to the word "outsourcing."

"Actually, we even had trouble with the word 'services' in the transition to the global business services model. This service mindset was still associated with low-level outsourcing work, so we needed to hear how it was going to be positioned differently at GBS than with an outsourcing model. People felt these words were demeaning and associated with low-end, disjointed processes and tasks. The company actually had to invest a lot of time in communicating that this was a significant change — that we would be doing the same GBS work as a colleague in Europe or the United States. We needed to see how our work fit into the bigger context of the organization. They told us we would now be driving the process, taking on leadership roles to drive excellence across the global organization."

From the pharmaceutical industry to the software, finance, and manufacturing sectors, strikingly similar transitions are described. An executive at a major management consultancy comments,

> *We are in the process of moving the global end-to-end solutions architect team to India. It will eventually be entirely driven by our team here. Currently, our European solutions architects handle the client interface and solution development, and then hand over instructions for the India team to implement the designed solution. But this will all change within the next 18 months. The team in Bangalore has been responding to requests from Europe, but now they will need to lead projects themselves.*

In many places in India, "outsourcing" and "BPO" are becoming terms used with ridicule and disdain. Infosys, once the shining beacon of India's globalization, has become the brunt of sarcastic slurs in the Indian papers: "Why is Murthy [former Infosys CEO] talking about Infosys and global leadership excellence in the same breath? It's just a BPO."

In Mumbai, some bankers have a visceral response to the suggestion that their work is "back end." An outspoken Mumbaikar (resident of

Mumbai) quickly corrects the mistake: "Actually, you misunderstand our organizational structure. The term you use does not relate to our situation since we are not a BPO."

India is in the middle of an identity shift, and the original stepping stone into the world of multinational corporations is now passé—even despised. India's growth has bred an elite generation of globally savvy bright-young-things with little tolerance for any whiff of second-class corporate citizenship as well as a reticence to identify with humble BPO beginnings.

For captive BPOs, the talent is actually integrated into the organization but retains a type of second-class citizenship, completing partial tasks in a process, often without full ownership, connections, relationships, or context. Captive BPO employees, however, are exposed to the organization's values, its talent expectations and opportunities. These often hit a nerve with intelligent, ambitious BPO workers who are trying to square the organizational rhetoric with the reality. The demand for development and full engagement from talent in India, the Philippines, and elsewhere either leads to change or disengagement.

THE BUSINESS CASE FOR A NEW GLOBAL TALENT MODEL

The smartest organizations understand that the key to this globalization game is talent: having the right kind of people in the right place at the right time to realize their growth goals. The right place is where the growth is happening now—and the right time is yesterday.

For many organizations, talent is the rate-limit on global growth, and the biggest challenge they face in moving toward a successful global model. Global leadership capacity, in particular, is the key binding constraint. In a recent survey, executives reported that "just 2 percent of their top 200 employees were located in Asian emerging markets that would, in the years ahead, account for more than one-third of total sales."[1] More broadly, CEOs in Western multinational corporations (MNCs) identify the ability to hire, develop, and retain talent in fast-growth markets as the main competitive differentiation in today's market.[2] Companies that get their global talent strategy right will set the course of their organization toward success and avoid becoming corporate dinosaurs.

More than any other factor, global talent has become the definitive gauge by which companies are measured and a key indicator of whether they will succeed or fail in the global market. Thirty percent of U.S. companies admitted in a survey that they have failed to exploit their international business opportunities "because of insufficient internationally competent personnel."[3] In another study, one in four global CEOs reported that they were "unable to pursue a market opportunity or have had to cancel or delay a strategic initiative because of talent constraints."[4]

Most business leaders recognize how critical it is to have a good global talent strategy. But many, if not most, are struggling to both define *what* a good global talent strategy looks like and *how* to implement it. In an executive survey, "76 percent believe their organizations need to develop global leadership capabilities, but only 7 percent think they are currently doing so very effectively."[5] The challenges in attracting, developing, and retaining global leadership talent are myriad and include inexperienced local talent in key growth markets, radical variance in leadership models across key locations (some models are difficult to transition to global roles), scarcity of globally experienced *and* locally savvy leadership talent, poaching, job-hopping, and increased competition from local companies in the war for talent.

BEYOND OUTSOURCING

Even though talent is widely recognized as a critical enabler or constraint for growth in global markets, many companies are still mired in unsatisfactory business process outsourcing models that produce mixed results—albeit at lower short-term cost—and confine workers to circumscribed roles serving counterparts and customers in developed markets. The outsourcing model's former sheen of efficiency has faded into harsh realities of miscommunication, poor handoffs, quality lapses, retention woes, disengagement, and a growing realization that a great deal of talent—not to mention time—is being wasted. For many firms, the BPO model has created a barrier between the organization and the very talent it needs to succeed in the future. For companies sending work to noncaptive BPOs, this talent actually works for another organization entirely.

A number of multinationals have taken steps to integrate former outsourcing partners into the daily flow of the business, and high-potential employees have begun to express their aspirations more openly. They are now becoming integral members and leaders of internal staff and engineering teams with labels such as Global Business Services, End-to-End Solutions, Technical Center of Excellence, or Global Product Development.

Another major change has been the realization that local markets in India, the Philippines, and other BPO locations in Eastern Europe and Latin America have strong growth potential. And the key to accessing growth markets is having local talent on the ground. The majority of the consumers of tomorrow will be located outside of today's mature economies. By 2020, the Asia-Pacific region alone is projected to make up more than 50 percent of all global consumption growth.[6] Reaching these new customers will require legions of talented people who cannot merely be in positions where they are executing strategies created elsewhere or doing back-end processing work. Rather, they need to have the ear of the organization and the ability to influence strategies that will position the company for success in these key markets.

Moreover, structural changes that reflect the impending primacy of fast-growth locations are essential. The markets are rewarding many companies that have moved their headquarters, key functional organizations, or business units from mature to fast-growth markets. These companies are seeing higher growth rates as they invest in local talent close to their key customers and begin to drive global strategy from their largest growth areas.

Challenges

Many companies have started to address the global talent issue by transitioning away from more traditional outsourcing models. As in the case of the pharmaceutical company mentioned at the start of this chapter, organizations are looking for ways to integrate their talent through both structural changes and engagement measures. The path toward a successful global talent management model has been one of trial and error for most organizations—full of painful transition periods, with many questioning the wisdom of the decisions. Here are comments from two other employees in a different firm who are working through nitty-gritty transition issues.

The Report: Michael

Michael, a marketing team head, is an American based in Europe. His confidence comes through over the phone, and he seems philosophically supportive of integrating the India team more fully. "We are trying to transition our Indian teams into greater leadership roles, giving them more ownership. We've got great talent there, and the lower cost of hiring that great talent is still a real advantage for us. But I will tell you that that transition has been and still is painful.

"I rely on the medical communications experts based in Surat for my marketing documents that I send out to doctors. Two weeks ago, I sent a report along to the team with the raw data and information on the target audience. I followed up with a check-in call to make sure that Jas, the guy in India assigned to this project, had gotten the documents and to see if he had any questions.

"I told him that, ideally, I needed the report in two weeks, and asked if he was okay with that. He said, 'sure.'

"Two weeks later, I got the report back and saw that, while Jas had integrated the raw data, the implications had not been interpreted at all. The key messages were not clear and the nuances in the

(Continued)

(Continued)

tone and language were just not right for my European audience. Actually, the report was unfinished in many ways. So it was now up to me to rewrite it, without any cushion time, which then impacted my deadline. I would say that this feels pretty typical of my interaction with the team in Surat.

"I expected Jas to take the data and interpret it based on his expertise. He should be able to discern which messages need to come across to the audience and then craft those messages in a way that will make sense to our customers and add value to me. I am not sure how much value these services are adding when I am the one who has to check and recheck and follow up constantly to make sure that we get the result we need. This wastes my time. It will be quicker for me to just do the rewrite now rather than spend so much time explaining all the changes. I expect another professional like me to be able to own the communication he is writing and deliver something that is complete, on time, and reflects a deep understanding of the material. We don't necessarily get that from our team there. If there is a question about something, I am always available. I am just an e-mail away. But those questions should come up early enough for me to address them, without impacting the deadline."

The Report: Jas

Jas is tall and bearded, mid-30s with a black turban and the silver bracelet signifying his Sikh identity. He seems tired and, when asked, says that he has been working long hours and then has to catch the late employee bus back to the city. He hasn't had much sleep lately.

Jas starts off with a sigh, "Yeah, the project with Michael could have gone better. When Michael called, I had not yet had time to look at the documents he had sent since I was working on a couple of other reports. So I didn't have any questions at that time and figured I could rely on my team in Surat to figure out any elements I didn't understand. The thing is, I can constantly discuss and get help with my local team if I have an issue, but how can I do this with Michael? I don't even know him. If I start out by asking a million questions, he will think that I don't know anything and I will lose credibility with him.

"When I finally got around to looking through the materials that Michael sent, I realized that it would take a lot of time to write this report. By that time, I only had a week left to complete it. I worked late hours trying to finish this document to meet Michael's timeline. I was hopeful that I could complete it, but I was only able to finish it to a certain level. Anyway, it's better that I get Michael's input on what I have already written and then make changes from there."

Jas sits back and slowly rubs his eyes, then shifts forward again and looks thoughtful as he continues: "You know, there is a lot of talk about this whole transition to more ownership, about integrating us into the global team. But the reality is that we are not one team. We are still treated like a service center and do not have as much say or respect within the organization. Ultimately, I am

(Continued)

(Continued)

working for someone else—so they have the final say in what is good or not. At the end of the day, it is their responsibility. They are paid the big bucks and work out of headquarters so they know what is needed. We are only providing a service; because they are driving the decisions, it is their responsibility to tell us what they need and to provide detailed requirements. Often they give us only a small amount of information and then get angry when we aren't able to read their minds. I am just responsible for doing the work I am given, to the specifications which have been outlined. Our client stakeholders determine those specifications. I am not in a position to argue with that. If they would give me more information or be more readily available—or if we had a relationship—that would be different. But the work is still just thrown over the wall to me and then there is silence. I try to match the specifications they send, but they often want me to make things up out of thin air. It is not my place to be offering my opinions in this kind of paper. I am just trying to give them what they want."

This dynamic between Michael and Jas points to the core struggles in play as organizations try to reposition themselves for global relevance. Most organizations recognize the trends and are in the process of aligning themselves to benefit from the global economic shifts. But they have found that their internal talent management processes are unable to keep up with, much less effectively drive, the organization's global growth. The transition to global talent sourcing, it turns out, is not just a matter of hiring more global workers. It requires a colossal mindset shift in the organization and new approaches to delegation, teamwork, employee engagement, knowledge transfer, performance evaluation, and developing the competencies needed to make all of these possible.

GLOBAL TALENT DEVELOPMENT: BOTTOM-UP AND TOP-DOWN

Global talent development demands commitment and change from both the current top decision-makers and emerging fast-growth-market leaders. We will focus in this section on the topics that individual leaders themselves can impact.

In one of the best examples of a holistic global leadership initiative, a global manufacturer made a commitment to develop its talent across all leadership levels. The company defined critical global competencies for all levels of the organization based on a global research framework.[7] It also built awareness of the cultural roots driving leadership expectations and norms across the organization's key geographies. Specific skills gaps were identified for leaders coming from all regions.

Fast-growth-market leaders focused on critical competencies for succeeding in a matrix environment with diverse global stakeholders. Across a two-year development program, these high-potential leaders honed skills tailored to bridge critical gaps for taking on broader responsibilities and influencing organizational stakeholders. The participants acquired tools and explicit leadership behaviors that would better enable them to gain a hearing for their ideas and expertise. They were given new job opportunities in which to apply these learnings regularly, including interaction with top regional executives. Key areas for skill development have been:

- Building credibility through owning the solution
- Communicating with impact
- Developing global business acumen
- Delivering a strong point of view
- Increasing advocacy and collaboration in global decision making
- Establishing a visionary leadership style
- Leading across cultures
- Positioning for visibility
- Managing upward effectively to change or challenge the process
- Navigating the global matrix
- Improving personal influence power versus position power

Development for the top 300 global executives, the majority of whom were from North American and European backgrounds, focused heavily on skills that would position them to receive critical business information from outside their normal frame of reference and to work effectively with global counterparts who used unfamiliar leadership approaches and communication styles. The initiative brought these executives to extended stays in the company's key growth markets in China, India, and Brazil. Here they heard perspectives from local leaders and employees, met with important customers and partners, visited factories and retail outlets, observed the competition in action, and experienced the realities of their global operations.

The goals of their developmental program included determining how leaders can create space for and utilize a variety of leadership approaches. It also built self-awareness around leaders' own natural tendency to assess highly and promote "like-me" leadership. The learning process contained many elements: experience on site in fast-growth markets, networking with global colleagues, strategic projects done at the request of the CEO, and facilitated sessions as well as personal coaching. Objectives included enabling these global leaders to adapt their leadership approach to skillfully navigate multiple cultures and markets, including their key locations in Asia.

There are several general developmental areas for each of the two groups—fast-growth-market leaders and mature-market executives—as they move toward a more global talent model.

Leaders from Fast-Growth Markets

Executive Presence

There are many components to executive presence, including posture, dress, gestures such as the form of one's initial greetings, and so on. The rules for these are largely unwritten and vary somewhat by culture. There are also important general skills required of people who aspire to join the executive ranks in most multinationals. For instance, there are clearly things that Jas could do in the report scenario just discussed to make the interaction more successful. Becoming a full-fledged global team partner brings with it a higher level of accountability. He currently appears to be expressing a kind of passive/aggressive attitude that is unlikely to establish him as an executive peer. If he wants others to see him as a true global partner, he needs to take more responsibility and initiative and step out of an outsourcing mindset himself. There is a danger that he will create a self-fulfilling prophecy: if he assumes that he is being treated as a second-class corporate citizen and acts accordingly, he may find that this is indeed the way that others treat him, even if corporate policy is to move away from outsourcing. How can Jas instead get a virtuous cycle going by altering his approach?

If Jas is unclear about his responsibilities, it's up to him to reach out and request clarification from Michael while expressing his intention to get the job done. It is not helpful to his reputation to provide a half-baked response and feel resentful about his role, especially if he is assuming that the ultimate responsibility lies elsewhere. Jas also needs to cultivate a particular skill of distilling and communicating key messages. Inexperienced people in his position tend to provide large volumes of detail without sufficiently digesting or interpreting the information. The term "executive summary" highlights the expectations of leaders who are exposed to large volumes of information on a daily basis. They want to know the main points and to have the option to drill down for further detail as needed; likewise, they expect their peers to be able to both synthesize and probe.

Several familiar cultural patterns were probably in the background of the initial response Jas gave to Michael: deference to hierarchy, a preference for relationship-based interactions, and reluctance to draw direct conclusions for others who will make their own inferences. For Jas to be effective at higher levels in this organization, however, he will need to understand these patterns and take steps to flex his own style. It is neither possible nor desirable for him to become a Westerner, but his current mentality will not serve him well in a global leadership position. Jas may find that Michael is amenable to meeting him partway if he asks him for help and expresses an eagerness to learn new skills.

Micro versus Macro Styles

Ingrid, the Swedish banker from Chapter 1 whose promotion we learned was postponed, goes on to describe what it was like to work for her new Indian boss in Bangalore.

> When I was passed over for promotion, there was a structural change and I started reporting to an Indian boss, Atul, for the first time. Atul was new in this position and also doing part of the role I used to manage. When I tried to give him suggestions on how the company worked, he would always respond, "Let's see what others say." He wasn't receptive to hearing things from me. Then he started micromanaging my team, and they came to me panicking because they were used to being very empowered with my leadership style. So I sat down to tell him that the team knows their priorities for a given day, and that he should trust them to do their jobs. He responded, "Ingrid, I've managed people for 10 years; I think that you are new to this." Any advice I offered was shut down because of the hierarchy.
>
> I really struggled during this time. I was blunt and outspoken and the Indian male managers there didn't know how to deal with me. I got a lot of "you need to be softer" from them. They also took away a lot of the responsibilities that challenged me and made me feel like I was growing. Even though I had more experience, my voice wasn't valued. It became all about my role and my place in the hierarchy versus what I knew how to do. These guys got very territorial and they were threatened by me because I didn't necessarily buy into the whole concept that I should respect you based on your role alone or that I should keep quiet if I know how to do something better based on my experience.

Many freshly minted leaders from India and elsewhere struggle when they start to interact with employees from other parts of the world. India is one of the most densely populated countries on the planet, and its offices are filled with young people who have little business experience and are climbing a steep learning curve. It is natural in these circumstances to work in close proximity with subordinates using a very micro, hands-on style. India has also traditionally been a relatively hierarchical culture in which respect is paid to people based on their status and titles, and the model boss, teacher, or master takes a stance of strict yet benevolent authoritarianism. Non-Indians from more egalitarian and individualistic environments are often quite uncomfortable with this style, as in Ingrid's case—particularly when it is applied by leaders who are still relatively new to the job themselves, insecure about their position, and inclined to feel threatened by people who are less compliant or even bold enough to challenge them.

In order to be successful in his new role, Ingrid's new boss, Atul, will need to step back from the micro style that has proven effective to this point in his career. He must recognize that he is now dealing with more experienced team members who have different, culturally based expectations and begin to experiment with more macro, or hands-off approaches, however nervous this makes him at first. Ironically, many Western expatriates must go through the opposite transition when they realize their local employees need and want more guidance—their finely honed delegation techniques are referred to disparagingly as "delegate and disappear."

To the extent to which he is able to grasp Ingrid and her team's background and training, Atul will be able to take her conduct less personally and experiment with different leadership approaches without feeling threatened. Working with the team to establish a vision for what they are trying to accomplish together could serve as a partial antidote to his tendency to micromanage; if he feels that team members buy into a shared vision, it may be easier for him to delegate work more freely.

Agile Leadership

There is also a second part to the story from Chapter 1 regarding Huang Shiguang's failed assignment to Germany. Huang's boss in China, a Westerner who has been his champion for years, describes what happened when there was a conflict between the company's China and Germany offices over the sourcing of high-tech equipment. The German offices were insisting that China operations would need to import the equipment from Europe in order to ensure quality.

Huang showed me the numbers and told me he knew his source in China was of equal quality and much cheaper. I believed him. But in the end, I was the one who had to escalate the issue to the corporate level and push through the decision. Huang didn't have the global network or the knowledge of the company's historical sourcing channels. And to be honest, he didn't have the stomach to go head-to-head with our German colleagues in order to push forward his point of view. I actually can't think of any of our current Chinese local leaders who would have been able to succeed in the same situation—but this is exactly what we need them to be doing. We're seeking people with the ability to leverage their in-depth local knowledge not just for the benefit of the local subsidiary but for the entire global organization.

During his time on assignment in Germany, Huang's tendency was to keep a low profile because he felt out of his element and was not sure how to behave. However, he would have benefitted by adapting with greater agility to his new surroundings and doing more to absorb and follow local patterns of behavior. He could have explored ways to position himself more visibly: reaching out to meet key individuals, asking his sponsors for introductions to executives, and participating in cross-functional meetings to demonstrate that he has wider interests and expertise beyond the finance function to which he currently belongs.

Along with his low profile, Huang's reticence to speak when he did not have a fully formulated expert point of view, combined with a reluctance to sing his own praises—modesty is normally seen as a virtue in China—led to his being ignored by German colleagues. Delivering a strong point of view requires not only marshalling evidence but clearly stating its implications and being prepared to respond to challenging questions and opposing views. Instead of avoiding or minimizing open conflict, which is a common cultural pattern throughout much of Asia, Huang needs to realize that conflict is expected among his German counterparts, who respect head-to-head advocacy as a sign of executive prowess. Learning the patterns of speech embedded in the phrase, "I disagree because . . ." is a good place to start, and is much better than "you don't understand this market. . . . "

Leaders in fast-growth markets have found many ways to get results. The energetic, data-based advocacy that they learn to exert in working with their global counterparts is sometimes combined with under-the-radar local pilot efforts to demonstrate that a different solution is possible. If their perception is that "headquarters will just slow us down," pressing ahead with an experiment that generates evidence and wins local executive buy-in can be the first step toward managing upward and challenging existing processes. This is a cross-border version of the innovator's admonition, "Act first and ask for permission later."

Leaders from Established Markets

Talent Recruitment

As we will discuss in more detail in Chapter 5, effective global leaders seek out diversity and ensure that unconscious bias—which we all possess in some form—does not distort hiring decisions. There is a particular variation of this problem in many multinational subsidiary environments today that is based on the tension between skill requirements for handling two kinds of audiences: global counterparts and local customers. Often job candidates or junior employees start with one capability or the other but not both.

It is important for global leaders to ask, "What kind of talent are we bringing in?" Finding this balance is critical in China, for example, and according to many Chinese businesspeople, the Western multinationals are doing it all wrong.

Hiring Locally Savvy Talent

John is a Chinese national who works for a European energy consulting firm. He is originally from Xi'an in western China, and now travels between Copenhagen, Frankfurt, Denver, and various locations in China. He uses American slang and moves fluidly between executive lunches and Karaoke bars. His regular travel to and from China keeps him up to date on what is happening there and its impact globally. John has inherited a northern European brand of black humor and a communication style that pulls no punches. He comments, "When the market is doing so well by itself, then the problems remain hidden. But once the economy experiences a bit of a lag, then the talent gaps really start to show up. Multinationals are up against very competent local competitors, and this lag can quickly equal failure. Chinese companies do customer service much better. They move more quickly, and the technology gap between local and global companies is shrinking fast. Often the people who are working for foreign ventures are the least competent in terms of what is needed for the Chinese market. They have been hired because they are very good in English and can speak in a way that makes their Western bosses comfortable, but they know nothing about how to create good local business relationships.

"These local hires can't actually solve the problems or deal with Chinese customers, and they are not encouraged to do so. MNCs simply do not prioritize the skills that are needed to do well in the Chinese market. Headquarters sets the strategy, and they do not even see the need for these skills. It was a great thing 20 years ago to work for a foreign venture. Now we are starting to see a power shift and it is the other way around. People are seeing better opportunities with local organizations. They feel like their skills will be more valued."

Leaders who want to make sure their organizations are bringing in the right talent are well-advised to review their recruiting practices for local market relevance as well as cultural bias. Here are some useful questions:

- Do our recruiting practices attract candidates who reflect a broad spectrum of local/regional diversity?
- Are our recruitment decisions based on "like me" organizational fit, or do they include a range of experienced talent from all key markets?

- Do our hiring practices support the company's global growth strategy?
- Do these practices reflect local market opportunities and priorities?

Another aspect of recruiting is defining a strategy for engaging with the many firms that offer to provide candidates in the whirligig Chinese job market.

The Recruiting Frenzy

Alvaro, an HR VP from a French electronics company, elaborates on the approach that the company's China subsidiary has taken based on its experience: "We actually went completely local with our hiring practices. We had to get a new strategy. The plan was completely alien to headquarters, but we eventually won out because global Human Resources is now based here in the region and the needs here are so great. This year we are recruiting 400 to 500 white collar workers in our business unit alone. We are almost 9,000 in China now. Not even 10 months ago, we only had 7,800.

"At one point we were working with 11 different recruiting companies. We would send the job spec to these headhunters, and then we would pay if we recruited based on one of the CVs they sent; if not, then no payment. It was a very opportunistic approach, and we would often lose the talent as quickly as it came to us. Especially at the upper levels, there is a small group of top leaders who are in high demand and just rotate to higher and higher positions along the MNC circuit, earning more with each new role. The recruiters have them on speed dial. As soon as they get into a job, the recruiters are there again trying to get them into another.

"So we hit on a new method. We are now working with only two or three headhunters with whom we have established a long-term relationship. We pay a bit more but are getting higher quality candidates and reducing our risk of failure as a result. Before we were trying to hire only a few very senior executives, but now we have opened the door for more local senior guys. They could be even more expensive than expats. And it is actually these people who help us attract strong employees from their previous companies. Good Chinese leaders tend to inspire a lot of loyalty. If the leader has high credibility, then he brings people with him."

Performance Management

In a recent Community Business study entitled "Adopting an Asian Lens to Talent Development," researchers found that local employees perceived leadership models and assessment processes used within global multinationals operating in the region to be "Western." The Indian study participants, for instance, agreed that "when assessing talent, this is done through a Western lens. They felt it was essential to redefine success . . . and adapt competencies to include the 'Indian style.'"[8]

Given the predominance of Western models for assessing talent within most multinationals, it is unsurprising that the focus is on leadership performance gaps. These gaps reinforce the view that the talent from the new markets is not ready for leadership in the organization. As a result, the voices of key individuals from global markets do not gain enough resonance in the organization to challenge the organizing structural biases that preclude them having a seat at the table and prevent the organization from transitioning to a truly global identity. Organizations that do not fundamentally reassess their performance management systems will continue to wander in this house of mirrors with no exit, wasting precious time on their path toward globalization.

High-potential Asian employees often express frustration at not being promoted, even though they execute perfectly the expectations for their role. Executives at headquarters and regional expatriate leaders tend to list a lack of several key competencies (global business savvy, strategic thinking, the ability to articulate a strong argument, out-of-the box problem solving and so on) that prevent these high-potentials from advancing. When asked if these competencies are explicit requirements on which employees are measured, leaders at most companies pause and then admit that at least some of them are not. The harsh reality is that many emerging leaders working for Western multinationals are being evaluated on a set of implicit leadership expectations that are so culturally embedded that they are often not even *articulated*, much less measured.

In the pharma example that describes the interaction between Jas and Michael, there is responsibility on both sides. Michael can help to break the destructive circular pattern of unarticulated expectations and critical performance evaluation by reaching out to Jas and learning more about his capabilities and developmental needs. They should get to know each other a lot better, and this is a worthwhile investment of Michael's time in spite of the geographical and cultural distance that separates them. It may be that Jas is not the right person for the role, but it is more likely that he needs hands-on mentoring, exposure to best practice models, and constructive feedback that will enable him to grow into his position. Jas will feel more comfortable discussing his developmental needs if he feels that Michael believes in him and is actively involved in providing support; Michael will also be better able to target what he delegates and to accurately anticipate and rely upon the work that Jas produces.

Another factor that keeps locally hired high-potential leaders from being favorably assessed and promoted is that it is safer to continue importing known leaders from mature markets. After all, these leaders have a network, years of organizational knowledge, and visibility with senior executives. Given the choice between sticking their necks out to advocate for a talented but far less visible local hire in a fast-growth market or simply bringing in a person the leadership team at headquarters already recognizes and likes, most expatriate leaders will choose the latter because it is safer and much easier to gain approval. "Promoting one of my Chinese team members into a critical role that is visible to regional and global leadership puts my career and reputation at risk," says an international assignee based in Shanghai. "It is much easier just to import a person who already has system-wide credibility, even though this is expensive and worse for our organization's future capability." Changing this dynamic requires a higher organizational tolerance for failure and strong support for helping non-Western talent succeed in stretch roles.

Leaders who are assessing the present performance and future prospects of individuals in fast-growth markets should consider widening their frame of reference to incorporate input such as the following:

- How effective is this candidate going to be in working with local customers and employees in comparison with expatriate candidates for the same role?
- How do local customers perceive the employee's performance?
- How do other local employees perceive the employee's performance?
- What are key needs for our organization to grow in the local market, and how is this employee contributing?
  - Personal network with customers, suppliers, government regulators
  - Sales and marketing skills
  - Ability and willingness to develop more junior employees
  - Loyalty of coworkers and subordinates (who might elect to follow this leader elsewhere in the event of a transition)
  - Ability to influence others within the local organization
  - Resourcefulness in getting things done regardless of obstacles

Succession Planning

The ultimate mark of effective leadership is finding and grooming a worthy successor, while ensuring that other leaders throughout the organization are doing the same. Corporate succession planning becomes critical when organizations are trying to create global leadership bench strength across all key markets. Current leaders must recognize that the most talented people in their pipeline may not look like them at all.

The 5-Foot 2-Inch Candidate

Evan is an American from the Midwest. His big-boned structure and farmboy accent are difficult to square with the fact that he is an old China hand, having lived and worked in the country for 25 years in a number of leadership roles. He currently heads up program management in Shanghai for a massive German auto parts supplier. "What I have found is that leadership back home really struggles to understand or support succession planning because they come at it with their own European perspective. They have a hard time understanding how leadership works here in China and expect people here to adapt to them and the way they work. That's where I think the problem lies.

"There is this automatic grading from the leadership that happens without them even realizing it. There are all these implicit leadership expectations."

Evan breaks the conversation to order another beer in perfect Mandarin.

"I had some conversations with my German boss. I work for the VP here who reports to the German president in Frankfurt. He has been with the company for 23 years, so he's not a new kid on the block. But he has very specific expectations. For example, I am responsible for program management in China. We are having a conversation around his vision for program management and he says, 'I want to put power and strength in program management here.' I ask him what that looks like. He replies, 'I want people to fear you. When you are there, they should be afraid because you will push them.'

"How do you think that is going to work in China? His paradigm is from Germany, where you aren't respected until you can confront others directly and even raise your voice. But you will never run into Chinese who will yell and scream. My German boss only respects people who push back forcefully and vocally. He will think others are weak if they aren't confrontational. Our leadership measures people in the first 15 seconds after they meet them—and they measure them on the wrong things.

"I have a 5-foot 2-inch Shanghainese lady here who really knows her stuff; I can send her to work on any JV or program issue and she can diagnose and fix it. She creates some magic and can get the different parts of the Chinese organization to start functioning together. My German VP took one look at her and said that she is not leadership material.

"My job is to come here and train my replacement, and I think this woman is the best candidate. But my VP doesn't believe she is right for the job based on his first 15-second impression. She can't go in and make people fear her. Well, you should go talk to the general managers of every one of the JVs she works for; they welcome her to come in anytime because they know they can trust her. Both foreigners and Chinese know that she will come in and tell them what the real story is and that she is going to fix it. This has happened again and again over the past five years. She is immensely competent. But my boss does not think this based on his 15-second impression. We are all guilty of that kind of snap judgment. But as leaders, we need to check ourselves. It is a huge stumbling block for foreign leadership going to China or India, because we bring this bias with us."

The power base in most Western multinationals still lies in Europe or the United States, but that model is growing increasingly outdated and irrelevant. As economic power shifts from west to east and north to south, organizations themselves must change to create room for new types of talent, and existing leaders must adapt to drive growth in a transformed environment.

Those leaders who currently operate within the comfort of their company's dominant leadership style need to push themselves out of their comfort zones in order to engage tomorrow's leaders—whose approach to business will be very different. They must also commit to supporting and growing future leaders as a strategic imperative, and provide them with the tools they need to succeed. The organization that insists on retaining a culturally narrow definition of talent will be less capable of leveraging the unique strengths of employees for competitive advantage in the markets that really matter.

GLOBAL TALENT'S IMPACT

Despite her painful transition to working for a local boss, Ingrid the banker returned to London from Bangalore a huge proponent of moving toward a global talent structure.

> *I am actually onboard with the move from outsourcing to more strategic roles. I saw it work well with my team. I was at the front of elbowing our India team into the global picture, putting people forward for projects with folks in London. By the time I left, my team in Bangalore had full ownership and responsibility. It created a high level of engagement because anything the business needed help with went straight to Bangalore—there was nobody in between. But in other functions, colleagues still went through London, even though the team in Bangalore was doing the work. They were still stuck in an outsourcing mindset. I saw a difference in connectivity, relationships, and visibility when the India team had direct communication with the business and they felt more empowered and excited, more involved in the business than the other areas. I try to drive this engagement now out of London and make the connections happen.*

Ingrid is already skilled at tapping the potential of newer talent, creating direct links between internal customers and employees who can meet their needs; indeed, she is now a leader in driving a change process that is vital to her organization. Getting talent right in today's global market equates to survival and sustainable growth over time. Once leaders throughout the company start seeing the impact of these global talent practices, the business case for change is no longer even questioned.

WHAT YOU CAN DO

- Be prepared to recognize high-potential talent from anywhere.
- Consider what you personally can do to enable the transition from an outsourcing approach to a global talent approach.
- For each project try to match the objectives with the right global talent, with as few intermediaries as possible.
- Identify and address your own skill gaps and/or blind spots.
  - As a fast-growth-market leader:
    Executive presence

    Micro versus macro

    Agile leadership
  - As a mature-market leader:
    Recruiting

    Performance management

    Succession planning
- Reach out to cultivate future leaders in your own country or in another global location who are not in the "like-me" category.

Global Mindset: Beyond Culture

When Cultural Awareness Is Not Enough

DEVELOPING A GLOBAL MINDSET

How can global talent be best positioned to succeed? It is worth stepping back from the breathless pace of fast-growth markets to consider the capabilities that are most essential for global leaders to fulfill their potential. Whether they come from west or east, north or south, current and future leaders like those depicted in earlier chapters must develop a global mindset that matches the geographical expansion of their employers.

Cultural competency is a vital ingredient for this type of mindset, and one of the master keys to unlocking global doors is a strong foundational capacity in this area. Acquiring a vital base of cultural knowledge and practical skills requires that leaders remain open to new learning, welcome a constant exchange of information and ideas, build a deep sense of common purpose with global counterparts, and embrace shared insights or "aha moments" that stimulate higher levels of performance.

Global mindset also entails looking beyond culture. For example, leaders must constantly assess economic, geopolitical, and technological changes as new and old powers compete in a rapidly transforming world. They need to find ways to anticipate and leverage fresh trends in order to innovate, inspire, and ultimately position their organizations to benefit as borders are redrawn and the epicenter of economic activity shifts. Ingrid the banker, for example, has discerned that her organization is in the midst of a major change process and has adapted both culturally and politically to become a skillful agent of change herself.

This chapter will define cultural competency, evaluate both misguided and more effective approaches to acquiring cultural knowledge and skills, and then examine other capabilities beyond intercultural skills that the most successful global leaders possess— capabilities that are also a primary focus of the rest of the book.

GLOBAL LEADERSHIP 101: CULTURAL COMPETENCY

In the new global reality, a high level of cultural competency is the starting point for addressing an evolving fabric of multiple value systems and cultural backgrounds. In contrast to previous eras in which one or two cultural paradigms were preeminent, multiple perspectives now coexist and jostle for dominance without a clear hierarchy of whose value system should define the standard.

Cultural competency reflects the degree to which differences are understood and effectively bridged and is demonstrated through both cognitive and behavioral adaptation. Cognitive adaptation is the ability to see the world through the cultural frameworks of diverse stakeholders, customers, or colleagues. Individuals with such a mindset display an unthreatened acceptance of cultural difference as natural and other cultural practices as legitimate and multifaceted in their own right. They are aware that their own culture comprises one of many ways of organizing behavior. While they may prefer some forms of behavior to others, all are seen as expressions of common human needs in a given context. Behavioral adaptation is the ability to adapt conduct and strategy to fit different cultural contexts and to move skillfully and authentically between them. This competency enables leaders to act in culturally appropriate ways to enhance performance, learning, and personal growth among employees from diverse groups.

People who lack sufficient knowledge about how to work with members of different cultures encounter costly, predictable negative consequences. These include direct costs along with hidden ones: missed deadlines, quality glitches, alienated customers, business lost to competitors, wasted time, mutual frustration, diminished trust, damage to personal and corporate brands, embarrassment for others, disengaged and discouraged local employees. And small-scale miscommunications that occur on a daily basis often grow into larger problems. The $39 billion investment and five years of wasted integration efforts that Daimler-Benz AG squandered on its failed acquisition of Chrysler Corporation can mostly be attributed to the companies' insufficient knowledge about one another before consummating the deal and the failure of national and organizational cultures to mesh.

Defining Culture

A worthwhile starting point for cultivating a global mindset is to learn about common differences between national cultures. Culture consists of "habits of the mind," or shared patterns of perception, thought, and behavior that are learned and passed on to others from one generation to the next.[1] On the most personal level, it is like the air that each of us breathes, or the water in which fish swim—invisible, yet essential for life.

Cultural boundaries may correspond with national or regional lines on a map; they are also likely to correspond with divisions between the hearts and minds of diverse team members who are sitting in the same room or communicating virtually via calls and e-mail. In either case, it is crucial to learn about culture, as different cultural habits have practical workplace consequences for joint communication, decision making, problem solving, conflict resolution, and so on. There are common and systematic ways in which cultural patterns differ based on the contrasting physical environments and historical contexts in which humans have learned to survive.

Cultural Self-Awareness: Five Dimensions

Becoming aware of one's own culturally based assumptions is an important initial step toward cultural competency. Decades of research in the intercultural field point to common contrasts between different perspectives. Five dimensions of culture are particularly critical in workplace environments: independent/interdependent, egalitarianism/status, risk/certainty, direct/indirect, task/relationship.[2] Figure 3.1 contains a list of these dimensions, along with brief definitions for each side of the cultural spectrum.

Understanding Others: The "Why" Behind the Behavior

These cultural differences are manifested in various ways in everyday workplace interactions. The next step beyond cultural self-awareness is to learn how our own basic assumptions and patterns of behavior contrast with those of others.. Reflecting back on several of the leaders from various locations portrayed in earlier chapters, it is clear that each of them could have benefited both from greater self-awareness

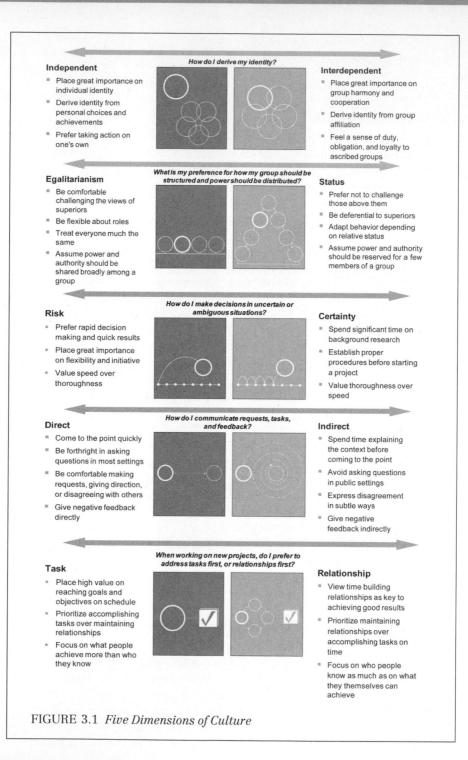

FIGURE 3.1 *Five Dimensions of Culture*

and from a deeper understanding of cultural influences shaping the behavior of their counterparts:

- Atul, the micromanager who became Ingrid's new boss, was using a hierarchical leadership style even when working with others such as Ingrid from more egalitarian cultures. (Dimension: Egalitarianism/ Hierarchy)
- Huang Shiguang, the Chinese expatriate who did not perform well in Germany, struggled in part because he did not adapt his relatively indirect communication style to a country where directness is valued. (Dimension: Direct/Indirect)
- Michael, the pharma executive in Europe who was disappointed with the contribution of his Indian counterpart, Jas, underestimated the importance of building a personal relationship that would help their communication flow more smoothly. (Dimension: Task/Relationship)

As the experiences of these leaders demonstrate, people who encounter different cultural patterns of behavior may all be looking at the same thing, but perceiving it in a completely different light. Culture shapes our perceptions and is often described as the tint of the colored glasses through which we view the world, or sometimes even as the box over our heads. How can we trade glasses with our counterparts to view situations as they do, or at least remove the box that is obstructing our vision? It is critical to understand *the "why" behind the behavior*—our own and that of our workplace colleagues.[3] Another example will help to show how shared perspectives could avert mistaken judgments and lead to a more flexible and efficacious approach.

Leadership Edge

Moses Macharia recently returned to a regional executive role based in Kenya, his home country, after a several-year developmental assignment in India. His employer, a Dutch consumer products enterprise, considers him to be a high-potential leader who could one day be among the firm's top executives. At the moment, however, he is struggling with the impact of his rapid promotions through the company system:

"I am younger than most of the managers on my team, and several of the people who are now working for me in Nairobi were formerly my bosses or even my boss's boss. It's hard to come back now and to be in charge of a regional function with a big change agenda. My job is to consolidate several functions that were formerly separate into a single department covering all of East Africa. I now have over 500 people working for me in this organization. With the individuals who were once

(Continued)

(Continued)

senior to me, I need to strike a balance between seeking their advice and opinions on the one hand, and acting decisively on the other. In fact, I already had to transfer one senior individual to another department because he refused to support the reorganization I am responsible for implementing. This was painful, as he had previously been a good mentor to me and was respected by others in the company. However, he was more comfortable with the previous organizational structure and accustomed to other people following his instructions, and having me in charge of this change effort was just too difficult for him.

"My boss in the region says that I need to balance careful listening with expressing a clear point of view and making hard choices. He tells me to ask tougher questions in meetings and to set a firm direction for the team. I find it a lot easier to do this in more private one-on-one settings than in front of a large group where I don't want to embarrass people, particularly those who have been with the organization for a long time. My last performance appraisal said that I need to demonstrate more 'executive presence' and 'edge.' I still don't know exactly what these mean in practice, although I'm confident that I understand our business and the direction we should take."

Moses is struggling in part with the cultural dimensions of egalitarianism versus status as well as direct versus indirect communication. If edge is defined as challenging the status quo in a provocative way that gets better results for the business, he may need to practice this in a style that is different from the corporate norm elsewhere. Most Kenyan workplaces are relatively hierarchical and indirect compared with the Netherlands, where his firm is headquartered (see Figure 3.2). Overt demonstrations of respect for elders are valued, and uncomfortable topics are often addressed in private rather than raising them directly in a public setting. At the same time, it is common for established executives in Kenya and elsewhere in East

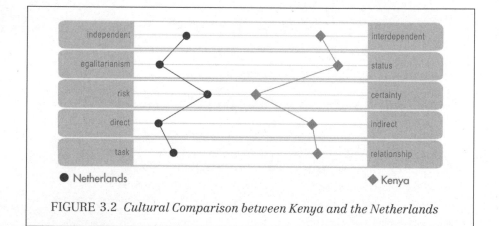

FIGURE 3.2 *Cultural Comparison between Kenya and the Netherlands*

Africa to lead in a forceful manner that many Westerners might regard as autocratic and not conducive to healthy debate.

Moses must learn to balance the local norms of public respect for elders and a top-down leadership style with the norms of his corporate culture and his current boss's expectations. Effective edge in this context may turn out to be less publicly direct and yet more status-oriented and directive than what his Western boss experienced in the Netherlands, where people tend to value open confrontation and employees expect egalitarian treatment as fellow professionals. To avoid creating a no-win cultural conflict between headquarters and regional perspectives, both Moses and his boss need to be very aware of the tint of each others' glasses—the why behind the behavior each considers to be optimum. Cultural competency in this case will require them to define and implement a version of leadership edge that is productive in the local environment, accomplishes the objectives of the organization, and also fits with Moses' own personality and background. Moses probably also needs to learn how to modify his style when he is dealing with executives from headquarters, "style-switching" between environments by engaging in the very kinds of direct public confrontation and debate that he is avoiding for good reasons in Nairobi.

ACQUIRING CULTURAL COMPETENCY: MISGUIDED APPROACHES

Because culture is a difficult concept to pin down precisely, leaders are often tempted to seek out shortcuts to handle it. Unfortunately, the seemingly easy solutions for working with people from other countries and cultures also tend to be excellent recipes for failure.

Expect Others to Adapt

The following are examples of flawed approaches that people have taken when they realize that they're operating with differing cultures. As the world's economic center of gravity shifts toward countries flush with an expanding sense of national pride and prosperity, such tactics and their underlying assumptions become even more damaging:

- "The world is gradually converging toward a common set of practices (mine), so it is not necessary for me to change."
- "We all work for the same company, and our corporate culture gives us a shared way of accomplishing tasks together."
- "In my function we all use pretty much the same methodology and think in the same way."

- "Others are learning to communicate with me, so I don't really need to adapt; I might confuse them by changing myself as well."
- "I've focused on learning our company's official language, and that is the most critical skill for me."

The common denominator for all of these approaches is a reluctance to change. This often stems from a feeling of being at full capacity already. Who wants to take on more complex challenges and more hours of responsibility in the day? Change is hard, especially when it involves the daily patterns, habits, and assumptions to which we default automatically much of the time. People who are living in a new country and trying to become part of the community often find each day to be both exhilarating and exhausting, as they must constantly pay attention to and experiment with unfamiliar practices. It is far easier to project one's own image on the world, to minimize any apparent differences (after all, we're all just human beings, aren't we?), and to succumb to the potentially career-limiting wish to adapt as little as possible. While these are natural human inclinations, they're also critically dysfunctional in a global context.

Employ "Universal" Techniques

Techniques of leadership and management touted as "universally effective" are often anything but and are frequently deeply embedded in a particular culture. "One-minute manager" or "authentic leadership" approaches can produce disastrous cross-border interactions if people do not adapt their styles and behaviors to different leadership contexts. Citizens of some parts of the world may see a one-minute manager as an insultingly superficial busybody who doesn't make the time for a genuine relationship, while so-called authenticity might easily become a pretext for "I can just be me, so my lack of knowledge about local business practices is no problem." People who handle global tasks as they would at home, using tried-and-true leadership approaches, typically stumble when working globally. Research increasingly stresses that it is critical to account for each specific global market context's distinctive features and to adjust one's approach accordingly, while being "adaptively authentic."[4] In other words, true authenticity requires a balance between what each person is already comfortable with and new behaviors he or she is willing to try that are better suited to a different environment.

Practice Do's and Don'ts

Nobody is gifted with an infinite set of lifetimes in which to master every culture or language. The "Kiss, Bow, or Shake Hands" type of book from a previous era that one can read on the plane is useful, but hardly enough. It is worthwhile to know a bit of local etiquette wherever you go in order to avoid immediately insulting your host. However, after the first 5 or 15 minutes, the discussion will soon move beyond those alluringly simple do's and don'ts. Going back to more kissing or bowing would appear strange or perturbing to the host at this point, and the person who aspires to be globally savvy needs to know what to do next.

Diet on Canned Culture

Cultural paradigms highlighting stark contrasts may easily become canned formulae that obscure as much as they help. A whole profession has developed around the task of delivering cultural training solutions for corporate clients seeking to work more effectively with people from other parts of the world; another related vocation prepares students for study or work abroad programs. Pressures to limit investments of time and expense can produce neat, packaged formulas for cultural learning that are often a poor fit with the realities that global leaders actually face. They sometimes even reinforce outmoded and inaccurate stereotypes that are offensive to people who have been labeled as members of a particular group. It is far better to start by speaking with the people involved on all sides of the cultural equation to gauge their work styles and task requirements, and then to offer customized recommendations and observations based on current data rather than on time-worn contrasts.

ACQUIRING CULTURAL COMPETENCY: EMBRACING NUANCE

An accurate and incisive approach to the topic of culture must also include individual variations, cultural change, history and paradox, and cultural units of different sizes and with different functions.

Individual Variations and Cultural Change

Although cultural patterns are consistent and predictable on a national scale, and individuals are always shaped by the cultures in which they are raised, it is vital to keep in mind that individual differences are present everywhere. Statements about national culture normally assume a range of behaviors in a bell curve of variations that include more atypical patterns: informal Japanese, risk-loving Swiss, chatty Finns, and shy Brazilians. Data-based generalizations can help us to recognize and respond to common forms of behavior, but they should not be allowed to harden into rigid stereotypes that smother individual variation.

Most people have a vivid sense of the many different personality types present in their own home town. Expatriates, too, usually realize that similar variability exists in their new home, with different body types, temperaments, levels of education, political persuasions, degrees of open-mindedness, and so on. Even in countries such as Japan that have a self-concept of national homogeneity, this alleged uniformity turns out to be more ideology than fact. In Japan's case, it was largely a product of historical efforts to unify culturally and linguistically diverse regions that once considered themselves to be independent countries and were often at war with one another.

An increasing number of people come from multicultural backgrounds or have been raised in multiple locations. They are in a unique position to fulfill "bridging" roles in corporate environments.[5] These individuals are not likely to fit the average profile for any single culture and are often quicker than others to notice changing circumstances. The current global economic transformation means that certain kinds of cultural knowledge are still relevant while others are already out of date, underlining the need to stay abreast of new developments.

Charlie the Chinese-Dane

Charlie sits across a table scattered with spicy plates at an upscale Sichuan restaurant in Beijing. It is mid-April and the sun pours through the floor to ceiling windows. Outside it is one of those days, rare now in Beijing, of bright blue skies and clean air. Charlie and his sister were the first two mainland Chinese children to immigrate to Denmark in the 1980s. He returned to Beijing 14 years ago and now works as the APAC representative for a multinational telecom company, Japanese-owned with European operations managed out of Denmark.

"You know, it is easy for me to talk to people about Denmark because the culture hasn't changed that much. When I meet people who are preparing to travel there for work, I know what they will experience there. I have this short little guide book to Danish culture, and I use it because the information is all still valid today. And this will probably be accurate in 30 years as well," Charlie says.

"You can't say this about China. Things that were true about China 10 years ago are not true today. If you are not here on the ground, with your finger to the pulse of these changes, you very quickly become irrelevant. Your knowledge is no longer valid. I read books written even five years ago, with examples about Chinese culture, and they are already out of date. They come across as very passé. And I think, 'Oh, this writer used to live in China, but he hasn't been back for a while.'

"For example, everything you learned at your company before coming to China about the importance of banquets, how to host here, how to toast your customers, and what gifts to give to develop the right relationships is much less relevant now. The current government's anticorruption

(Continued)

(Continued)

campaign means that government officials and top executives do not want to be drawing attention to themselves. Far fewer people are going out for banquets at nice hotels, and they will probably not let you take them out for a flashy occasion.

"All the companies and officials have quickly erected a no-gift policy. The luxury goods industry has been impacted. Macau has taken a huge hit. Conspicuous consumption is completely out, and no one wants that Macau stamp on their passport because they could face questions about where they got the kind of money you need in order to gamble at those VIP clubs. So companies are scrambling to recalibrate their knowledge about how to operate and to maintain their relationships with important contacts.

"This is just one example of how China is changing. If you are far away and relying on an outdated version of how this country works, then you are making all the wrong decisions."

Changes like the ones Charlie is describing are difficult to fully assess while they are in process. The importance that Chinese businesspeople place on close personal relationships is likely to continue, but this will be expressed in different ways, and there may be considerable variation depending upon location—Beijing is the seat of China's government, but other parts of China have sometimes lived according to the adage, "Heaven is high and the emperor is far away." As government policies evolve, it is possible that the country will revert to previous patterns or discover new ones. The only certainties are the need to stay on top of these changes and the value of intercultural bridge persons like Charlie in explaining them to others.

History and Paradox

Cultural learning also needs to be more historical and alert to contradictions. Most Chinese families carry memories—seldom discussed outside a small number of close relatives—of where their original homes were located and the deeply traumatic struggles of their grandparents or great-grandparents to stay alive during the Japanese invasion, the civil war between communists and nationalists, and subsequent social upheavals during the Great Leap Forward and Cultural Revolution. The war, genocide, famine, and chaos of the twentieth century have left an imprint that may be reflected in the attitudes of even the most polished and privileged young employees in a modern city like Shanghai. Members of China's urban professional classes, for example, were persecuted and sent to the countryside for reeducation during the Cultural Revolution—using pickaxes to break up ice in irrigation ditches rather than playing the piano or practicing medicine. Surviving members of their families eventually returned to the cities, and their grandchildren are now part of the workforce. So even the well-meaning parental advice that a young person might receive from parents to seek out a stable government job or profession holds echoes from a previous era.

There are similar nuances and points of emphasis in any given culture. It is impossible to fully understand the tensions between Russia and Ukraine, for example, without knowing the history of two invasions of Russia from the west—one led by Napoleon in 1812 and the other ordered by Hitler in 1941—that resulted in desperate wars for national survival and became part of every Russian schoolchild's education. During the Crimean War of 1853–1855, which has been largely forgotten outside of Russia, hundreds of thousands of Russian soldiers also died fighting against France, Great Britain, and Turkey over control of some of the same areas that have recently been under dispute again.

Culture is also replete with paradoxes that are often lost in simplistic comparisons. Each dimension of culture actually has many subcategories that open up further questions. The United States is commonly labeled as an egalitarian culture, but the gap in compensation between ordinary employees and top executives is far wider than in other advanced economies. Although major cities in China, including Shanghai and Guangzhou, have become hotbeds of entrepreneurial activity, economic risk taking is balanced with an understandable longing for stable prosperity and certainty on the part of people who retain their elders' memories of life-threatening insecurity. Families who have more recently arrived in urban areas also retain nostalgia for their agrarian roots, even if they have voted with their feet in favor of the faster pace and higher risks of city life.[6]

Culture and Concentric Circles

Culture itself is better understood as a series of concentric circles denoting groups of increasing scope. Its manifestations range from the habits of a family to those of a community, team, organization, country, or region. The nesting of such interrelated cultural units according to size is not a new idea. Confucius noted the relationship between families, states, and kingdoms, and advised that the health of a kingdom is grounded in the health of the families within it—that is, the most basic cultural microcosm.

In today's world, each individual is probably engaged with at least several of the circles shown in Figure 3.3 during the course of daily life. The same person may take on different roles and patterns of behavior depending on the cultural context. There are other more thematic or specialized cultural units as well: schools, churches, the

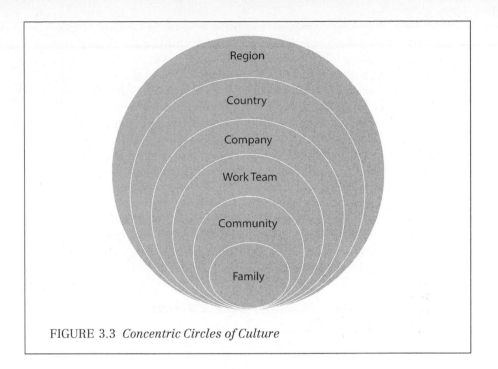

FIGURE 3.3 *Concentric Circles of Culture*

military, and professional groups such as engineers, accountants, or lawyers.

National culture is one among various sources of cultural influence; people may identify more closely with their family, community, or profession, each of which impacts and is impacted by national cultural norms. Civil strife in many conflict zones such as Nigeria, Egypt, or Sudan can be attributed in part to the fact that some residents identify more closely with a particular religious group, ethnicity, or tribe than with the nation as a whole.

A major cross-border acquisition typically involves multiple layers of culture, each of which needs to be handled in different ways. People from different national cultures are suddenly thrown together and asked to function at higher levels of performance; they urgently need to acquire cultural competence of the kind described earlier in this chapter. Meanwhile, corporate cultures frequently come into conflict, business units are modified or eliminated, work teams and functions must integrate new members belonging to complex matrix structures, and local communities are affected. The merger itself could be derailed because one or more functional "tribes"—say R&D, manufacturing, or sales—rebels against the new ownership structure, or the organizational cultures and their embedded systems turn out to be incompatible.

Cultural transformation occurs most readily in smaller groups. Organizational change initiatives have the best chance to take root initially within smaller-scale teams; as time goes on, a snowball effect can ultimately extend to larger business units and, eventually, the entire organization. National cultures normally change at a more glacial pace; many expatriates who seek to alter their host country's practices have learned to their dismay that such a goal is not feasible. Social crises or new technologies—railroads, automobiles, the Internet—may provide the impetus for larger numbers of people and even whole countries to change their daily habits and perspectives, but the process is seldom swift and in some cases requires centuries. And even with such changes, underlying cultural patterns often remain consistent; for example, cars have reinforced individualism in countries where most people drive to work alone, while serving literally as a community vehicle in other places where extended families ride together in the back of a single truck.

BEYOND CULTURE: OTHER PUZZLE PIECES

Recent research by the Corporate Leadership Council (CLC) confirms the value of cultural competency, but also emphasizes that this alone is not enough to succeed as a leader in today's global environment. In one of the largest and most recent empirical studies on the characteristics of global leaders, the CLC collected data on 11,500 leaders from around the world—all of whom were serving in roles with strategic, profit and loss, and operational responsibilities across more than one country. The CLC's research found that lack of intercultural skills does, in fact, impede aspiring leaders and their organizations. Leaders with lower intercultural skill ratings were significantly less likely to be identified as high-performing global leaders. However, it appears that there are also limits to the positive impact of higher levels of cultural competency, as indicated in Figure 3.4. According to the CLC, "Although not having intercultural skills can derail a global leader, it does not differentiate good and great global leaders."[7] In other words, simply being a master at working with foreign counterparts does not guarantee that you will flourish in a cross-border leadership role.

What is it then that enables global leaders to perform at the highest level? Culture *is* an important piece of a larger puzzle. When global leaders analyze any business problem, they must consider a broad range of factors that could include individual personalities, functional specialties, levels of skill and experience, gender and generational differences, technical issues, resource constraints, political power struggles, and methods of corporate governance. Figure 3.5 illustrates the types of issues that frequently have a causal role along with culture.

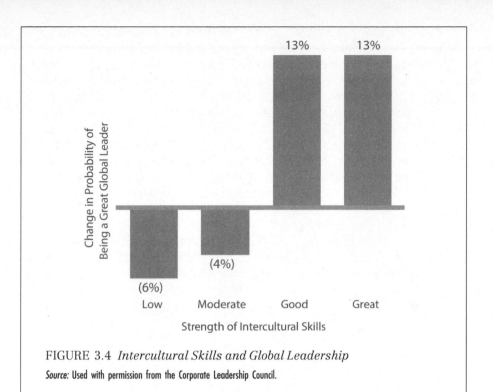

FIGURE 3.4 *Intercultural Skills and Global Leadership*
Source: Used with permission from the Corporate Leadership Council.

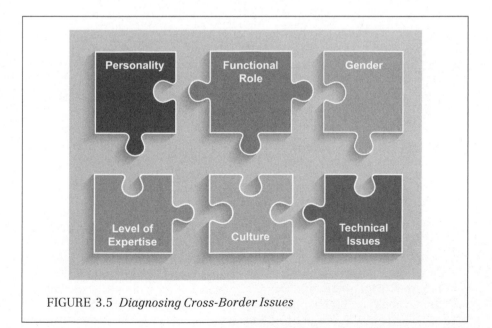

FIGURE 3.5 *Diagnosing Cross-Border Issues*

In addition to cultural competency, leaders in global roles must develop a keen awareness of the dynamic nature of the global markets described in Chapter 1. Shifting global power relations are upending systems that have been used to define and make sense of the world for generations. Today many geographical borders are increasingly permeable, and personal identities are often more fluid and less tied to a specific culture or nationality. New markets are forming, connecting in different ways, and transforming the way business takes place. Technological advances are rapidly flattening economic opportunity, creating more borderless connections, and shaping consumer demands. Within this changing mix, cultural influences may belong more in the foreground or in the background when diagnosing root causes and formulating viable solutions.

It is tempting to either trivialize the impact of culture or to make it the single prism through which events are interpreted. Both approaches are flawed and reductionistic. One such viewpoint minimizes the significance of culture altogether, depicting it with quaint images such as folk costumes, indigenous foods, and exchanges of name cards. Culture is seen as separate from "business," which is considered to be more serious and practical: "Now let's get down to business." The problem with this perspective is that nearly every aspect of business is permeated with cultural attitudes and behaviors. "Common sense" forms of buying and selling, managing employees, communicating important messages, providing customer service, transferring knowledge, and negotiating agreements differ considerably from one environment to the next, and are shaped by organizational, national, and industry cultural norms.[8]

Those who are convinced of the importance of culture, on the other hand, tend to be reductionistic in their own way, interpreting nearly every cross-border business challenge in terms of national cultural differences. Like the government-run shop in a totalitarian state where, regardless of what the customer requests, the owner slaps the same ugly fish on the counter, a passionate interculturalist may attempt to address every problem with the same set of national culture dimensions. Many issues have multiple causes, and it is useful to do more than just wield the same cultural hammer that makes every problem look like a nail (although the hammer is also quite handy when you need it).

In fact, some differences in national cultures appear to have greater significance than others. Data from the more than 64,000 people who have filled out the current version of the GlobeSmart Profile[SM] indicate that South Korea, Japan, and China are the most different from other countries in the world across all of the cultural dimensions combined in terms of their average profile results—they are also quite different from each other. There are clusters of countries that are much more alike, such as the United Kingdom and its former colonies Canada and Australia, or near neighbors like Denmark and the Netherlands.[9] Depending on the national origins of people involved in a particular cross-border interaction, these kinds of similarities and differences could make cultural contrasts more or less striking or critical.

Other causal factors besides culture are typically important as well. Cultural influences—in the form of distinct "habits of the mind," shaped by interactions with particular environments and passed down across generations—affect all human activities, including politics, education, the military, governmental institutions, and the economy. Even a country's tax laws and the responses of citizens to them, for example, provide rich indicators of cultural norms. But if a given cross-border business challenge is analyzed and broken down into the various ingredients that comprise it, culture may or may not turn out to be a primary causal factor, and is most likely one among several. There are other perfectly reasonable explanations for common business issues.

Oven Delivery in Shanghai

A current resident of Shanghai, who formerly lived in the U.K., describes her recent experience in ordering a new oven for her apartment:

"Most multinationals don't understand the pace of this market or their competition here and what they are up against. I get up on a Sunday morning and decide I need a new oven for my kitchen. I go online and choose one. The next step in the process asks me, 'When would you like that delivered? In a couple of hours?' I click the yes button, thinking, 'Yes, please.' 'Would you like to pay by cash, credit, or debit card on delivery to your home?' 'I will pay with my debit card, thank you very much.' So within three hours on a Sunday, I have a new oven delivered to my place, carried up four flights of stairs, and then the delivery guy swipes my card and I am done. Oh, and all of this delivery work was for free.

"The same is true for my groceries—for anything I want. The e-commerce business has gone wild in China and is combined with uniquely local service expectations and offerings. There are actually very few multinationals that can compete on this basis. They don't know what hit them. If I had to do the same thing in the U.K., they would deliver as far as my John Lewis store and tell me I could pick it up in four days' time. I would pay by credit card online and there would be a fee in place for anything faster than four days. If I wanted someone to deliver the oven to my house, they would tell me that the road is too narrow to drive the delivery truck through and charge me as much as the oven itself in delivery fees, and then I would need to make the delivery men a cup of tea and thank them so much for walking up the three steps at the front of the garden. And don't even think of asking for any of this to happen on a Sunday."

What accounts for this stark difference in the process for oven ordering and delivery in Shanghai versus the United Kingdom, and how could a multinational company go about making itself more competitive? Causal factors behind the Shanghai scene described here are likely to include the quality of infrastructure, both online and in the supply chain (software, networking, warehouse logistics, delivery vans), proximity to manufacturing facilities, population density, economies of scale, labor costs, and the purchasing power of the Chinese currency. There are probably also causal factors more directly influenced by culture—although not just national culture—such as consumer expectations, customer/vendor relationships, holidays, work habits, and existing corporate processes and procedures.

It appears that relationship-oriented Chinese companies, presently constrained by government policies that discourage lavish social events, are finding new ways to create tight bonds with customers through user-friendly online interactions and hassle-free delivery service. Such bonds are further intensified because their web-based platform serves as a means for customers wary of official pronouncements to build virtual relationships with each other and get the real story about products and events. The sense of status some individual Chinese feel *vis-à-vis* other countries in the world has undergone a reversal as this transformation continues. Another person living in Shanghai comments:

> *We used to worship foreigners and their status was very high. So these foreigners came in and were treated very well; we admired and wanted to learn from them. I remember I used to go online on Western sites and just be in awe. But now the things and the people that I used to look up to no longer seem so special or worth my time. I never look at them anymore because they seem slow and outdated to me. Instead I do everything on Taobao (Alibaba's consumer megasite), and it is a million times faster and easier; the service is also far better.*

With the oven delivery example in mind, a company seeking to be competitive in both China and the United Kingdom would need, first and foremost, leaders who fully comprehend both environments as well as circumstances in other major markets. It is particularly difficult to cultivate such leadership if the organization's headquarters is located in a slow-growth market. Company leaders must also be able to bridge the gap between the two locations, weighing both how to deliver prompt, superb service in Shanghai and how to bring best practices to other locations in ways that raise its global standards without adding a prohibitive level of cost.

The CLC study cited at the beginning of this section reinforces these points and provides useful hints as to other key capabilities for global leaders who seek to perform at the highest level. In general, the CLC's findings fall in the area of "expertise." Activities and competencies beyond intercultural skills found to be strongly correlated with successful global leadership include:

- Having ready access to information about global market and organizational issues.
- Spending more time with global peers and clients.
- Focusing on strategic talent management.
- Exerting influence effectively across geographical, functional, and business lines.[10]

Previous research by the authors has confirmed the need for global leadership expertise in various forms that include but also go beyond cultural fluency. Successful global leaders do more than just adapt; they also add value based upon their functional knowledge and leadership experience in accomplishing key tasks around the world.[11] Each of the individuals portrayed so far—Ingrid, Alan, Shiguang, Sohail, Atul, Jas, Michael, Moses, and Charlie—will be at their best when they combine cultural competence with a keen awareness of changes in global markets as well as their own subject matter expertise.

Subsequent chapters will explore other specific cross-border challenges that most leaders are likely to encounter—global teams, inclusive leadership, mergers and acquisitions, innovation, and ethical dilemmas—as well as hard-won learnings from companies and individuals that have struggled to address them. Culture will continue to be a theme in each chapter; however, we will seek to neither overestimate nor underestimate its role. Habits of the mind are ubiquitous and inescapable, yet cultural patterns can be altered. It is important to analyze global business challenges using the full puzzle set of possible causal factors, and to formulate solutions that incorporate a range and depth of task-based expertise.

WHAT YOU CAN DO

- Complete your GlobeSmart Profile[SM]. Compare your profile with a country or countries in which you have an interest; click on gaps between your profile and selected country profiles to receive advice about how best to bridge each gap. (http://learning.aperianglobal.com/go/profile).

- Ask another person—a counterpart from another culture or country, a workplace colleague from a different function, a teenager at home, or a significant other—to complete the profile and compare it with yours.

(Continued)

(Continued)

• Go beyond national cultural comparisons to find out more about your counterpart's background, personality, and other kinds of cultural affiliations at work or at home.

• Consider what additional factors along with national culture may be important for leadership issues that you are dealing with—and the relative weight of each point:

  ▪ Individual personalities

  ▪ Functional specialties

  ▪ Levels of skill and experience

  ▪ Gender and generational differences

  ▪ Technical factors

  ▪ Resource constraints

  ▪ Infrastructure

  ▪ Supply chain logistics

  ▪ Political power struggles

  ▪ Methods of corporate governance

Global Teams: Beyond Facilitation

Why Matrix Teams Fail and How to Get Better Results

WORKING IN THE MATRIX

One of the biggest visible impacts of the world's shifting center has been the transformation of organizational structures from centralized, hierarchical models to fluid, matrixed organisms. The transformation has been an evolutionary necessity for organizations trying to scale their operations across multiple geographies.

The matrix structure is a technique for managing an organization through a series of overlapping reporting relationships to create balance between the needs of various functions, geographies, business units, and product groups. Figure 4.1 depicts these common elements of many matrix organizations—some may have two or three and others all four. This structure is designed to facilitate rapid response to change in two or more environments, while flatter structure and multiple reporting lines permit a freer exchange of information. All these elements are critical to organizational agility within a fast-paced global economic reality.

Matrix organizational structures are commonly deemed the best antidote to unhealthy silos that isolate groups of employees from one another in separate units. Such silos are conducive to finger-pointing—engineering blames sales for not selling great products, but meanwhile sales blames engineering for not making what customers want—along

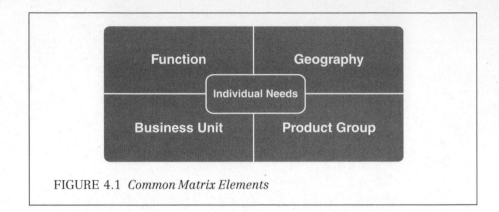

FIGURE 4.1 *Common Matrix Elements*

with decreased accountability for collaborative efforts, and fragmented decision making. The intentional tension built into a matrix organization is designed to ensure that employees take into account a broader set of information and priorities beyond their own roles. Every matrix team has the ultimate goal of serving the best interests of the company as a whole.

Matrix Challenges

Although matrix structures have proven their value in breaking down silos, employees in such organizations face a variety of challenges. They must serve the various and sometimes conflicting needs of numerous stakeholders. Moreover, they are often widely dispersed, which can mean that matrix team members and stakeholders rarely, if ever, have the chance to meet. There can also be fragmented accountability and confusion around priorities and procedures for joint decision making. An Italian functional head for a German manufacturing components supplier describes his organization's recent transition to a global matrix model:

> *We have to learn to live with potential conflicts between local and corporate structures. This is difficult to navigate because the responsibilities and lines are more complicated. The tension of the matrix is always there. There is constant ambiguity. Now, we all have at least one functional boss, if not two. And then, on top of that, we have a local boss. So every employee needs to navigate between many bosses and priorities and conflicts of interest. We may be pushed in two or three different directions. How should we navigate in this new, ambiguous world?*

LEADING A MATRIX TEAM

A matrix structure's success, or lack thereof, is primarily a function of team health and team members' ability to navigate its complex reporting lines. Any matrix is really a collection of interconnected teams. Each team needs to operate at peak efficiency, and the collaboration between teams needs to be equally efficient in order for the organization to run well.

For team leaders in a matrix, what are the critical competencies that will ensure success? Previous team development efforts have focused on better intercultural facilitation, project management, and technology for virtual communication. However, our research shows that a leader's ability to correctly position the team in a matrix environment is a more critical factor for success.

A Software Development Team

Rick is a UK-based project manager, heading up a short-term software development initiative with a team in India. The team lead in India is Bhavesh, who is Rick's main point of contact for the initiative.

FIGURE 4.2 *Software Development Team*

Rick: Hello, this is Rick Schaeffer. Is anyone on the line?

Bhavesh: Hello Rick. I am Bhavesh Chatterjee, and I have with me Azim Ahmed, our developer; Priya Vikram, our designer; and Sanjay Ramaswamy, our test engineer.

Rick: Hi everyone, I'm Rick. I'm the project manager for the F-17 expense tracking tool. Now this is a kickoff meeting to discuss the development of the reporting mechanism. Did you receive the documents I sent?

Bhavesh: Yes, we did.

(Continued)

(Continued)

Rick: Good. I'd like to use this hour to go over the functional spec and let you guys ask questions. Okay?

Bhavesh (unvoiced thought): I wonder what the priority of this project is? I will check with Manish, my manager.

Bhavesh: Okay Rick.

  After reviewing the specifications in detail and talking through project milestones and deliverables, Rick wraps up the meeting.

Rick: So those are the features and functionality that we need in this reporting tool. Do you have any questions?

Bhavesh (unvoiced thought): The requirements are clear, but there are many ways to interpret this information. I don't want to ask detailed questions because when I have done so in the past, senior people were very impatient and told me I was "overthinking."

Bhavesh: No . . . no—they seem very clear.

Rick: We need to get this developed by October 14th. That gives you about a month. Do you think you can do it?

Bhavesh (unvoiced thought): I need to check with Manish. We have other work, and Gandhi Jayanti and Ramzan are coming up. But I don't want to sound as if I am unwilling or making excuses.

Bhavesh: Yes . . . we will do our best.

Rick: I will be checking in with you for our first milestone meeting in two weeks. In the meantime, if you have any questions, or if there are any problems, please don't hesitate to call or e-mail me.

Bhavesh: Yes, definitely!

  Two weeks after the initial meeting, Rick has the first scheduled update meeting with the team, during which Bhavesh assures Rick that the development is progressing. After that, Rick hears nothing. He e-mails Bhavesh to confirm their next meeting on October 4th, when they are scheduled to review a sample. Rick receives no response to his e-mail to Bhavesh, so he calls him. But the previous day was the birthday of Mahatma Gandhi, a national holiday known as Gandhi Jayanti, and Bhavesh is away briefly enjoying time with his family. When Rick can't reach Bhavesh, he tries calling Azim.

Rick: Hello Azim. This is Rick Schaeffer.

Azim (unvoiced thought): Why is he calling me? He should be talking to Bhavesh; he's the team lead.

Azim: Oh, hello Mr. Rick.

Rick: Listen, I haven't been able to reach Bhavesh to confirm our meeting tomorrow, and I just wanted to find out what's going on. Over here, we have the saying, "No news is good news"—but I'm not sure if you have the same saying over there?

Azim: Er, I didn't get you.

Rick: Never mind. Um, how's everything going?

(Continued)

(Continued)

Azim (unvoiced thought): It is really not my place to make this report.

Azim: Okay . . . yesterday was a holiday—Gandhi Jayanti, as you may know—and it is almost the end of Ramzan.

Rick: Right, right—but are we on track? We're less than two weeks away from the deadline, and I haven't gotten the sample for tomorrow's meeting.

Azim: Yes, Ramzan is an important time of year for many of us.

Rick: That's nice, Azim, uh, but can you give me an update regarding the reporting tool?

Azim (unvoiced thought): Bhavesh is the team lead; if I talk to Rick about the problems we are having, Bhavesh will lose face, and besides, we may be able to fix them before the deadline.

Azim: Yes . . . we are working very hard to meet your deadline.

Rick: Can you send the sample? I'd feel better if we had something to look at before we meet.

Azim (unvoiced thought): I don't think Bhavesh would be happy to know that Rick bypassed him with this request.

Azim: I will tell Bhavesh your request.

Rick: Excellent, if you can get that to me before the end of your day, I'd appreciate it.

Azim (unvoiced thought): I will tell Bhavesh, and he will decide what should be done.

Azim: I'll do what I can.

Rick doesn't receive the sample, and is asked to reschedule the meeting. After another frustrating teleconference that takes place the following week, he finally gets a functional reporting package one week after the feature was due, but there are still several significant problems with it that could have been resolved through better teamwork.

Common Best Practices

There are many steps that Rick could take as the overall head of the team in this scenario to facilitate more productive interactions:

- Travel to India to meet the team members in person and learn more about them.
- Provide a big-picture introduction to the team's efforts.
- Set more tightly spaced milestones during the early project stages.
- Check in with Bhavesh and other team counterparts more frequently.
- Schedule one-on-one conversations with Bhavesh so that he can raise issues without losing face in front of his team members.
- Ask open-ended rather than yes/no questions. For example, "What do you think is a feasible time frame for completing this project?" "What other priorities do your team members have?"

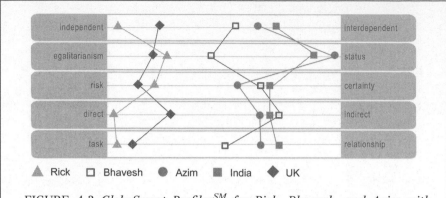

FIGURE 4.3 *GlobeSmart Profiles^{SM} for Rick, Bhavesh, and Azim with Country Averages for India and the United Kingdom*

- Use reflective listening, paraphrasing, and summarizing what others are saying to further draw out team members who show signs of uncertainty or hesitation.

All five of the cultural dimensions we introduced in Chapter 3 are relevant to this team as well. Figure 4.3 compares the profiles of individual team members along with the country averages for India and the United Kingdom. The contrasts between the team members, whose profiles correspond roughly to their country profiles—with some individual variation, as is normally the case—are easy to discern in the team members' interactions. Each team participant needs to "style-switch" in order to be more effective.

If Rick were to recognize the more interdependent and hierarchical nature of the Indian team members, their hesitation to take risks and to share problems directly, and how their comfort level is enhanced once they establish a personal relationship, he would probably alter his approach. For instance, when Bhavesh responds, "Yes, we will do our best," in their initial team meeting, Rick would be less likely to take this response at face value. Instead, he'd recognize it as an expression of discomfort, and find ways to explore possible underlying issues. He would also be better able to recognize Azim's hesitation in responding to questions that he feels should be directed to his boss Bhavesh, and he might try a different approach that does not put Azim on the spot.

Indian team members such as Bhavesh or Azim could also contribute to more productive teamwork. To the extent that Bhavesh understands Rick's independent, egalitarian, risk-oriented, direct, and task-focused tendencies as culturally-based, he will find it easier to anticipate and respond to Rick's requests without being offended or appearing evasive. He, too, could take constructive steps such as suggesting that Rick come to India to meet the team, budget permitting, or that they schedule regular one-on-one calls that would allow him to speak more frankly. Likewise, he might be more direct in offering realistic deadlines for project completion and in describing problems with competing priorities. And when any of the Indian team members encounter unexpected obstacles and delays, they could reach out to Rick in order to keep him in the loop, even though they might normally avoid bringing nettlesome problems to a more senior foreign counterpart.

GLOBAL TEAM PERFORMANCE: BEYOND FACILITATION

Yet even with all of the improvements that the team can make through culturally savvy facilitation on the part of the team leader and mutual style-switching, there is a deeper issue that could still derail the team completely. As we can detect in Bhavesh's unvoiced thoughts, he is not sure whether this project is a priority for Manish, his local manager. If he goes to Manish and is instructed to put other projects first, Rick is going to receive limited cooperation no matter how hard he tries or how many excellent facilitation techniques he uses.

A first step for any leader or potential leader of a matrix team, including Rick, is to ask, "*Is this team set up for success?*" The checklist of questions in Sidebar 4.1 is a good place for the team leader to start before even agreeing to take on the job. For any significant team initiative, the answers to all of these questions should be positive in order for the team and its leader to have a strong chance of succeeding.

SIDEBAR 4.1   GLOBAL TEAM LEADER CHECKLIST: SEVEN KEY QUESTIONS

1. Is there executive sponsorship for the team?
2. Have the team and its goals been established with buy-in from key people in each relevant part of the matrix: geographies, functions, business units, product groups?
3. Are there other key stakeholders (customers, suppliers, different parts of the organization), and do we have their support as well?
4. Is it possible to establish a shared vision and common objectives for team members?
5. Is there a shared sense of urgency and level of priority among team members?
6. What percentage of their time will team members be devoting to this effort?
7. Are other resources essential to the team's success, and are these available?

Each team needs effective executive sponsorship and organizational alignment in order to function at its best. In the absence of this kind of supportive context, the ties between team members, subgroups, and stakeholders are likely to be fragile and also to entail divergent objectives. The team leader will have to invest considerable time and effort identifying sources of misalignment or resistance, shepherding various stakeholders, and seeking buy-in without any direct authority. This is an uphill battle at best. An effective team sponsor can be instrumental in gaining stakeholder support across the matrix and orchestrating a collaborative rollout of the team's efforts.

Negative responses to the seven checklist questions may be a critical indication that more groundwork needs to be in place before the team's efforts are kicked off, or that the project itself should be reconsidered. Warning signs for prospective or current team leaders might include replies from team sponsors such as:

- "I haven't had time to speak to the other geographies yet, but it's a terrific idea for you to do that!"
- "I'm not sure what else your team members will have on their plates in addition to their work for you."
- "At this point we can't change anybody's annual objectives except for yours, but you're very persuasive. I'm sure you can convince your team members of the urgency of this project!"
- "Just make it work somehow; this is an important initiative for us!"

Here is the kind of meeting that should have happened *before* Rick, Bhavesh, and the rest of the development team had their first team call.

Andrea, the business unit head, anticipates that the upcoming software development project will be a matrix effort, and organizes a videoconference with Rick Schaeffer, Manish Gupta, who runs the IT operation in Noida, near New Delhi, and Bhavesh Chatterjee.

Andrea: Thanks for joining me. First I'd like to introduce everyone. Manish and I worked together last year on a big project for the sales team. Manish, it's good to see you again on the videoconference screen! Please allow me to introduce Rick Schaeffer, whom I've selected to be the project manager for this new expense tracking project.

Manish: Good to see you again as well, Andrea! It's a pleasure to meet you, Rick! This is Bhavesh Chatterjee, one of our most experienced software developers, who is currently running several projects. Bhavesh will be working with you as the new team lead here in Noida.

(Continued)

(Continued)

Andrea and Rick: Nice to meet you, Bhavesh!

Andrea: Before we get started on this new team effort, I'd like to make sure that we're all on the same page about what we're trying to accomplish. You've received information on the new expense tracking tool and its importance for our business unit's objectives to improve operating efficiency. Any questions about this?

Manish: If I understand correctly, IT's role here will be to build the product based on specifications that have been outlined, so the scoping has already been done. Do you anticipate any further scoping issues? We are juggling a number of different priorities at the moment, so it would be good to know the priority of this project relative to the security software that we've been asked to upgrade.

Andrea: I'd appreciate it if you could ask Bhavesh and his team members to devote at least 50 percent of their time to this project over the next month. We don't want to derail the security software, but as you know, that is a longer-term project that people will be working on for the rest of the year. What do you think about the scoping, Rick? You've looked through the specifications. Do you think any modifications are required?

Rick: It seems relatively straightforward, although I am sure Bhavesh will have a number of questions about the project details. It would be good for Bhavesh and me to set up a one-on-one call before we bring in the rest of the team.

Manish: This sounds like an excellent idea. Bhavesh, it's fine to go ahead and schedule to meet with Rick, and please let me know immediately if it looks like your team will require more time for the development. We'll have a lot of schedule juggling to do if this takes any longer than six weeks.

Bhavesh: Happy to do so. Yes, I will keep you informed regularly. Rick, shall we communicate by e-mail to set up a separate time?

Rick: Sure, that would be great.

Manish: In the future, perhaps we could consider a simpler project setup. I know how busy our good project managers like Rick are, and it's challenging to run a team that is far away. Bhavesh might be able to help at an earlier stage with the scoping, and then he and his team could take more responsibility for the project from end to end.

Andrea: Thanks for the recommendation, Manish. Perhaps we could work toward this through the current project. Rick, please help us and Bhavesh to think about any skills he would like to build, both on the technical side and in stakeholder management, and work with him to get to the next level in terms of end-to-end accountability.

THE DATA ON GLOBAL TEAMS

In order to understand the factors underlying the scenarios above, it is helpful to take a closer look at the data available on global teams. Over the past decade, the authors have gathered survey results from 2,240 teams and a total of nearly 17,000 team members located around the world. This is one of the largest available sources of data anywhere regarding the performance challenges global teams encounter.[1] Figure 4.4 depicts the seven survey elements, while Sidebar 4.2 shows their ranking from highest to lowest scoring. Cultural diversity is at the center of the model, surrounded by more process-oriented stages of team development; the outer layer juxtaposes virtual and face-to-face forms of communication.

Contrary to what some professional facilitators or consultants might expect, global team participants see themselves as being relatively skilled at virtual communication methods and at communicating with remote team members. Items from these survey elements are generally rated at the top end of the scale. Team members give

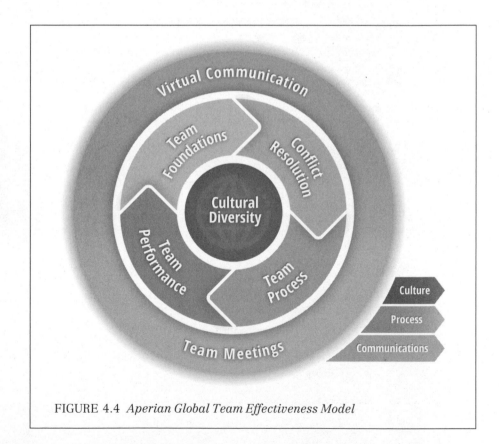

FIGURE 4.4 *Aperian Global Team Effectiveness Model*

SIDEBAR 4.2 GLOBAL TEAM ELEMENTS RANKED FROM HIGHEST TO LOWEST SCORING

- Cultural Diversity
- Virtual Communication
- Team Performance
- Team Foundations
- Team Meetings
- Conflict Resolution
- Team Process

---

themselves high marks for effective virtual communication and for refraining from negative judgments based on overt differences in culture and language. The top-ranking survey items across this very large set of responses, with their corresponding elements, can be seen in Sidebar 4.3.

The most challenging global teamwork elements turn out to be team process and conflict resolution. Specific items that survey respondents gave the lowest ratings focus on systemic issues such as rewards, collaboration with other parts of the organization, and metrics. It also appears that team members can rely too easily on virtual communication and lack an effective balance of virtual and face-to-face contacts. Finally, they struggle to solve problems together when conflicts arise. Sidebar 4.4 shows the items consistently rated lowest by survey respondents.

Each of these global team weaknesses can be directly linked to characteristics of matrix organizations. As with Rick's project team depicted at the outset of this chapter, teams with matrix structures that harbor clashing priorities and reward systems are likely to have a hard time achieving their performance goals. All team members need to

---

SIDEBAR 4.3 HIGHEST-RATED SURVEY ITEMS (STRONGLY AGREE)

- Team members effectively use e-mail, voice mail, and other virtual methods of communication (virtual communication).
- Team members are able to communicate with team members in distant locations (virtual communication).
- Team members avoid making negative judgments about other members because of cultural and language differences (cultural diversity).

SIDEBAR 4.4   LOWEST-RATED SURVEY ITEMS (STRONGLY DISAGREE)

- The team's reward system encourages cooperation and shared effort among team members (team process).
- The team receives the resources and cooperation it needs from other parts of the company (team foundations).
- The team has accurate and objective metrics in place to measure the results of its work (team process).
- The team effectively combines face-to-face interactions with virtual communication (virtual communica-tion).
- The team has an effective procedure for resolving problems among team members (conflict resolution).

---

know where in the matrix their most critical stakeholders are located in order to receive the resources and cooperation they will need. Should they focus on the interests of particular functions, geographies, business units, or product groups? The metrics upon which team members are evaluated must be aligned, even though annual objectives are typically set within the context of different organizational silos. And although team members may be highly skilled at virtual communication, getting together in person—particularly at the outset of the team effort—can help build personal relationships, develop a shared understanding of diverse stakeholders, and create an aligned set of team processes. With so many diverse team interests and countervailing matrix pressures, it is essential for global teams to cultivate shared methods of problem solving that enable them to view issues collaboratively rather than antagonistically.

Personal Differences?

Vasilis is a burly engineer and outdoorsman with a gray-speckled beard who is a global team head in a major high-tech equipment maker. He is much admired by colleagues for his technical expertise, and speaks with a wry and self-deprecating sense of humor.

"In the early days of our team project, there was not a lot of rapport among team participants. In fact, it would be fair to say that we didn't like each other very much. There were several team members based in other locations with whom I just seemed to be at odds. I attributed this to their abrasive personalities and stubborn adherence to personal agendas at the expense of the team. Frankly, I thought they were being selfish.

"We finally met face-to-face and began to more carefully analyze the chronic conflicts that were impeding our progress. We discovered that negative behaviors we had previously attributed to other team members—being unreliable, untrustworthy, or selfish—were not a matter of personal character or lack of good will, but rather the product of many forces that tended to pull team members apart. The members of our team each have their own place within a matrix organization

(Continued)

(Continued)

composed of various business units, functions, and geographies. We were being drawn in conflicting directions by the demands of different strategic objectives, stakeholders, reporting relationships, and metrics. When we began to look at these systemic issues more closely, we realized that most of our conflicts were due to such underlying causes. Soon we stopped finger-pointing and actually started to like each other! And although we still have plenty of challenges today, we have much stronger relationships and work together far better as a team."

Many leaders of dispersed multicultural teams eventually express frustrations similar to those experienced by Vasilis. Figure 4.5 portrays the divergent matrix influences he described that can undermine trust and alignment among team members without careful handling.

ORGANIZATIONAL ALIGNMENT AND TEAM FOUNDATIONS

Many team leaders have been thrust into their roles without the time or political latitude to work through checklist items such as executive sponsorship and organizational alignment. In addition to escalation strategies, which may or may not be feasible for leaders whose teams are

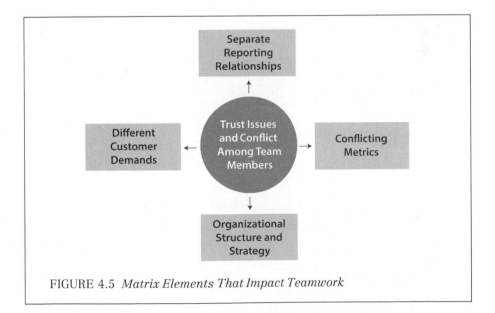

FIGURE 4.5 *Matrix Elements That Impact Teamwork*

already in motion, Figure 4.5 provides a simple analytical framework to begin to sort out possible reasons for conflicts between team members.

Our survey results strongly suggest that global team leaders also need to pay special attention to creating a sound "container" that they can use to align team members' efforts. A shared vision and business objectives—standard business guru prescriptions for teams getting started—are particularly difficult to establish and maintain if collaboration among team members is undermined by crosscurrents between different reward systems, stakeholder demands, metrics, and so on. Ingrained habits, whether they are process driven or formed based on organizational or national cultures, tend to be most tenacious and reflexive when conflicts occur. The more complex and matrixed the team structure, the more probable it is that such issues will surface. Although the need to balance competing interests is deliberately built into matrix organizational designs—the intentional tension referred to previously—most team leaders are thrust into their roles with minimal preparation (they literally "didn't get the memo" with the rationale for a matrix team) and must learn to navigate the matrix on their own.

One further set of data from the global team survey, the items rated by respondents as having the highest importance, offers insight for matrix team leaders about where else to focus in the early stages of team development besides on the Global Team Leader Checklist shared earlier. High-priority items identified in the survey results underline the value of paying special attention to the building blocks of team development, as four out of five items come from the Team Foundations element of the survey (see Sidebar 4.5). In other words, matrix teams are likely to face strains and struggles that homogeneous groups can master more readily, and they require foundations built on bedrock rather than on sand.

Wise team leaders will begin with extra attention to these items, and will go back to basics when conflicts emerge to reinforce a shared

---

SIDEBAR 4.5   FIVE HIGHEST PRIORITY ITEMS (MOST IMPORTANT)

1. The team receives the resources and cooperation it needs from other parts of the company (team foundations).

2. All members of the team are clear on their roles and responsibilities (team foundations).

3. There is a high level of trust among team members (team foundations).

4. The team's reward system encourages cooperation and shared effort among team members (team process).

5. All members of the team support and understand the team's goals (team foundations).

platform for all team activities. These priority items may include resource or systemic elements that are partly out of the team's control, but there are steps that team leaders can take with respect to each of them. (See Appendix A for a set of recommendations for what team leaders can do to address each item.)

Ironically, looking beyond the immediate task of facilitating interactions between team members makes for more effective facilitation in the long run. Knowledge of the wider matrix environment in which the team functions—and especially how this influences individual team members—will enable leaders to understand their team's dynamics more deeply, to address underlying structural issues where feasible, and to focus team-building efforts where they can have the greatest impact.

ENABLING NEW MATRIX LEADERS

Looking toward the future, it is important for global companies to position leaders from all backgrounds for success. This is true both for developing team leaders like Bhavesh or people such as Huang Shiguang, the Chinese expatriate in Germany portrayed in Chapters 1 and 2.

The matrix structure itself is particularly challenging for leaders from more hierarchical and relationship-based leadership cultures such as India and China for two reasons. First, the model creates ambiguity around who is in charge, and the "leader" or decision-maker can change on a project-to-project basis. Multiple reporting lines also create competing priorities and confusion around whom one should ultimately seek to please. One Chinese leader describes his perplexed response to a matrix organization:

> In China, there is always a head and this person is always the one with the authority. Everyone recognizes whose position is highest. But in Western countries, the authority or the head isn't always the person with the highest position. Many times someone is given the title of being the facilitator or coordinator and they have the authority in this certain situation. Authority often shifts in a matrix environment.

In addition, the matrix structure often strips leaders of their local relationship networks and asks them to do the same level of work leveraging a group of foreign strangers whom they may have never met face to face. One Indian leader compared this experience to having his limbs cut off. In response to these factors, many leaders prioritize their local business context, in which they often thrive, and withdraw from the global, matrix dynamics of the organization.

A global manufacturing company recently reorganized, deepening its matrix structure, taking decision-making power away from country directors and putting it with global functional councils. The leadership skills needed to operate within these councils are vastly different. As one leader put it:

Before, country-level leaders needed to be experts and made decisions with relative independence. They are now just one voice seeking to influence a joint global team decision. They have to understand the global business context and advocate decisions that are best for the entire global organization, not just their local context.

Matrix leaders are expected to articulate their points of view in the context of the holistic global business. This requires a cross-functional and cross-regional breadth of knowledge and experience, which is rare in certain locations. As a result, some leaders are perceived to favor the business needs of their region or country. This, in turn, damages their credibility at the global decision-making levels and leads to accusations of "lack of global or strategic mindset" or "lack of global business acumen." The vice-president of a global organization noted that an overly local focus damages a leader's ability to influence:

An influential leader is open-minded about whose idea may be the best idea, regardless of where it comes from. Influence is not just about pushing one's own idea onto others—because your idea may or may not be the best idea. Share the ideas, listen to others' ideas, then try to sell your idea if you have the best one. A good leader is one who is able to get the best ideas on the table.

What makes leadership in a global matrix particularly difficult for client-facing employees in fast-growth markets is the need for a high degree of competence in the *local* market coupled with *global* business skills and acumen. Local business acumen is nonnegotiable in these fiercely competitive environments. At the same time, leaders must be able to run regional operations or global business units as well as align with and drive global strategy in an integrated matrix environment. But the transition from the local-only leadership role into regional or global matrix roles is a big leap, and the skills needed to be successful in each role are often at odds with one another. Sometimes the very competencies making leaders indispensable in their home markets are also inhibiting their growth inthe global matrix.

New Competencies Required

Making the matrix work is all about getting the balance right. A regional HR director for a global manufacturer describes the new talent requirements she is trying to build as a result of the matrix demands:

> We live in a 3M world: Matrixed, Multicultural, and all over the Map. So your supplier is sitting in one continent, your employer in another, you are sitting in another, and your customer and supervisor are somewhere else. What we need to look at is: What are the global competencies needed to be successful in a 3M organization?

Enabling this balance requires both a different approach and a very different set of competencies. A regional head for a heavy machinery company describes the shift in this way:

> Our organization needs to grow leaders who have the maturity and ability to work in a variety of local environments and across cultures. Traditional organizations were structured "vertically" around functions and geography, but work is becoming more "horizontal." Cross-functional teams deliver complex products and services to and through global customers and supply chains.

> Each of us must reach out to other parts of the organization to solve problems for our customers, and this often requires us to understand different values and interests. In a matrix organization, this decentralization is particularly important because if the individual at the point of intersection of the reporting lines cannot exercise influence to get things done, then they will constantly be escalating for decisions. Constant escalation undermines the confidence of their managers and leads to a negative spiral of increasing control and escalation.

Bhavesh, Huang Shiguang, and other high-potential leaders from fast-growth markets face a crucial choice: Do they want to serve in global team leadership roles or focus on their home market? If they select the former, then they and their employers must systematically go about the task of cultivating three interlinked assets that will position them for long-term success. These are advantages that all team leaders need to acquire, but team leaders from newer markets must cultivate on an accelerated learning curve.

- **Cross-border relationships:** Developing a relationship strategy is just as vital as having a solid business strategy.

Questions for matrix team leaders: Who do you know already across the global organization? Who else do you need to know, including people in other functions, geographies, business units, or product groups? How will you get to know them?

- **Organizational savvy:** Determine whether your team is positioned for success in a matrix environment, and, if not, immediately address the problem areas.

    Questions for matrix team leaders: Is your team positioned for success within the organization (use the checklist in Sidebar 4.1)? Have you created a strong foundation for your team's success by placing special emphasis on key building blocks such as shared knowledge of team stakeholders, clarity about roles and responsibilities, and trust among team members (see Sidebar 4.5 and Appendix A)?

- **Influencing skills:** Critical abilities include being able to style-switch or frame-shift, adapting to new environments while remaining competent at home. Effective influencing means being able to serve as a shuttle diplomat between locations, helping people in each place to understand the other, and to accomplish tasks through integrating the work of different functions.

    Questions for matrix team leaders: What is your current repertoire of influencing skills and how could you augment it? For example, are you overly dependent on one strategy such as logical persuasion, asking people you know well for help, or trying to trade one favor for another? What will actually be most persuasive to your audience—what drives their behavior—and how can you adjust your current influencing style with your counterparts in mind?

WHAT YOU CAN DO

For Team Leaders

- Address the seven questions for matrix leaders in the Global Team Leader Checklist in Sidebar 4.1 on page 61.
- Focus on building and maintaining strong team foundations, including all the high priority items listed on page in Sidebar 4.5 on page 68.
- Implement the common facilitation best practices listed on pages 59 and 60.
- Create a GlobeSmart Profile^{SM} for your team and consider whether profile gaps between team members could be contributing to team challenges; discuss how the different cultural perspectives of team members could be leveraged for the benefit of the team.
- Use the GlobeSmart Teaming Assessment to diagnose team issues related to cultural diversity, team process, and communication; implement follow-up steps based on the results. You can learn more about this assessment at www.aperianglobal.com/learning-solutions.
- Ensure that you have the three assets effective team leaders need: cross-border relationships, organizational savvy, and influencing skills.

For Team Members

- Understand the matrix reporting lines of fellow team members with whom you are working most closely.
- Clarify roles and responsibilities between yourself and other members of the team.
- Build shared awareness of the competing priorities that may impact the ability of team members to focus on this project or team.
- Consider involving other matrix managers in the prioritization of the team tasks, timelines, and goals.
- Examine whether any current team challenges are based on personality conflicts or on underlying matrix tensions. Take a proactive role in building trust among team members.
- Support team leaders from other locations to cultivate the assets and skills they will need to be effective.

Global Inclusion: Beyond Race and Gender

Inclusive Leadership for Competitive Advantage

TAKING A BROADER APPROACH

Diversity and inclusion (D&I) initiatives are taking on different forms and must constantly renew their relevance as the world's economic center shifts. With the center of economic gravity moving east and south, the most visible manifestations of diversity—race and gender balance, for instance—are changing. In addition, companies are increasingly finding value in taking broader approaches to inclusiveness that embrace perspectives from different generations, functions, and thinking styles.

Diversity in Asia-Pacific

Alvin Wong is an R&D team leader based in his company's regional headquarters in Singapore. He is originally a Hong Kong Chinese—when he was 12 years old his family immigrated to the United

(Continued)

(Continued)

Kingdom, and he later went to graduate school in the United States. The mid-sized multinational that he works for assigned his team the task of designing a localized version of the company's best-selling product, a modular solar panel array for homes and apartment buildings.

Alvin speaks quickly and with a wry smile: "I assumed that our main challenges would be technical, but we keep running into roadblocks, and some of them seem to be more personal than technical. This gives me a big headache. Two of our team members from mainland China don't seem to get along well with the Singaporeans on the team or even with each other. After a dinner and a few drinks the other day, one of the mainland Chinese on the team told me that his Singaporean colleague is too relaxed about taking time off and is overpaid for the work he is doing—I think our whole team has figured out that there is a different pay scale here. Meanwhile, the Singaporean team member he was complaining about confidentially approached me to question the technical capabilities of this same guy who was talking about him.

"But that's not all," Alvin continues. "During our meetings, one of the Indian team members always seems to dominate the conversation—his English language skills give him a big advantage over the rest of the team. I know that some of the others who are less fluent are unhappy about this, and sometimes they have side conversations in Mandarin that exclude him. Rahul, the other Indian team member, is from the south of India rather than the north, and is much more cautious about speaking up. I think he is a bit intimidated because he is younger and attended a less elite school."

Alvin smiles with a touch of sadness. "The team is also pretty tough on me. I work hard to keep things going, but sometimes feel that because I am ethnic Chinese, they judge me more critically and are more jealous of my position than they would be toward a Caucasian team leader. I speak some Mandarin and Cantonese, but for business I am actually more comfortable in English. I've been in Singapore for two years but I still don't really feel at home anywhere, including here."

He laughs ruefully, looking at the conference room table where the next team meeting will start in 30 minutes. "When this team was created, I told my boss, 'Because we're all engineers, we speak the same language and will get along fine.' But it turns out that even our different kinds of engineers don't agree with each other: the chemical engineers want to focus on the materials we will use and their properties; our mechanical engineers are concerned about the assembly process and manufacturing costs; the designers want to create a package that is physically attractive because people will be able to see it everywhere on top of roofs in cities and neighborhoods; and our field support engineers keep talking about ease of installation and maintenance, which they think should be a priority because it affects our long-term profitability.

"We've already missed two key milestones, and keep getting bogged down in technical arguments and bickering, although there are no open personal conflicts during our meetings. I'm going to have to work extra-hard to get everyone realigned around a common set of objectives and a process for analyzing trade-offs, and to draw out the contributions of the less vocal team members. My boss told me, 'Alvin, you were born to do this. You know the region and can be a great bridge to headquarters R&D.' But now I'm not so sure."

Alvin is running a very diverse team, although it may not look diverse to a first-time visitor to Singapore. Asia now has over half the world's population (51.4 percent according to a recent count),[1] and individuals from countries within the region consider themselves to be at least as different from each other as would Germans and Brazilians, or people from the United States and Egypt. Moreover, enormous countries like China and India contain a degree of internal ethnic, socioeconomic, and linguistic diversity often compared with that in all of Europe. In this environment, many corporate approaches to diversity that have their origins in the United States or Europe still appear to be woefully one-dimensional and incomplete, with limited relevance to local circumstances.

A Question of Focus: Part I

"I will make it really easy for you this year. Women! You only have one metric you need to focus on. Get our representation of women in the organization up from 15 percent to 20 percent."

Derrick felt his emotions rising as he listened intently to Jean, the primary executive sponsor of the diversity and inclusion initiative in the U.S.-based manufacturing company where he worked. He felt immense pressure in his role as the head of diversity and inclusion for his organization—leading a team of one. He was not only determined to succeed professionally, but felt a personal obligation to make an impact and effect change.

Derrick's parents immigrated to the United States from Ethiopia before he was born, and he identifies himself as black. Issues of diversity and inclusion are very close to Derrick's own experience. He is deeply committed to making changes not only in his organization but in the world. He feels strongly that most challenges are very systemic—that it is not about numbers but about inclusion of the variety of voices and perspectives that can drive innovation and help the organization make better business decisions. Therefore, when Derrick's executive sponsor gave him his simple directive—although stated in an upbeat voice intended to make him feel motivated and committed—he could not help but feel frustrated and discouraged.

Derrick knows the representation of women within the company is below industry average. This is an important issue, both in terms of overall numbers and also their roles within the organization. There are a few senior women in the company, but not many. He knows from his everyday experience in the company that ethnicity is still a significant issue as well. In fact, in some ways it is even more awkward and loaded than the representation of women in the workforce because minority percentages are particularly low among the company's technical employees. But most critical from Derrick's perspective is that a focus on any single dimension of diversity is not going to bring about significant and sustainable change. His objections are truly not because the current focus is on women instead of ethnic minorities. From Derrick's perspective, real diversity and inclusion are about leveraging the backgrounds and skills of people of all types. In the end, that is what is important. Why doesn't his executive sponsor get this? Yet Derrick worries that if he tries to push back against an

(Continued)

emphasis on achieving better representation of women, his executive sponsor and others will misinterpret his response due to the color of his skin.

Later that same day, when Derrick speaks with a few women who have heard rumors about the new focus of his diversity efforts, they raise yet another issue that he is all too familiar with based on his own background: "We do not want to be singled out. We have worked so hard to attain what we have, and we would never want people to wonder if we got here based on our competence or based on our gender." Derrick feels like he is being set up for failure—and worst of all, he feels misunderstood and powerless, the very things he is trying to counteract in the organization.

FROM REPRESENTATION TO LEVERAGE

Derrick is struggling with a boss who has positive intentions but has unfortunately taken a one-dimensional approach to diversity. The approach that Derrick would prefer—to focus on inclusion from a wider perspective—is better suited to the current and future global workforce that includes employees like the members of Alvin's R&D team. Global companies first need to fully assess and comprehend the range of diversity that already exists in their ranks.[2]

Diversity initiatives in some multinational organizations are shifting, influenced in part by the changing profile of their employee population. They are moving beyond a focus on numbers and having diversity *represented* in the workforce, to fully *leveraging* that diversity through inclusive leadership practices. Most corporations still need to hire more people from underrepresented groups. However, many organizations are now also working to create a culture that enables all employees to draw upon their various backgrounds and capabilities to advance their business goals. In fact, a number of companies have renamed their diversity and inclusion departments or initiatives as "inclusion and diversity," reversing the word order to symbolize this change in focus. There has been an important shift toward building an environment where multiple voices are *invited* and *utilized* to make better business decisions.

RACE AND GENDER STILL MATTER

Although D&I efforts have broadened, race and gender continue to be important, even as the approach shifts toward leveraging diversity of all kinds. D&I practitioners have learned that improvements in race and gender representation can lead to broader representation in other areas of diversity; for example, minority and female employees often bring with them other differences, such as their generational group or socioeconomic background. Organizations tend to focus on race and gender representation because they want their employees to reflect the society in which they and their customers live. Many also believe in providing equal opportunities to groups that have traditionally been excluded or consigned to more subordinate roles. Race and gender demographics are visible and therefore easy to track and compare with the broader population to assess progress—a characteristic that helps to account for the appeal of gender statistics to Derrick's sponsor. Of course, the extent to which minority and female employees are actively included in formulating strategy and making decisions matters as well.

Race and Ethnicity on a Global Scale

On a global scale, 90 percent of the world's children under the age of 15 live in developing countries, so racial and ethnic diversity are built into our collective future.[3] Moreover, places like India, China, Indonesia, Nigeria, and Brazil, for example, each have their own significant internal ethnic differences—sometimes reinforced by religious, educational, political, and socioeconomic factors.

The R&D team portrayed at the beginning of the chapter holds racial differences between Indians and Chinese and ethnic contrasts among the Chinese and Indians themselves. For D&I efforts to be relevant worldwide, they will need to encompass, for example, the 56 official ethnic groups in China and the more than 2,000 groups in India, plus less formal differences based on regional cultures and dialects. There are also many tens of millions of overseas Chinese and Indians who have taken on characteristics of their adopted homes. A team leader like Alvin who seeks to unlock the full potential of his team must understand the backgrounds of each individual team member more fully, including his own, and consider how these might shape preconceptions and biases that impact their work with each other.

It is also true that the workforces of many advanced economies are becoming more ethnically diverse as a result of immigration and birth-rate demographics. For instance, one study showed that half of all infants in the United States under one year of age were members of a racial or ethnic minority group. In the United Kingdom, the percentage of workers of European ancestry within the total work-force has fallen by almost 10 percentage points in the past decade. And women comprise almost half the workforce in both the United States and the United Kingdom.[4]

Opportunities for Women

Creating greater opportunities for women is another workplace challenge nearly everywhere in the world. However, as with race and ethnicity, the relevant issues can be quite different depending upon the country setting: access to education, taboos on women in the workplace, working conditions and physical safety, the types of jobs open to women, social norms that prevent women from working long hours, equal pay for equal work, or access to jobs in the executive suite.

Working 24/7

Corina is a 30-something Romanian based in Belgium and heading up new business development for the health care division of a global tech firm. She notes, "In the sales environment I come from, there is a 24/7 style of working and being available. But you cannot demand that 24/7 accessibility from everyone because by doing that, you actually exclude valuable people from key roles where they would perform well. Sometimes this is also a gender issue because women have more responsibilities at home.

"It took me a while to understand that I was assessing people poorly even though they were doing a good job because I was expecting them to be on call 24/7. So I took a step back and met with each of them one-on-one and said, 'let's make an agreement about how we want to work together and when I can reach you.' Some people who were, in my mind, performing badly and would have eventually been driven out or left, have actually turned out to be among my best performers. I got to a point of mutual understanding with them and found a way to work together within certain hours of availability. So I was able to change my assessment criteria and create a more balanced approach. Especially on a multinational sales team, this becomes critical. You get these situations where there is an office manager, who is female, and these four sales guys. And then I get angry phone calls from the sales guys wondering why the office manager is unavailable. So you have to educate them as well about how they are assessing performance. They need to readjust their expectations. The leader is responsible for creating an environment where different kinds of people can thrive."

Diversity's Value

The economic value of workplace gender balance is being borne out by a growing body of empirical evidence. A McKinsey study authored by Michael Landel cites the example of Sodexo, a firm working to ensure gender balance in its organization. The company explored the correlation between gender-balanced management teams and key performance indicators such as employee engagement, brand awareness, client retention, and financial metrics. It analyzed data from 50,000 company employees across 90 entities around the world—and the results were compelling. Teams with a male–female ratio of between 40 and 60 percent reportedly produced positive, more sustained and predictable business results than those of unbalanced teams.

This finding on the value of gender diversity is reinforced by another McKinsey study that cites a strong correlation between the proportion of women on executive committees and financial performance. The researchers collected data on more than 200 companies located in the BRIC countries (Brazil, Russia, India, China) and six European countries. Companies in the top quartile for women's representation on their executive committees showed a 47 percent higher average return on equity in comparison with companies in the same industrial sector with no women on their executive committees.[5]

The better performance of organizations with more diverse leadership compared with other companies in the same industry and same country suggests that diversity is a competitive differentiator that shifts profit gains toward more diverse companies.[6] Other studies further support the positive correlation between increased diversity and improved performance. The relationship is consistent regardless of the type or dimension of diversity. So the key question in a changing world is not whether diversity has value, but how to cultivate and deploy it effectively on a global scale.

Shared Principles, Local Relevance

The most successful diversity and inclusion initiatives in global organizations today both incorporate shared underlying principles and implement solutions with local relevance. We cannot assume, for instance, that the challenges of race and gender are the same globally. It is important to be aware of the biases that our own point of view may create when trying to understand these challenges on a global scale. Challenges that minority groups and women face must be defined locally. When this does not occur, others who do not share the same historical and social context may react with irritation, skepticism, or apathy. Take, for example, the situation at a pharmaceutical plant in a small town in India.

Leadership at the Plant

Sandeep calls in from a shaky line in Gujarat, where he is the plant manager for a major pharmaceutical giant. He speaks frankly and focuses on the practical issues, without getting mired down in the philosophical elements behind the lack of women in leadership at his plants.

"Getting women into leadership at the plant is a challenge. And the reasons vary from demographic to geographic. Where we are located in India is not the best in terms of work/life balance. The plant is in a small town for India. It is difficult for spouses to find work here. For young people to get good job opportunities here is hard, for that matter. The challenge is especially difficult for married women. We have had some success with attracting single high potentials, but for married women, it is not easy to find opportunities for their spouses and so we tend to lose them. Women get married and leave the organization and move with their husbands. It is relatively easier to get female talent in other roles, but not so much the factory, not here.

"If I were to look at sites worldwide versus sites in India, we need to do a little more upgrading of our sites in India so that women will feel comfortable here. Better facilities are needed. We need a crèche, employee welfare facilities. If we can do this, we could attract more women. But the location is still difficult. In India, the chances of finding a woman working in the supply chain business are also limited because it is not a traditional area that women go into. Women and men are more separate here. We struggle to get resumes of women because in India, women tend to stay away from factory environments like this one.

"I don't think that security is a concern because our location is fairly secure for women. Transportation is provided. There are certain rules which don't allow women to stay late at the factory in India as well. It is the sheer nature of the work that is the issue. My reports are more than 90 percent male. So employees might be reluctant to have a woman manage them, and there is also a concern for the woman as well. It would be tough for women managers to be out there on the shop floor. Getting mechanical engineers who are women is hard. Part of the issue is cultural and another part is the feeder pools. In our leadership positions, we have not had a lot of women, so there is no precedent, and we don't have a model for them, either. There are so many factors involved here.

"But, practically speaking, we need to focus. If we can incentivize spouses, this would be the place to start here in India. Because of the plant locations, if we can support both members of the couple with roles at the same site, this would help."

The local response to a diversity and inclusion initiative implemented in Japan further underlines the importance of having a global perspective.

Women in Japan

A large, successful U.S.-based IT company was committed to having an increased number of women in leadership positions worldwide. To this end, it initiated and rolled out a global gender initiative. The presentation given to offices around the world included statistics (primarily based on U.S. research) regarding significant inequities for women and the discrimination that they endured.

What was interesting was the reaction this information provoked among women in the Japanese office. Although they were working women themselves, they felt the presentation was extremely U.S.-centric because it assumed that women in Japan who stayed at home rather than having paid employment felt like victims who had been excluded from the workforce. This seemed condescending and based on a misunderstanding of women's lives in Japan. "Here in Japan," they were quoted as saying, "We do have challenges with women rising to leadership positions. We admit that, but we feel far sorrier for American women, who don't seem to have a choice about whether to work or not. They are asked to do everything—to have a career, to raise children, and to run their household. In Japan, there are many women who do not work outside the home but who have a great amount of power and influence in their families. They manage the household finances and are in charge of the bank account. Their husbands work many hours, but the wives have a lot of decision-making power at home. They have different roles, but this does not mean they are unequal or feel victimized."

BEYOND RACE AND GENDER

In addition to race and gender, there are many factors that define diversity for a group of people or an organization. Data from the GlobeSmart Profile^{SM}, which was outlined in Chapter 2, confirm the importance of national culture. When we analyzed data for 20 countries with large sample sizes, an individual's home country emerged as the greatest single predictor of differences across all five Globe-Smart® dimensions. Further examination of the data produced statistically significant differences underlining the vital role of other elements of diversity:

- **Generation:** Contrasts between direct and indirect communication are most impacted by age, with younger people in general being more indirect. Survey respondents under age 35 were also more status-oriented and less inclined to take risks.

- **Functional role:** Job type is the strongest variable in determining whether people across all countries are more risk-oriented—particularly in terms of favoring rapid, timely decision making—or inclined to favor certainty based on more complete data and analysis. Job type also seems closely correlated with whether respondents focus first on tasks or on relationships. Senior executives tend to be the most risk-oriented; people in process-driven roles such as IT, engineering, and manufacturing are the most task-focused.[7]

In addition to contrasts based on generational differences and job type, other research points to cognitive diversity or differences in thinking style as a relevant diversity factor, especially for driving innovation in organizations.

Generational Differences

Many organizations have increased their focus on work-style differences between generations. They point to contrasts in preferred modes of learning, motivational factors, and management styles, and seek to address workplace generation gaps. As the workforce ages in industries such as oil and gas, aerospace, and financial services, such differences are critically important because younger employees must absorb vital skills and information quickly from senior workers. This is particularly true in organizations that have age "troughs," created when few employees were hired during periodic economic downturns. There may be a cohort of highly skilled engineers or other professionals nearing retirement age who have a limited time window in which to transfer their accumulated knowledge to employees in their 20s and 30s, with relatively few mid-level managers in between. Motivating and retaining younger employees and transferring knowledge to them becomes even more vital under these circumstances.

Employees who joined the company decades ago to have a steady job, were happy with the prestige of its name brand, and learned their skills through a long apprenticeship in several different roles are sometimes shocked by the attitudes of younger company colleagues. Members of this younger generation may have a thinner attachment to the company, are looking for rapid career advancement, and expect to have access to high-tech learning resources. In other cases, the attitudes of people from different generations may turn out to be more similar.[8] Careful inquiry will bear out how important the differences could be in a particular situation.

The characteristics and terminology best used to define each generation are linked to important historical events within certain countries and regions. It is essential to avoid assuming that the characteristics of age cohorts in one country will be consistent with those in another. An increasing number of global D&I initiatives are seeking out locally relevant classifications of generational groups as well as other diversity dimensions. For example, many global D&I professionals refer to the research report from Deloitte, "Talking About Whose Generation?"; a sample of its findings is depicted in Figure 5.1. Gaining a more complete picture of a talent pool requires

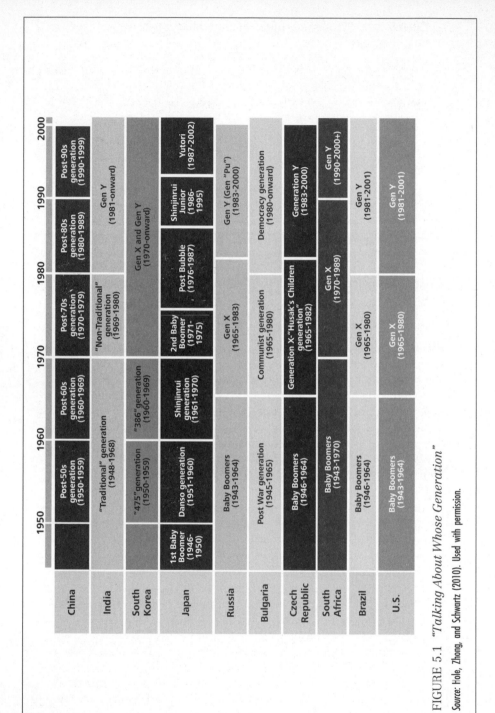

FIGURE 5.1 *"Talking About Whose Generation"*

Source: Hole, Zhong, and Schwartz (2010). Used with permission.

companies to understand the generational composition of their entire global workforce.[9]

Perplexed by Prague

Nigel, an expatriate from the United Kingdom, leaned back in his chair and looked out the window onto the cobblestoned streets of Prague. Though he had lived here for almost two years, this country still surprised him. As head of the Business Service Center in the Czech Republic for a large insurance company, he had a big job to do: he needed to leverage the team here for the best business results, yet employee engagement seemed low. His company's Learning & Development Department had mandated a team-building program to help improve engagement and performance. One element Nigel was focusing on was generational differences, but he was quickly realizing that his concept of Generation X and Y did not really apply here in Prague.

There was a huge difference between generations here, but it seemed to have much more to do with those born as a part of [former Secretary General of the Communist Party] Gustav Husak's effort to create a population boom (a common strategy employed by other communist leaders such as Romanian leader Nicolae Ceausescu to create a vibrant and plentiful workforce), and those who were born after this boom ended in 1983. It seemed that what motivated employees born after 1983 was far different from what was important to those born previously. The assumptions his European and U.S. colleagues made about the workforce here were just not correct. He had received so much information that suggested the employees were risk-averse, hierarchical, and needed structure. Although this was true of the pre-1983 generation, it was not at all the case of the 20-somethings he was meeting. Nigel felt that in some ways they were far more adventurous and entrepreneurial than he was as a 50-year-old from London.

As evidenced by Nigel's experience, generational groupings referred to in the media, workplaces, and popular conversation vary significantly by country and exhibit very different workplace behaviors. The Czech Republic is only one of 10 countries on the chart in Figure 5.1, and there are far more countries with their own unique generational patterns.

Close scrutiny reveals generational differences within countries that some might find surprising. For instance, our GlobeSmart Profile[SM] data for China indicate that younger people are the most indirect in their communication style, whereas each more senior generational cohort becomes more direct; this pattern did not emerge as clearly for other countries.[10] In contrast to the view that younger Chinese are becoming more Westernized, this evidence appears to indicate that they support traditional Chinese values of respect for age and hierarchy.

Functional Differences

Leaders in some global organizations note that, for them differences across job functions seem to be even more significant than the differences between people from various countries. As organizations expand globally, their structure is typically altered from a more traditional hierarchy to a matrix. Matrix structures, as discussed in Chapter 4, intentionally integrate job functions, product groups, and geographies to break down silos and encourage holistic thinking across boundaries. As a result of this growth in matrix structures, it has become more necessary for employees of different job types and functions to interact in order to achieve business goals together. Just as inaccurate stereotypes can impact the interactions of people from different national and cultural backgrounds or genders, so stereotypes exist as corporate scientists interact with the finance and legal departments, or people from sales and marketing interact with engineering.

Fixing the Sales Team

At 37 years old, Avi heads up global sales for an Israeli technology firm. He calls in to Shanghai from Tel Aviv, where he is based, at a ridiculously early hour. "Don't worry, I am usually at work by this time. I get my best work done in the morning before anyone else wakes up," he says. He speaks in rapid-fire phrases and with a lot of confidence.

"If we are talking about inclusion, then we should talk about how different functions are treated in this company. See, we have always been this very innovation-focused company, and we are very proud of our history and the things we build. Sales is a dirty word here.

"We just hired a consulting firm to do research on sales at the company because we were having so much trouble. The sales department here is treated as an afterthought or a necessary evil. People struggle because we don't have support or even a basic level of respect. We don't value sales as a company. In order for us to really excel, the sales team needs to feel that we have the support of the organization behind us. It should be everyone's job to make sure that this team is successful, but we feel like our opinions are not valued, and we are constantly second-guessed.

"It has been in the organizational culture so long. We are a tech company, and so engineers are revered and pull a lot of weight in the organization . . . 'oh, and then someone needs to go sell it.' But actually, you can't do one without the other. We don't want to lose the technical expertise, but the company won't exist if we don't make some money.

"You walk down the halls in the engineering wing of our building and you overhear things like 'Avi said we need to make a product like this, but he's in sales so what does he know?' or 'we can't give that product plan to him because he is in sales and he will sell it before it is ready.'

"So the result of the research findings by the consulting firm is that now we are going to spend 90 percent of our time fixing the sales team and change us rather than change the organizational culture itself."

Technical versus Nontechnical

At a Seattle-based IT firm, a continent away from Avi, a similar set of issues emerged. Employees complained about the bias that existed between technical employees in IT or engineering functions and non-technical functions such as HR and marketing. Fifty employees came together in a room, and those who self-identified as technical employees were asked for adjectives they would use to describe nontechnical colleagues. They used words like illogical, fuzzy, uninformed, uneducated, ignorant, and useless. Similarly, self-identified non-technical employees described their technical peers with terms like socially inept, passive-aggressive, self-absorbed, arrogant, territorial, and black-and-white thinkers.

The starkly negative perceptions each group held of the other highlighted the importance of exploring this functional dimension of diversity within the organization. Functional differences were clearly linked with an unhealthy dynamic that was impeding collaboration between different parts of the company. Surfacing negative stereotypes sparked constructive discussion about how to build mutual respect and improve working relationships.

Greater awareness of the biases toward others held by people in different functions can be a first step toward increasing their ability to collaborate effectively. Addressing such biases often highlights the need in the company for technical and nontechnical perspectives as well as the value of each functional role, and fosters a renewed commitment to joint efforts for the company to reach the next level.

Diversity of Thinking Styles

Another key dimension of diversity pertains to thinking styles. Many models have explored this over the years, including Edward de Bono's Six Thinking Hats and the Hermann Brain Dominance Instrument created by William Hermann. Maxine Williams, Facebook's global head of diversity, frames discussions of diversity around what she calls cognitive diversity—in other words, engaging people with different perspectives and approaches to problem solving. A primary focus on gender or race may seem to leave many people out of the discussion. Williams argues that cognitive diversity, on the other hand, engages a broader cross-section of people and promotes the sense that diversity is a common challenge. She suggests that nearly all people have had the experience of feeling like they were an outsider based on their thinking style or point of view—for some this is a brief instant and for others a whole lifetime—and seeks to build understanding and connections based on this shared sense of having been excluded.[11]

Models related to thinking style usually include thought patterns such as analytical, imaginative, intuitive, critical, passionate, integrative, and so on. Building greater awareness of contrasts in thinking styles can help team members to avoid battles between people who are entrenched in clashing styles. This allows them to instead approach issues in more flexible and creative ways that leverage multiple approaches. Each style has valuable characteristics as well as potential blind spots, and may be more or less relevant depending upon the type of problem the team encounters. Whether you are the kind of person who typically focuses on concrete facts, or one who prefers minimal structure and going by gut feel when searching for solutions—each has something unique to contribute.

The Strategic Planning Team

The team sat together around a large conference table for its annual strategic planning session. While this had become a tradition in the three years since the merger, and the team members now had quite a lot of experience working together, somehow these exercises were still fraught with tension. Each person had such a different way of approaching the same task, and this seemed to send them off on tangents that were not always the most productive.

- Daniel usually wanted to start with a clean sheet of paper and/or brainstorm using the *Apollo 13* metaphor of building a solution by combining the collection of parts on the table; he derived a lot of satisfaction from the energy of that kind of discussion.

- Peter insisted on looking carefully at accumulated data regarding the company's track record to date and the competitive environment, believing that such knowledge would ensure deep and meaningful discussion. He had worked with the company's finance and marketing departments ahead of time to ensure that good information would be available for the meeting.

- Katherine was doing her best to shepherd, facilitate, and make sure that everyone got along well; she cared deeply about the people in the room and saw the value that each one could add, seeking constantly to build bridges between them. She felt that the success of the plan they produced would depend as much on the quality of the relationships they were building as on the specifics in the plan itself.

- Pascal was very task-focused and concerned primarily with his own function. He was an intuitive decision-maker with a short attention span and a desire to get things done. In many cases he had either made up his mind on an issue already or wanted to move on as soon as he had heard enough about the next topic. If the discussion was complete in his mind, he would be ready to walk out the door with his briefcase while others thought the meeting was not yet finished.

The team needed to come up with the next strategic plan for their growing business, but these differences often seemed to hinder more than help. What aided them most was when they decided to

(Continued)

(*Continued*)

revise the planning agenda to explicitly include activities that appealed to each team member's style: brainstorming, data analysis, relationship-building, and nailing down conclusions and action steps. Each style added something useful to the overall mix, and it was easier for team members to contribute constructively to other parts of the agenda when they knew that the session they had designed was coming.

It is challenging for any team to cultivate a shared understanding of differences in thinking styles—with all their unique individual variations—and to leverage these differences to drive innovation and better business performance. As with the other dimensions of diversity, it is critical for team members to know their own styles, to understand ways in which they are similar to and different from one another, and to make strategic choices together about which style is appropriate for a particular purpose and/or how to bridge these differences to win in the marketplace.

INCLUSIVE LEADERSHIP: THREE STEPS

The types of diversity that matter most in a global setting can be defined based upon the nature of the employee population, current social issues, and business opportunities. Most organizations want to uphold certain core values. In addition, it is worth asking, "What elements of diversity are most relevant to a particular business unit, geography, or function?" Defining a clear value proposition is the first step toward building a successful diversity initiative. Based on this kind of prioritization process, inclusive leadership practices can be deployed to fully leverage diversity for business results. These efforts form a three-legged stool, with each leg supporting the others to promote systemic change:

1. **Seek out diversity.** Recruit using methods that increase the amount of diversity represented in the pool of applicants and new employees.
2. **Create more inclusion.** Build awareness of individual unconscious bias within the organization and how it impacts decisions to ensure that such bias does not lead to poor business results.
3. **Drive accountability.** Create an environment where employees can act as change agents by "saying the unsaid" and expressing themselves openly when they feel that others' comments or actions might be rooted in a biased view.

Seek Out Diversity

In addition to seeking out the diversity already present within the existing workforce, another step is to look critically at recruitment pipelines. Increasing the number of diverse applicants can reduce bias, and many factors can impact an organization's ability to attract a pool of diverse candidates for open positions. For example, if a tech firm advertises open positions through blogs that attract readers of a certain type (for example, race, gender, generation, function, thinking style), the choice of media format will have a heavy influence on the makeup of the pool of candidates. This may seem like common sense, but given how stretched many organizations are with regard to resources, it is only natural that taking the easy and known path seems most efficient. Once the candidate has applied, practices such as removing names and other identifying details from resumes prior to screening have also proven helpful in reducing the impact of bias.[12]

Because previous patterns and experiences influence hiring decisions, organizations need to assist hiring managers in reviewing their criteria for decision making to ensure there is an inclusive process. A set of practical and fairly simple questions, building on the general queries about recruiting practices posed in Chapter 2, can help them to think through more consciously what key qualities are important for a specific job description:

- What do you value in a good candidate based on your own identity?
- How much of this definition of a good candidate is relevant to the job description? What is most relevant?
- In what ways could your own cultural background or biases impact your ability to find what you value in candidates?
- Do you need to adjust what you look for in a candidate to be sure you are not over- or underestimating a person's ability to do the job?

Figure 5.2 suggests a further set of steps for recruiters to identify and avoid potential sources of bias.

Create More Inclusion

Organizations have learned that it is not enough to merely have people of varying backgrounds walking the halls of their offices or dialing into conference calls. When an organization can recruit more diversity, more perspectives become available, but how often do leaders and individuals call upon and utilize these diverse perspectives to actually *make* important business decisions? In order to truly realize the advantages of a diverse workforce, there must be significant focus on inclusion practices that express and leverage multiple perspectives.

1. Identity Groups	2. Qualities of an Ideal Candidate	3. Job Description Filter	4. How will you determine if the candidate has these qualities in Column 3?
What groups do you belong to that make up your identity?	*Based on these groups, what do you value in a candidate?*	*Based on the job description, which qualities (from Column 2) are relevant? What additional qualities do you need to add based on the job description?*	*What questions will you ask or behaviors will you look for during the interview to determine if the applicant has the qualities of an ideal candidate?*
Company/Division ABC Tech	• Initiative • Leadership • Deadline Oriented • Outgoing	• Initiative • Deadline Oriented • Problem Solver • Works in Teams	Describe a project you have worked on: • What was the process? • How important were deadlines? • How many people did you have to communicate with? • How did you make decisions?
Profession:			
Family:			

FIGURE 5.2 *Avoiding Recruiting Bias*

In his article "Why Is Diversity Vital for Innovation?," Steve Dennings notes that cognitive diversity—that is, the diversity of thought that happens when teams and organizations incorporate members from different groups—doesn't improve performance on routine tasks. But when dealing with complex tasks like engineering problems, other challenges requiring creativity and innovation, or managerial issues, cognitive diversity is a key explanatory variable in levels of performance.[13] Two main obstacles prevent many organizations from better leveraging cognitive diversity:

1. *Unconscious bias*, resulting in overestimating or underestimating a person's ability or idea.
2. A corporate culture that makes people less open to *say the unsaid* and express unpopular opinions.

Superstars versus Everyone Else

A Boston-based high-tech company had grown quickly through a remarkable series of innovations. As it expanded throughout the world, the company's leaders recognized that their more global presence had gained them a diversity of thought that could be a huge advantage to continuing their tradition of innovation and high performance. These were smart, ambitious, and forward-thinking people; so what was getting in the way of their truly being able to leverage the ideas and thinking of their workforce?

Employee interviews uncovered a culture in the organization that was only open to the ideas of those "superstars" who had been successful previously in product development and who were primarily based in the United States. Ideas from others were viewed with much greater skepticism, regardless of their value. In principle, people agreed that "we want an environment where all ideas are considered," but in reality, this was not happening.

Many employees attributed the second-class status of other workers to bias. They wanted strategies for how to overcome it, yet the sources of the bias were not at all obvious. The problem seemed to be ingrained habits of behavior that were grounded in the company's own DNA and reinforced by its successes over time. Most participants in the system considered themselves to be open-minded and without any particular bias—yet there was a pervasive but unconscious bias against those who weren't the acknowledged superstars.

Overcoming Unconscious Bias

Bias was previously equated with more overt forms of racism, sexism, and ethnocentrism; as a result, many countries have taken important actions to protect groups that historically bore the brunt of such prejudice (such as scheduled castes in India, native peoples in Australia and North America, Turkish immigrants in Germany, and African Americans in the United States). Most people assumed that bias was a matter of conscious, deliberate choice, and that good people were not biased.

However, more recent neuroscience research has confirmed that bias is often unconscious—and we all have it in some form. Our brains are wired for prehistoric times, when it was critical that we swiftly assess whether an approaching person, animal, or new environment represented a life-threatening danger. For our ancestors, the ability to make quick and accurate decisions was essential for survival. Neuroscience has found that the oldest parts of our brain, the two amygdalae, are extremely powerful in times of stress because they are involved with emotional responses and decision making.

By placing subjects in a variety of situations and then analyzing the impact, researchers have confirmed that if another person is perceived as being different from the subject, he or she is often viewed in negative terms, while those seen as similar to the subject are judged in positive terms.[14] In a global work environment, this kind of unconscious bias can lead to poor business decisions and inaccurate assessments of others' abilities and ideas when such negative or positive associations are attached to people of particular nationalities.

How can organizations overcome unconscious bias if it is, indeed, unconscious? Bias—particularly in its more subtle forms—can have a significant impact on whom we evaluate favorably or whose voice we choose to hear. The first step in overcoming such bias is to make unconscious or at least unintended default tendencies available for more conscious examination and assessment. Sidebar 5.1 offers one tool for this purpose.

SIDEBAR 5.1   EXPLORING UNCONSCIOUS BIAS

If everyone has some form of bias, how can you explore yours? One interesting exercise is the Implicit Bias online survey; the survey's Implicit Association Test offers a way to probe unconscious biases. This 10-minute test will present you with words or images and ask you to respond as quickly as possible. At the end, your responses will be tallied so that you can see how your score compares to others and to your own expectations. This test has been taken more than one million times, and the results usually reveal varying types and degrees of bias. Your test results will include interpretations based on research done with more elaborate versions of this test. However, the parties who have contributed to this particular online instrument make no claim regarding the validity of suggested interpretations (www .understandingprejudice.org/iat/), so the results should be used only to stimulate self-reflection.[15]

Another good tool for exploring these personal patterns is to take a critical look at your own network—specifically, whom you currently seek out for advice and consultation on important decisions. As you

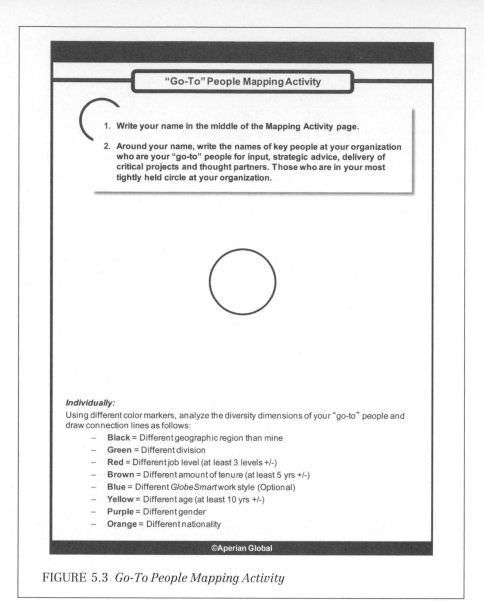

FIGURE 5.3 *Go-To People Mapping Activity*

complete the assessment in Figure 5.3, note what voices you are inviting to participate in your decisions, and whose input you aren't requesting. How might this be impacting the breadth of your perspective and the outcomes of your choices? What obstacles are getting in the way of inviting other perspectives—and how could you seek input from additional sources? Thinking about whom you invite to the table when making decisions and whose perspective is missing is a good way to begin to make your unconscious bias more conscious—and to ensure you have fewer blind spots.

Saying the Unsaid

Each person negotiates his or her involvement with the work environment, deciding how much insight to offer based on environmental cues and responses. Individuals may be particularly reticent about expressing themselves if their insights are informed by ways in which they are different from others and are thus possibly vulnerable to exclusion.[16]

Inclusive Leadership: An Aha Moment

Gabriella is a successful, high-potential leader at a growing global pharmaceutical company, and is proud to have been named the new team leader for a global marketing team. She has been extremely successful on a team with a similar function in the United States and is well known for her technical expertise and ability to get the job done. She is confident she knows the rules of the game—her past success has proved this.

As she began working with her new, global team, Gabriella clearly spelled out the business processes she wanted to implement. Her team members seemed to be in agreement with her direction; she received little resistance to the changes she was trying to implement and was pleased with the progress.

A few months later, Gabriella realized that in the Asia-Pacific region there were distinctive local features of the relationship between pharma companies and doctors, who work under a different legal framework concerning generic drugs. The processes she was trying to implement were not going to work as she had originally expected. She was shocked and frustrated—not only about her own ignorance of these differences and the questions she did not ask but also that the members of her team with more knowledge of the region had not spoken up.

"They just went along with what I said. They did not question me!" she exclaimed. Gabriella went back to her colleagues and asked, "Why did you go along with me? I was the one who was wrong!" The others explained, "You seemed so sure you were correct that we were afraid to question you." Gabriella became quite serious and reflective and then said thoughtfully, "Wow! I wonder how often that happens—that people have ideas or the information we need but do not speak up?"

Gabriella's global team members did not speak up, even though the changes she was trying to implement were likely to fail in Asia. A critical factor in leveraging diversity of thought is creating an environment where people are willing to say the unsaid. This could mean disagreeing with the views of a forceful leader—as in Gabriella's case—or expressing an unpopular, minority opinion to peers. Leaders can shape this kind of environment by inviting and rewarding diverse perspectives.

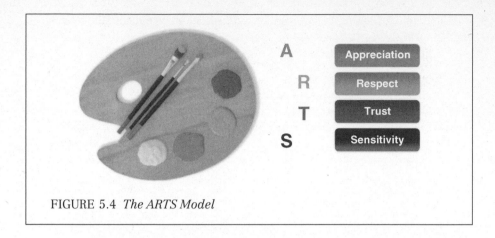

FIGURE 5.4 *The ARTS Model*

In global team settings, establishing ground rules for participation is one way of fostering inclusion. The intended message sent is not always the message received. Spending time at the outset of a team interaction to acknowledge differences and then devise guidelines for working together helps to transform conflict into "creative abrasion."[17] Figure 5.4 offers an effective model for this.

When team members come from different cultural backgrounds, it is important to recognize cultural differences that may impact what respect and appreciation look like and what behaviors are most effective in promoting open communication. Having shared operating principles that promote each of these ingredients fosters an environment where people are more willing to express unorthodox opinions.

Creative team interactions often involve noticing value that others have missed—what has thus far remained unsaid. Fanning the sparks of just-forming thoughts can lead to new achievements. The ability to take many different ideas and bring them together into a collaborative solution that no one could have created on his or her own is one of the most important links between diversity and inclusion and business results. Here are suggestions for leading a team dialogue that includes divergent thinking or the expression of different perspectives:

- Ensure that every person in the room feels primed to contribute because the logic of the process and the scope of the work are explicit.

- Consider assigning one or more roles for divergent thinking to provide legitimacy and to uncover richer solutions; actively solicit the voice of the outlier.

- Learn to feel comfortable with the time-consuming dynamics of divergent thought and guide the discussion without moving too quickly *or* too slowly.

- Once different viewpoints have been expressed, help the team to change its focus to jointly crafting solutions.
- To weave participants' ideas together, use inclusive communication techniques such as paraphrasing ideas, pointing out common threads, and providing clearly articulated criteria to evaluate solutions.

Leaders who accommodate dissent and acknowledge the voice of each individual can meaningfully include diverse ideas for the good of the whole.

Drive Accountability

The last component to truly embracing inclusion and diversity in an organization is creating a culture of accountability. In order to do so, leadership must make it not only acceptable but *expected* that employees say something when they feel they have observed bias that has a negative impact on business results. In order to embrace inclusion, organizations need to undergo a culture change that allows every employee to serve as a change agent. To accomplish this, there needs to be buy-in on the business case for inclusion as well as skills for successfully intervening in situations where bias appears to be present. Though necessary, this process can be slow and challenging.

As the culture of inclusion starts to take hold in an organization, it may initially appear that there is little or no change. In fact, it may even seem as though some people or barriers in the organization are working as roadblocks to change. These barriers can appear as angry e-mails or blogs, lack of participation in scheduled events, or even open hostility toward the initiative. But champions may also emerge who are supporters of the effort, recognizing the potential of inclusive leadership and offering their support in a variety of ways.

The most significant changes occur when everyone in the organization is empowered to act. This means that they are not just taking individual accountability for implementing more inclusive behaviors. They also feel accountable to the organization to speak up when they see a situation where biased decision making appears to be producing less than optimal business results.

Organizations often struggle with determining how to implement this type of environment without creating a confrontational, combative atmosphere that negatively impacts productivity and employee engagement. A best practice is to have people use a collaborative and solution-oriented technique for saying something when they feel a colleague has acted in a way that may be reflective of a biased opinion.

The DESO model outlined by Jonamay Lambert and Selma Myers[18] includes the following steps:

- **D**escribe the Behavior
- **E**xpress Personal Impact
- **S**pecify the Business Impact
- (Explore) **O**ptions for Managing the Situation

See Something, Say Something

The departmental meeting had just begun. People shuffled in with their coffee cups and laptops. The conference room phone was dialed into a shared line to include the team members in other locations. The latest challenges in the new product development project were reviewed and discussion began. Sarah, a mid-level manager, began her presentation, passing out a thick packet of slides filled with data and research—her second report this week. "I'm sorry," said Anton, rolling his eyes as he took the handout, "we just don't have time for this. I feel like we are constantly getting slowed down by too much research. Can't we just brainstorm here about next steps?"

David felt uncomfortable and wondered why Anton had cut Sarah off and discounted her presentation so directly. Later in the day he happened to meet Anton in the hallway, and they walked together to the break room.

David: Anton, do you remember what you said to Sarah in the meeting? (**D**escribe)

Anton: Oh yes. Sorry if I seemed abrupt, but all that research is just not going to get us ahead—we need creativity here!

David: I could see you were trying to encourage a more open dialogue, but I also think there are a number of different approaches and thinking styles on the team. It made me uncomfortable to see her presentation cut short. (**E**xpress)

Anton: It seemed to me that everybody on the team was feeling pretty impatient at that point. Sarah tends to drown us all in data.

David: I'm afraid the team might make the wrong choices if her research is neglected. (**S**pecify)

Anton: Sometimes she does make valuable points, although it takes her too long to get there and having too much information can confuse the team as well.

David: Would there be a better way to integrate her point of view? I wonder if her material could be sent out electronically in advance, with time during the meeting focused on questions and ideas related to the data. Is there anything you could do to partner with her and help her make her presentations more concise? (**O**ptions)

Anton: Maybe. She always asks for my input while she is putting together her materials.

David: I know it wasn't your intention to shut her down like that.

Anton: Thanks for mentioning this. I didn't mean for what I said to come across that way.

David has followed all four steps of the DESO model in the example above. However, speaking up is difficult, and it is even harder to not create a confrontational situation. Not every employee will be as open to feedback as Anton was. It's common for people to become defensive or blame others for being too sensitive. Yet organizations that have successfully implemented this kind of discussion have found that it is most effective to create an environment where everyone feels responsible to address bias that appears to be impacting business results. Employees are more likely to change their behavior and to become more aware of impact of their own biases when a *peer*, rather than a manager or supervisor, points out the situation. This kind of accountability at all levels of the organization will help inclusive leadership practices become a reality.

The ability to provide constructive feedback to others who act in a way that does not leverage diversity to its fullest can be one of the most effective ways to create culture change within an organization. Inclusion must ultimately become part of the essential fabric of the organization, and not just a training program or a set of recruiting targets. Inclusive leadership requires a clear commitment from senior executives. Employees at every level in the organization can also take ownership both to change their own actions and to assist others in recognizing how they may need to shift and change their approach as well.

A Question of Focus: Part II

Derrick felt a surge of pride and relief as he sat across from his executive sponsor Jean, reviewing the key accomplishments of the diversity and inclusion efforts in his organization. The number of women had, indeed, increased over the course of the past 12 months; but so much more had happened that he felt confident he was impacting the business significantly.

Collaboration between the technical and nontechnical functions within the organization had increased. This had led to better outcomes for key projects and initiatives, such as the recruiting initiative that had broadened the company's network to attract more diverse candidates—and, yes, more women. Better collaboration between regions was making it easier to come together around common objectives.

There was now less open conflict in the internal blogs and more open dialogue to resolve differences in opinions, thoughts, and ideas. There had also been a slight but noticeable uptick in retention rates for younger employees. It was too early to say if this would become a trend, but Derrick thought that this might be because they were feeling it was easier for them to speak up and contribute. While there was still a long way to go, these signs of change had made everyone more confident about the future.

WHAT YOU CAN DO

- Start with your own awareness. Be mindful of values, biases, and beliefs that affect your relations with others. Rethink everyday interactions to better understand the potential impact of unconscious biases and stereotypes.

- Identify the kinds of diversity that are most important or relevant for the particular environment in which you are working.

- Do not assume that the diversity dimensions that are most relevant to you are relevant to your global counterparts.

- Address bias that may be impacting the recruiting and hiring process to ensure you are seeking out a diverse workforce.

- Expand your network beyond the usual go-to people (based on habit and comfort) to ensure broader input and different perspectives.

- Proactively seek out ideas, approaches, and perspectives from people who do not think as you do, and express appreciation for their input even when you disagree.

- Question evaluations of people from different backgrounds or work styles when told they are not ready for new assignments, projects, or promotions.

- Put yourself in the position of colleagues, customers, and stakeholders from different backgrounds and ask:

  - How would they interpret this message?
  - How would they approach this issue?

- Address the situation when a colleague makes inappropriate comments or decisions that appear to be based on bias—conscious or unconscious. See something, say something.

Global Mergers and Acquisitions: Beyond Diligence

The Real Work Needed to Bring People Together and Make Any Deal Worthwhile

THE CHANGING LANDSCAPE

Mergers and acquisitions are a primary growth strategy for companies domestically and worldwide. Although the decision to take such a step is typically left to a small circle of top executives and specialists, the implementation of a major transaction requires that leaders and employees at all levels collaborate effectively. Most members of today's corporate world can expect to experience a merger or acquisition sooner or later. Some will go through the process many times—which makes it especially important to foresee what can go wrong as well as how to obtain more positive results.

Industries old and new have been transformed as foreign suitors continue to purchase firms or major business units with distinctive identities. Such purchases include, for example:

- The European steel giant Arcelor by India's Mittal Steel
- Sweden's Volvo by Ford and later China's Geely
- U.S.-based Chrysler by Daimler-Benz of Germany and later Italy's Fiat
- Luxembourg-based Skype by eBay and later Microsoft in the United States
- IBM's personal computer and server divisions by China's Lenovo
- G.E. Plastic by SABIC of Saudi Arabia

Chagrin in Chicago: Part I

It was another cold March day in Chicago. The gray skies and dim light made it feel like once again winter would go on forever. Inside a large modern building on the outskirts of the city, however, every office was buzzing with conversation. The unexpected sale of the company had just been announced, and rumors were flying. Employees were grappling with what they had just heard from their CEO. Starting soon, they would be making a radical transition from a proud and aggressive medium-sized medical devices start-up—still run by its original founders and famous for its leading-edge technologies—to a newly acquired part of a large South Korean multinational company.

Among the many small knots of people who had gathered between their cubicles to discuss the announcement, there were intense exchanges of questions and comments:

- "I heard the CEO's explanation, but wish I had a better sense of why it was necessary for us to sell out."
- "Yes, the presentation was pretty high level. I hope they'll give us more of the details soon."
- "The CEO said that our new owners are anxious to learn from us. Will this mean that they take the technology and discard the employees, or will they really integrate us? I'm not sure how much we have to learn from them. Maybe they'll be sending some of us to work in Korea."
- "The markets here and in South Korea are so different—government regulations, the approval process, customer relationships. I hope our new owners know what they're doing in trying to bring us together."
- "I hear they already have a subsidiary here in the U.S., based in North Carolina. Looks like we've got another integration task with Raleigh as well as with Seoul. They'll probably want to move whole functions from Chicago down south because it's less expensive."
- "I don't think our sales function will be affected very much. We're so local in our approach I imagine that we won't be doing much more than integrating new products into our portfolio, and maybe printing new name cards. The merger could even help us if their products sell well here."

(Continued)

(Continued)

- "It might be a totally different story for those of us in R&D. They will want to integrate development projects to avoid duplication and probably to absorb a lot of our technology as well."

- "We still have our day jobs. How are we possibly going to pull off all the systems integration the CEO talked about and still keep our current projects going?"

- "I just volunteered to coach my daughter's soccer team, but now I imagine I'll be spending a lot of time in Seoul. I wonder how that's going to work . . . I've heard that the Koreans work crazy hours, and they'll probably expect that from us, too."

- "Did you see the head of manufacturing who was standing next to the CEO during the announcement? She was looking pretty queasy. Everybody said she was the top successor candidate for the CEO's job before the merger. Where does this leave her now? She's either dusting off her resume or about to launch a new campaign or two to prove to our new owners how valuable she is — maybe both!"

BEYOND DILIGENCE

Firms working on mergers or acquisitions commonly focus on immediate strategic and financial issues; these concerns shape the questions asked during the due diligence process:

- What is our acquisition target's financial condition?
- How well do our product portfolios mesh?
- How much overlap is there between our customers and theirs, and how will customers react?
- Will we have new market opportunities?
- What cost savings can we extract from the combined operations?

While busily searching for information in response to such questions, M&A teams often underestimate or mishandle the more subtle issues. Industry experts are increasingly recognizing that lack of cultural fit is the primary reason that an estimated 70 percent of mergers and acquisitions either fail or underperform.[1] When a very large company acquires a smaller one with the primary focus on obtaining the smaller firm's technology, everyone is clear about which culture will dominate, and retaining the acquired personnel is neither vital nor even perhaps desired. It is a different and more challenging situation, however, when the transaction's success depends upon meshing organizational systems and cultures and retaining key employees. There are often significant corporate cultural differences, for instance, between smaller, more entrepreneurial firms and large corporations. What could appear to a larger acquirer to be systems that increase efficiency, such as implementing a matrix organizational structure or creating shared services for functions such as Finance and HR, may seem extremely inefficient to employees of the smaller firm that has been acquired. Including national cultural differences in the mix along with differences in organizational culture introduces complexity of an additional order of magnitude.

CULTURAL FACTORS

Global leaders who face the task of combining company operations must consider carefully how culture comes into play and how to address cultural issues, while building expertise specific to mergers and acquisitions. As indicated in Chapter 3, culture can be defined as "habits of the mind" passed on from one generation to the next, and as ways of solving problems in a particular environment. It is best understood not as a fixed pattern of behavior, but rather as a dynamic, many-layered series of interrelated concentric circles—family, community, team, company, country, industry—in which people tend to follow certain norms of thought and action. Three aspects of culture are worth particularly close attention in a cross-border acquisition, corresponding with the country, company, and team layers of culture shown in Figure 6.1.

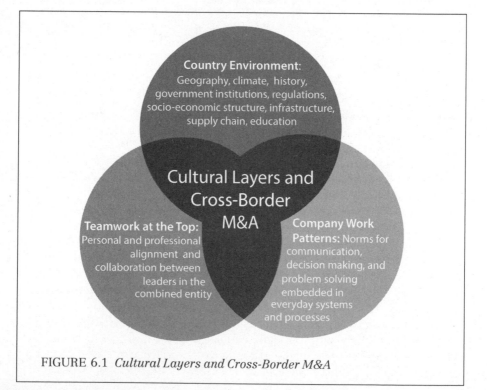

FIGURE 6.1 *Cultural Layers and Cross-Border M&A*

Problem No. 1: Reading the Country Environment

Niccolo Machiavelli is perhaps best known for his stern advice that it is better for a prince to be feared than to be loved, but there is much more to his writings. In his treatise *The Prince*, Machiavelli also notes that a ruler should "learn the nature of the terrain, and know how mountains slope, how valleys open, how plains lie, and understand the nature of rivers and swamps; and he should devote much attention to such activities."[2] In a modern corporate era where organizations still compete energetically but mostly without physical combat, the concept of "terrain" is still relevant and easily overlooked, especially in cross-border transactions.

Example: Bharti Airtel Invests in Africa

Krishna Palepu and Tanya Bijlani have authored a richly textured case study about how Bharti Airtel, India's leading provider of cellular services, sought to grow beyond its home market. The company had reached a position of domestic dominance through a unique set of strategic choices: outsourcing the building of infrastructure such as cell towers and its digital network, focusing on the use of prepaid charge cards, and radically lowering prices to bring tens of millions of new customers into the market. Based on analysis of many different global opportunities, Bharti Airtel executives selected Africa as the best location outside of India to extend their business model. After failing to come to mutually acceptable terms with MTN, Africa's largest cell phone business, they purchased Zain Telecom, the continent's third-largest cellular company, based in Bahrain with operations throughout much of the African continent. When the acquisition was consummated, it became the largest ever cross-border deal in an emerging market context.[3]

The Indian expatriates who were sent to Africa to upgrade the new local Bharti Airtel subsidiary quickly ran into a variety of issues. They encountered an unhealthy organizational legacy of the prior structure in which expatriates from Europe and the Middle East made key decisions, leaving local employees disempowered and poorly motivated. In terms of culturally based work patterns, they reportedly found their employees in most African countries to be more indirect and emotional in their communication style. By comparison, the Indian expatriates were relatively direct and objective when communicating.[4] African authorities have continued to criticize Bharti Airtel for being overly dependent on expatriates, citing an "expectation gap" based on cultural differences, and calling for greater localization.[5]

However, the most fundamental set of problems that Bharti Airtel encountered in Africa was based on its strategic misreading of the continent's business environment. The company's leaders initially failed to understand this new cultural context because of the pervasive way that that their prior experience in India, including their remarkable successes, shaped their assumptions about what would be viable in a different location. Simply put, they assumed that Africa would be a lot more similar to India than it actually turned out to be and that they could easily replicate their previous formula for success. Once on the ground, Bharti Airtel's assignees from India experienced the potentially destructive lure of entrenched habits and assumptions. As a result, they made a series of painful discoveries as they attempted to implement their business model in a new location. These included:

- **Country and regional differences:** Bharti Airtel assignees had to learn how to cope with different political structures, social attitudes, regulatory structures, tax regimes, and languages across the 17 countries where they were doing business in Africa. The differences between these countries turned out to be far more challenging than first assumed. Broadly speaking, they found the most significant contrasts between Anglophone and Francophone environments, with stiffer labor laws and regulations in the latter.

- **Infrastructure:** Limited availability of efficient transportation or a viable infrastructure for overland transportation meant that in some locations cell phone towers had to be brought in by helicopter or even by elephant. At times, the company had to build and maintain its own roads.

- **Supply chain:** Bharti Airtel suppliers in Africa, including some of the same firms that were already serving them in India, had less robust operations than in India but were accustomed to charging stiff European prices. Outsourcing turned out to be both difficult and more expensive.

- **Employee response to outsourcing:** The company underestimated the extent to which local employees would object to being second to employers they perceived as less prestigious; this actually led to worker protests and strikes in Nigeria, and a black eye to Bharti Airtel's brand image when Nigerian workers protested and shut down part of its network.

- **Competition:** Local competition proved to be formidable, tenacious, and well-established, with a first-mover advantage in key markets. Competitors also had developed attractive cell phone applications such as a mobile money transfer service that encouraged customer loyalty and less responsiveness to aggressive pricing.

- **Socioeconomic structure:** Aggressive price decreases by Bharti Airtel, part of the company's core strategy to "manufacture minutes" by stimulating ever increasing demand and economies of scale, failed to produce the anticipated results. Price changes were matched by some competitors and also failed to generate the huge expansion in demand that occurred in response to lower prices in India. Cell phone prices seemed to be a bigger obstacle than the cost of a phone call. Possible reasons for this may include greater concentration of wealth in a number of African countries, particularly those run by the most corrupt and kleptocratic regimes, with a lack of prosperity filtering down to rural areas.[6]

Bharti Airtel continues to struggle to make its acquisition in Africa a success. After buying Zain's operations, the company as a whole suffered through a long period of declining net profits, dragged down by losses in Africa and other overseas ventures. In a recent year, Bharti Airtel lost over $100 million in Africa alone and has still failed to reach any of its initial acquisition goals for revenue, earnings, and subscribers announced at the time of the purchase. More than five years after the acquisition, performance in Africa is labeled as the "biggest key negative" for the company as a whole.[7]

In spite of these setbacks, Bharti Airtel continues to forge ahead with fresh investments in infrastructure and by doubling down with additional acquisitions of smaller telephony firms in markets such as Uganda, the Democratic Republic of Congo, and Republic of Seychelles. It has also hired away a key executive from its largest African competitor to become its CEO for Africa, and restructured first into Anglophone and Francophone units, and then into units based on market position.[8] As the fundamental assumptions behind its original business model in India have proved to be problematic in this new environment, Bharti Airtel has been forced to adapt. In some markets, the company has chosen not to be the low-price leader and is building key infrastructure instead of outsourcing. In addition, to increase the appeal of its services beyond price, it has rolled out cell phone applications such as mobile payment and information for farmers on weather, crop prices, and cultivation techniques.

The jury is still out on whether the Bharti Airtel will learn to run the operations it has acquired in Africa profitably and without compromising its own core competencies. If its executives and employees had known more about the 17 countries they were getting themselves into, they might have reconsidered their approach and at least gotten off to a better start. They are now committed to a long and expensive road, paying a heavy price to learn along the way.

Why Diligence Falls Short

Due diligence for a merger or acquisition is often considered to be a business task that is independent of culture. Yet classic elements of research on culture help to explain why Bharti Airtel executives overlooked so many factors critical to the success of this pivotal cross-border transaction. Nancy Adler, an expert on international organizational behavior, describes the phenomenon of projected similarity, or the assumption that other people or situations are more similar than is actually the case: "Projecting similarity involves assuming, imagining, and actually perceiving similarity when differences exist."[9]

Projection of similarity is tied to underestimation of differences. Milton Bennett and Mitchell Hammer have defined the intercultural development stage of "minimization," in which similarities are recognized but differences are underestimated. This is the stage in which the temptation to project similarities is most likely to be the strongest, also making it easy for executives conducting due diligence to dismiss any perceived differences as minor. Data gathered over many years indicate that the majority of corporate groups are in the stage of minimization.[10]

The Bharti Airtel executive team perceived more similarities between the Indian and African markets than were actually present, and failed to recognize significant differences in ways that residents of various African countries were solving problems in their own particular environments. They probably made assumptions such as the following:

- India and Africa both have large numbers of poor people who will respond to lower prices by increasing their cell phone usage. *(Yes, but wealth in Africa is less well distributed, and many people still lack even the means to purchase cell phones.)*

- India and Africa both have vendors to whom key functions can be outsourced. *(Yes, but many of Bharti Airtel's outsourcing partners had African operations that were less robust and more expensive than in India.)*

- India and Africa both have infrastructure challenges. *(Yes, but Africa's land mass is nine times the size of India's, with many areas that are far from the coastline.)*

- India and Africa are both diverse, and we know how to handle diverse customers. *(Yes, but Africa consists of many different countries with separate governments and regulatory structures; it also lacks unifying cultural influences with the impact of Bollywood or cricket.)*

- India and Africa both have many languages. *(Yes, but Indian professionals have English as a common unifying language, while Africa has Anglophone and Francophone regions, plus other countries that fall in neither category.)*

- India and Africa both have colonial heritages. *(Yes, but during the century prior to its independence, India was ruled primarily by one country, wheras Africa has the recent legacy of many different colonial masters, including Great Britain, France, Belgium, Germany, Portugal, Italy, Spain, and the former Ottoman Empire.)*

Another common challenge in intercultural contexts is groupthink, or the tendency for homogeneous teams to converge prematurely on conclusions as a cohesive in-group, striving for unanimity without sufficient reality testing. Adler's description of what can happen when a team acts this way sounds like what seems to have occurred as Bharti Airtel's Indian leadership was analyzing the potential Zain acquisition, largely in the absence of input from local nationals:

The consequences of groupthink include incompletely survey-ing objectives and alternatives, failing to examine the risks inherent in preferred choices . . . conducting poor information searches, introducing selective bias in processing available information, and failing to work out contingency plans.[11]

There were undoubtedly other reasons for Bharti Airtel execu-tives to make their giant bet on Africa without knowing the local terrain as well as Machiavelli would have recommended. Some of these might have been a strong sense of self-confidence and faith in their own business acumen based on prior successes in their home market. Executives who have invested large amounts of time in the hunt for an acquisition target may also loathe returning home empty-handed. Their pride is at stake, and they want to get tangible results to justify the investments in time and money already incurred.

Bharti Airtel's situation is by no means unique. Any successful team considering an acquisition in an unfamiliar place can readily fall into these same snares of projected similarity, minimization, and groupthink, fueled ironically by the very successes that have gotten them to this point. Such pitfalls exist not only for top executives who commit to a merger deal or an acquisition but for every other company employee who then is tasked with implementing their decision. When an increasing number of people are heavily commit-ted to emphasizing similarities, persuading them that differences are also important becomes a pervasive organizational challenge that sometimes can be addressed only after a direct collision with the facts on the ground. The issues that Bharti Airtel encountered—including the unique local characteristics of political and regulatory structures, infrastructure, supply chain, human resources, and so on—should be part of an expanded due diligence checklist for cross-border M&A that considers the distinctive environment of each country and the cultural habits it has helped to shape.

Problem No. 2: Integrating Cultural Patterns

Once the deal has been signed, various teams are normally created in order to integrate organizational processes and systems. This nitty-gritty implementation phase can be very unsettling for team members. In retrospect, many merger veterans cite their work on small project teams as a critical part of their journey toward a unified corporate culture. Such teams force people from both organizations to collaborate on a specific, outcome-driven project, overcoming obstacles together along the way. But this is often not how people feel in the beginning of the process. They typically see acquisitions in very black-and-white terms, with winners and losers. The acquirer is at least temporarily the winner that exerts the most control, and employees of the acquired firm know that big changes are probably coming soon. They are likely asking themselves the most common question, "What will this mean for me?" while polishing their resumes just in case. The acquirer's employees may also be uncertain of their own futures. Cross-border transactions contain many ironies:

- *The Taller Little Sibling:* The national subsidiary of an acquired firm may be many times larger than the subsidiary of the buyer in that country.

- *The Golden Child:* Subsidiary employees of the acquirer are now jealous of the new "golden child" that has been purchased in their country with great cost and much fanfare, and they are uncertain about what this will mean for their own roles.

- *Outnumbered:* Employees of a division in the new parent company are anxious because there are far more employees in the same division of the foreign firm that has been purchased.

- *Outsourced:* Employees of the new parent company surmise that their jobs could soon be relocated to less expensive locations abroad where the acquisition has operations.

- *Untouchable:* In some cases, the acquiring company intentionally wants the acquisition to retain a large degree of autonomy and separateness in order to preserve its brand recognition. In this situation, integrating operational systems becomes even more complex.

- *Culture Change:* A smaller company in a foreign market has been purchased to spark culture change in the new parent company, which means that unfamiliar executives suddenly take on key roles and begin to implement their own policies and ideas.

Facing an existential threat such as loss of one's organizational status and sense of certainty, people typically respond with variations of "fight or flight"—going on the offensive to strive for dominant alpha status, hunkering down in a resistant defensive posture, or looking for outside job offers to escape the situation altogether. None of these responses is conducive to constructive collaboration among new coworkers. Even the term "synergy," which originally had the cheerful and optimistic 1 + 1 = 3 connotation of a dynamic combination of forces, has been co-opted by merger specialists to refer to cost savings, and more specifically to reductions in head count following a merger or acquisition. Under strained circumstances when everyone knows that the dreaded synergies are on the way, there is a strong temptation for employees to be on their worst behavior, especially when dealing with potentially threatening new colleagues from a different part of the world.

Yet this is the time when close and effective cooperation is most essential. The companies that have come together probably have been using different organizational structures, software, financial systems, sales incentives, marketing brands, manufacturing processes, human resource practices, quality metrics, and so on. In addition, each legacy organization had its own informal patterns of communicating, planning, problem solving, making decisions, and resolving conflicts that are still mostly implicit and taken for granted. Often, even the same terms—for instance, "commitment," "entrepreneurial," or "compromise"—used by two organizations are interpreted differently by each one's employees.

National and organizational cultures are frequently intermingled, and the choice to adopt one way of doing things or another can have huge symbolic significance. In the wake of a transaction, everyone is watching intently for the degree of consistency between public pronouncements and everyday operating decisions. Below are examples of style and terminology clashes that have occurred in post-merger integration settings involving Asian, European, and North American participants, with representative voices from each side, along with a brief description of how the conflict was addressed. Relevant national cultural dimensions include attitudes toward risk taking versus certainty and independence versus interdependence.

Example: Definition of Commitment

A. "Commitment is a firm promise and a fundamental matter of trust. If you commit, you are held accountable. Commitments should be ambitious and realistic, and not meeting them is grounds for removal."

B. "Commitment to revenue targets incorporates stretch goals and is deliberately ambitious. Not reaching a stretch target is okay as long as your performance is acceptable and you are making money."

Resolution: The acquirer's definition of commitment (A) is regarded by top executives as being a core element of their organizational culture, and lax attitudes toward meeting commitments are seen as one of the problems with the acquired organization that led to its sale. Leaders from the acquired organization must learn to make and achieve clear commitments—or be removed from their roles.

Example: We Are Entrepreneurial

A. "Our company is highly entrepreneurial. We move quickly, take risks, and confront each other directly when our opinions differ— we are always striving to make things better. Our employees are passionate and dedicated to their work."

B. "Our new parent is autocratic, bureaucratic, and process-oriented. Now we are being forced to implement global processes that do not really fit us. For example, the processes we must use for new product testing and marketing are cumbersome and time-consuming. We also need to pay out of our budget to implement these processes, which is very frustrating. How can we be profitable with these increased costs for processes that do not add value to achieving our business objectives?"

Resolution: Feedback from employees in the acquired organization caused headquarters executives to reflect and realize that they were not as entrepreneurial as they had thought, and could do more to streamline their processes and act more nimbly. Key individuals from the acquired organization were promoted to executive positions at headquarters and asked to be agents of organizational culture change. This was difficult at first both for these leaders and for employees at headquarters accustomed to their legacy processes, but over time it has had a real impact in cutting unnecessary bureaucracy and speeding up the time in which new products come to market.

Example: The Value of Compromise

A. "Our product must be differentiated in the marketplace. Too many compromises undermine the integrity of product design and our brand. People who are uncompromising in their standards make great products rather than mediocre 'me too' devices."

B. "Compromise is a fundamental requirement for working together. Each part of the organization has to compromise for the good of the whole. People who don't compromise are selfish and obstruct progress for their own personal reasons."

Resolution: The members of the new integrated executive team recognized that they were interpreting the same word differently, and that each interpretation had value. True innovation generating that produced unique value in the marketplace was important (A), as was close collaboration and alignment to achieve common goals (B), even if it meant sometimes giving up a cherished idea. Team members sought to integrate both kinds of value, using a broader range of terminology that defused emotional clashes around the word "compromise" by stressing the simultaneous needs for innovation and for flexibility.

Problem No. 3: Teamwork at the Top

Perhaps the most acute challenge in integrating two organizations, especially when they are headquartered in different countries, is a very personal one. People who are used to being in charge commonly have trouble letting go. Some executives, particularly those from the acquired entity, are likely to be stinging at the loss of their previous status and wrestling to retain as much authority as possible. They may also conflate their own quest for continued relevance with a stalwart defense of others from their own home country or organization, adding a kind of righteous fervor to their actions. Executive teamwork is undermined when one or more members of the team are actively lobbying for greater control.

Sergio Marchionne, head of Fiat Chrysler, emphasizes that getting clashing personalities to fit together can be the most difficult aspect of a merger. Individuals who feel who they have suddenly lost control can become dysfunctional, and the effect of a punctured ego is like having what he describes as an evil spirit in the building.[12] Long-time Chrysler employees know well what Marchionne is talking about. Daimler-Chrysler AG, their previous merger with another automotive giant, was plagued by ego clashes and lingering ill will throughout its sorry lifespan, ultimately resulting in an expensive failure. The conduct of executives striving to be at the center of things, refusing to acknowledge the fact that their world has shifted, has a divisive influence that is mirrored at other levels of the organization. The allegiances they still command lead to fragmentation, conflicting loyalties among subordinates, competing cliques, redundant review processes, reopened decisions, and widespread resistance to meaningful integration.

Senior executives are typically the ones who find it hardest to adjust to new realities because they were part of their legacy organizations for many years and were probably instrumental in shaping its corporate culture. This previous culture is embedded in their everyday actions, and each work habit they have to alter or give up can be felt as yet another loss of identity, comfort, and status. Whether the required change is perceived as a pinprick or a body blow, resistance is often tenacious. The executive fighting for relevance is engaged in a symbolic battle fueled by deep emotions and may be willing to persist even in the face of a solid business case for doing things differently. Well-intended but unclear messages about a "merger of equals" can make things worse; this implies that authority is still up for grabs, though even mergers between entities of roughly equal size almost always result in a controlling side. When authority is ambiguous, ordinary business decisions suddenly become more complicated as people who don't actually need to be involved try to demonstrate their ability to have an impact. On the other hand, entry-level employees tend to be the quickest to adjust to post-merger realities. They are still learning new habits anyway, and as time passes, a growing number of them know only the merged entity because they were hired after the transaction.

Bruised egos, lack of alignment, competing factions, resistance to change, and unnecessarily complicated decisions all make it harder to focus on customers and on achieving business objectives. The post-merger integration process drags on, and too much energy is absorbed by internal friction. In this situation it is vital to enable the organization to move forward and coalesce around a shared direction. There are only a few options for handling the aggrieved parties:

- **Feedback:** Top executives who are disgruntled by what they perceive to be a diminished role in the combined organization may respond favorably to a frank discussion with the new CEO. It is hard to achieve a real meeting of minds and hearts when the CEO and the executive are from different countries and speak different native languages, but it's possible. The message "We value your expertise and want you to have a key role in the new organization" could be just what is needed to smooth ruffled feathers and bring a different tone to the relationship. This kind of declaration must then be followed up by additional actions from the top, drawing out the desired contributions, giving public credit where it is deserved, and also holding the wayward executive accountable for any further foot-dragging.

- **Coaching:** There are executives who have thrown themselves completely into their roles for many years and have had little time to self-reflect or to consider the consequences of their actions. They are operating in ruts worn deep by the power of habit, and resist paths that lead off in uncertain directions. Yet they are sometimes willing to listen to other voices they respect and are sufficiently adaptable to change under the right circumstances. A gifted coach may be able to create a safe environment for the executive to mourn the death of the old organization, to step back from entrenched habits or grievances and reflect on personal goals, and to embrace the new reality with a fresh attitude.

- **Removal:** Post-merger integration teams seek to retain key executives from the acquired organization for a variety of reasons: skills and experience, technical or industry knowledge, close ties with other employees, the desire to present a face of continuity to the outside world, or the need to preserve important customer relationships. If the person is incapable of changing to serve a new top leadership and its vision, however, such factors are outweighed by other negative consequences that undermine the integration process. Ongoing dissatisfaction and resentment, and the ripple effect this has on others, usually have a far greater cost. When attempts have been made to provide feedback and/or coaching and the divisive conduct continues, it is best to act quickly and to send the person looking for another job. This might ultimately be better for the individual who is removed, and it will certainly help the integration to move on.

INTEGRATING CULTURES: SUCCESS STORIES

There are a precious few real success stories among large-scale M&A transactions across borders. Big companies can more readily absorb smaller ones. It is clear who will be making the decisions, and the employees who have been acquired have little choice: adapt or leave.

Marriages between major industry peers are a different story, however, because of the delicate balancing act involved in combining operations in an efficient new structure while preserving valuable people and practices from both legacy organizations. Many mergers struggle along for years and achieve partial victories without clear-cut success; others are eventually undone. Similar challenges can occur when a company acquires a smaller firm based in another country with the aim to build a presence in the country or region through the acquisition. In this case, as in a transaction between industry peers, there is usually a need to preserve both key personnel and cultural characteristics of the acquired entity.

The automotive industry has provided instructive examples—not only of high-profile and expensive failures like the aforementioned DaimlerChrysler case, but also positive surprises such as Chrysler's more recent tie-up with Fiat. The most high-profile success story, the Renault-Nissan Alliance, was initially labeled a marriage of the poor, and few predicted that it would prosper. Even Carlos Ghosn, who was to become the celebrated leader of Nissan and later both companies, put the chances of success at no better than 50 percent, according to a colorful account by Kannan Ramaswamy.[13] Although Renault-Nissan stopped short of a full-scale merger, the companies have taken a number of steps together to address common M&A problems described earlier in this chapter.

- **Reading the environment.** Renault and Nissan engaged in an unusually extensive due diligence process. They had both been rejected by prior suitors and understood the importance of cultural fit. While the transaction was still under discussion, they already had 21 joint study teams examining various aspects of both firms' operations, priorities, and organizational cultures. Just as importantly, this team activity was already building mutual trust even prior to the actual transaction.[14] As one company leader stated, "In many marriages today, people [jump in] without knowing each other well. There was a good personal relationship before we started."[15]

  As soon as the deal was signed, Carlos Ghosn embarked on an exhausting travel schedule. He visited all of Nissan's major sites and spoke with employees at every level, including shop floor employees and dealers who transacted directly with customers. Ghosn was consistently curious and respectful in these early dealings, listening and learning carefully before moving on to make difficult choices.[16]

- **Integrating cultural practices.** Ghosn had lived abroad for much of his career, spoke four languages, came from a bicultural family background, and was himself a veteran of previous mergers. Over time, he implemented almost every conceivable strategy for integrating the cultures of Renault and Nissan (see Figure 6.2):

  A. **Adapt:** Ghosn was quite aware of the Japanese cultural patterns embedded within Nissan's daily operations and took care to alter his own style as needed. He comments, for example: "The French way of managing and leadership in France expresses itself in completely different terms than in Japan. I knew it from in the beginning. . . . You have some fundamentals which are the same . . . but the ways you exercise these fundamentals are completely different. In Japan, I don't run meetings the same way that I run them in France. I don't reward people the same way that I do in France. What is expected even in terms of communication [differs from one place to another].

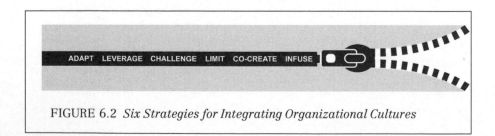

FIGURE 6.2 *Six Strategies for Integrating Organizational Cultures*

The tools are not the same, the words are not the same—the way even you shape your strategy is not the same."[17]

B. **Leverage:** As COO of North American operations for his previous employer, Michelin, Ghosn had integrated the operations of fellow industry giant Uniroyal Goodrich after Michelin acquired them. A key strategy he developed in the course of this prior experience was the use of cross-functional teams to pursue various elements of the integration process. These teams were tasked with generating proposals to improve targeted aspects of the business by tapping the knowledge and experience of employees themselves.

In the case of Renault-Nissan, Ghosn utilized two types of teams: cross-company teams (CCTs) that sought ways to combine the two companies' operations, and cross-functional teams (CFTs) that focused on Nissan's recovery by stepping out of formerly siloed structures and thinking together across departmental lines. Ghosn was involved in the selection of team members, and he and the rest of the executive team had the ultimate say over their recommendations, but the proposals for Nissan's successful transformation came largely from team members. The fact that major reforms at Nissan were proposed by the company's own employees helped in communicating difficult messages and in building the commitment to act.

Ghosn also sought to leverage what he saw as positive aspects of Japanese society and of Nissan's corporate culture: "A good corporate culture taps into the productive aspects of a country's culture, and in Nissan's case we have been able to exploit the uniquely Japanese combination of keen competitiveness and sense of community . . ."[18]

C. **Challenge:** Paradoxically, Ghosn's respect for Nissan and its employees and his readiness to listen also helped the organization to modify traditional Japanese management practices. Rather than reflexively defending the status quo, the cross-functional teams, consisting mostly of Japanese participants, challenged the standard pillars of Japan's lifetime employment system. They proposed addressing Nissan's dire financial condition through a massive headcount reduction (although without direct layoffs) accompanied by plant closings, promotion of younger managers based on performance rather than seniority-based promotion, and more substantial performance bonuses. Another very controversial measure was selling Nissan's *keiretsu* (industrial conglomerate) cross-holdings in its partners to raise cash to pay down debt and make new investments.[19]

Japan has a historical pattern, demonstrated in its transition to the Meiji Reformation in the mid-1800s, of using pressure from abroad (*gaiatsu*) as a pretext for carrying out changes desired by factions within the country. In one sense, Ghosn benefited from having proposals for radical change come from Japanese employees themselves, but his presence as a foreigner also provided Nissan employees with a rationale for doing what they knew was necessary, yet had been constrained by long-standing traditions and social ties from implementing on their own.

D. **Limit:** While seeking benefits for the combined Renault-Nissan enterprise, Ghosn and Renault deliberately steered away from full-scale assimilation of Nissan on the grounds that this would cause unnecessary confusion; Ghosn felt that they could not create a unified team of Japanese and French running a company that was neither Japanese nor French.[20] His original boss, Louis Schweitzer, also expressed the view that culture is quintessentially local and that arbitrary assimilation would undermine brand value. At times Ghosn actively defended Nissan when managers from Renault demanded changes to conform to their systems that offered no clear value, had the potential to distract employees, and might sap Nissan's identity.[21]

Ghosn also grasped the feelings of humiliation and loss of autonomy involved in any takeover, stating, "Every single time you make a merger, somebody is losing his identity . . . and saying something different is rubbish." He sought to limit changes to what was essential for restoring the business while focusing instead on rebuilding the company's sense of pride along with its core strengths.[22]

E. **Co-create:** The Renault-Nissan Alliance produced a string of significant benefits through careful joint planning and investment. These created broader synergies than simply cost-cutting, although they achieved greater efficiency as well. In fact, better performance in some areas made it possible to invest more in high-priority initiatives. Here are a few examples of co-creation:

- *Mutual learning:* Nissan absorbed new ideas from Renault's strengths in design and purchasing, while Renault learned from Nissan's manufacturing prowess, inviting Japanese experts to teach workers on its factory floors in France and elsewhere.

- *Combinations of existing resources:* Combined purchasing efforts and sharing of vehicle platforms resulted in economies of scale and enormous savings. In addition, Renault's use of an underutilized Nissan factory in Mexico increased plant utilization from 55 percent to almost 100 percent and enabled Renault to return to an important market with a relatively small investment.

- *New efforts with combined resources:* Joint investments were made in a new commercial vehicle assembly plant in Brazil, facilitating Nissan's entry there, and in R&D investments to build the next generation of fuel cell technology.[23]

F. **Infuse:** Ghosn has had a tremendous effect on both Nissan and Renault through the influence of his personality and leadership style, and has undoubtedly shaped both organizational cultures over time. He describes his own leadership agenda as making a lucid diagnosis of the state of the business ("No sugarcoating!"), prioritizing employee recommendations, and rallying people around the common goal of reviving the company while persuading them to take difficult steps.[24] Ghosn's leadership brand of clear rationality, toughness tempered by congeniality, and manifest passion—attributes of his own cultural heritage and personal style—were powerful medicine when combined with the proposals of Nissan's employees and healthy aspects of the rebounding corporate culture. Ghosn notes that "as Nissan's identity strengthens, the North Americans, Europeans, and Japanese working here are becoming much more alike than they are different."[25] Ghosn's respectful yet demanding leadership style has had a lot to do with this alignment of approaches.

- **Teamwork at the Top.** Another positive feature of the Renault-Nissan enterprise was the close relationships between top executives on both sides. Louis Schweitzer, Renault's CEO at the time of the merger, had come to know the chairman of Nissan, Yoshikazu Hanawa, quite well. He also took the unusual step of appointing Tsumoto Sawada, Nissan's respected head of engineering and manufacturing—powerful functions within the company—as a senior vice president and personal advisor at Renault. As Mr. Sawada said, "My main responsibility is to provide advice to Mr. Schweitzer and to his senior executives about how best to work with Nissan. . . . I know most of the key people and I can talk to them quite openly. My primary [job] is to make sure that there are few surprises between the partners."[26]

Thus, when it came time for Carlos Ghosn to consider the input from the CCTs and CFTs and to make difficult decisions, he could generally be assured that he had the support of top executives at Nissan as well as Renault. Such alignment was crucial for the drastic steps he would take to revitalize the organization.

Every M&A success story is still a moving target that merits ongoing scrutiny. Renault-Nissan is no exception, even after more than 15 years. The combined enterprise now ranks fourth in the automotive world in terms of global vehicle sales volume, a status that neither company could have achieved on its own. Yet the value of the alliance must be renewed on a regular basis to keep it healthy. Additionally, some parts of the operation—such as core engineering functions—are likely to be better off retaining a measure of autonomy in order to preserve their brand identity and their ability to serve critical customer segments.

Probably the single biggest challenge the combined entity faces is grooming a viable successor for Carlos Ghosn. It is not easy to step into the shoes of a celebrated CEO who has sometimes been called "superman," and is now running not just one Fortune 500 company but two, having taken on the role of CEO at Renault as well. Renault-Nissan's alliance structure is notoriously complex. Ghosn is constantly in motion from one continent to the next, and is said to live like a monk or a Knight Templar, with a strict regimen for diet and sleeping to offset his incredibly demanding schedule.[27] Several people once touted as potential successors have left the company and landed in executive positions with automotive industry competitors. It is hard to imagine any other one person who could run both companies simultaneously, although the combined enterprise will need to address these questions soon.[28]

Chagrin in Chicago: Part II

Mergers and acquisitions tend to be a work in progress for far longer than most participants would expect. They require sustained effort and an increasing sense of shared trust in order to succeed. Since the acquisition described at the beginning of this chapter was announced, collaboration and planning on the management level have been going on for almost a full year, and the next stage of full-scale integration is about to start. The mood has changed considerably; some issues have been addressed, while others linger. Here are comments from executives and team leaders in the now-combined organization about what has been most helpful and what still needs to be done.

- "Our joint efforts have helped us come together as a unified team with shared goals and systems for working together. These have become the starting point for all of our discussions. The next phase is to expand our positive team dynamic to a broader circle of people."

- "We now have the common objective of being the fastest in the world at bringing high quality new products to market—using a 24-hour, round-the-clock development cycle."

(Continued)

(Continued)

- "Initially we were concerned that some people would be more vocal than others and that Korean team members would not express their opinions openly. We are now having discussions which are more balanced and productive."

- "The business case for the acquisition has become clear at the leadership level. Employees in the field are still not fully convinced, although they have heard the explanation on multiple occasions. They need a more complete understanding and a more tangible sense of the benefits to the company and to them in order to become more open to changing their daily work patterns."

- "You can't just push a button and have an aligned global team across the organization and at every level. It is not feasible to change everything simultaneously, so we are moving forward step by step."

- "Becoming one company has different ramifications for different business units and staff functions. Some departments are more localized and domestic than others. It is important for us to be clear and coordinated going forward."

- "There is ongoing concern from those whose work can be globalized that our new partners might take this over. There are many decisions yet to make about what should be done jointly or locally, and people want to know how they can influence the outcomes."

- "Now we need to help each individual team member understand how the integration will affect their own work, and to ensure that their personal performance objectives are aligned with the objectives of the combined organization."

- "Everybody in the new company needs to clearly understand the 'what,' and also to have some freedom to develop the 'how' that fits their particular function and market circumstances."

WHAT YOU CAN DO

(either as a member of the acquirer or the acquired party)

- Avoid the due diligence pitfalls of projected similarities, underestimated differences, and groupthink.

- Ask due diligence questions that go beyond the usual financial and strategic concerns. (What about factors such as country and regional characteristics, infrastructure, human resources practices, and the differences in competitive environments?)

- Be alert for key M&A problems related to national, organizational, and team cultures.

- Go out of your way to demonstrate respect for and to learn from your new partners.

- Consider using some or all of Carlos Ghosn's strategies for cultural integration: adapt, leverage, challenge, limit, co-create, infuse.

- Help the new organization to build a unified team atmosphere at every level.

- Keep the focus on setting shared goals and executing them effectively, avoiding prolonged distraction with internal struggles.

- Look constantly for mutual benefits and what is best for the combined organization; stay away from win/lose integration scenarios where possible.

7

Global Innovation: Beyond Products

Agility to Innovate on a Global Scale

INNOVATION: THE NEW PLAYING FIELD

Michael Porter once said that innovation is the central issue in economic prosperity. Over the past decade or more there has been a growing body of evidence that innovation is coming from outside of the developed countries, with significant implications for global organizations. Opportunities for innovation are rapidly evolving in many other marketplaces around the world, including Asia, Africa, and Latin America.

China's Automotive Market

The center of gravity of the world's automotive market has shifted dramatically. China's automotive market is now the largest in the world, with close to a quarter of global volume. Stepping out onto the noisy streets of Shanghai, you will be greeted by a fleet of Land Rovers, Porsches, and Maseratis, mixed in with Volkswagens, Buicks, Toyotas, and so on. Every major carmaker in the world is represented here, and many of them are currently making more than one-third—some almost two-thirds—of their profits in China.[1] The number of vehicles sold in the country surpassed the U.S. sales volume during the recession in North America and Europe, and though the rate of market growth has slowed in recent years, sales remain far higher than those in either the United States or Europe.[2] Within five years the Chinese automotive market could be more than 30 percent larger than that of the United States.

The structure of China's automotive industry is a petri dish of intermingled joint ventures and alliances, with new facilities sprouting up all over the country.[3] Non-Chinese automakers are required to enter a joint venture with a Chinese partner and may have up to two of these partners. There are several dozen Chinese automakers with names less well-known outside of the country, but many of them have huge capacity and ambitious plans to expand both domestically and abroad: Shanghai Automotive, Dongfeng Motor, Chang'an Motors, Guangzhou Automobile, Chery, Brilliance China Auto, BYD Automobile, and Great Wall Motors. Domestic manufacturers are often owned by a branch of the Chinese government; others are controlled by provinces—this would be the equivalent of a Texas Car Company in the United States, or a Bavarian Motor Works in Germany that was actually owned by the state of Bavaria.

Innovation in this environment comes in various forms, many of them counterintuitive to people from other parts of the world. Take the brand image of Buick, often characterized in its U.S. home market as a mediocre, mid-range car driven by aging grandparents. General Motors has leveraged the car's historical associations—respected former premier Zhou Enlai had a Buick[4]—to position it as a luxury brand for dynamic businesspeople. Buick in China is seen as a car for the "big boss," or at least a person who aspires to that status. Its Chinese owners are almost half the age of those in the United States. However, this dissonance between types of customers in different markets no longer matters, as GM makes close to 80 percent of its Buick sales in China.[5] Even the mini-van Buick model in China appeals not to soccer moms but to executives, and General Motors has designed an especially roomy and comfortable minivan for these high status customers, resulting in a huge boost in sales.[6]

There are many other opportunities for innovation in China's car industry in addition to distinctive brand positioning. Here are a few examples:

- **Luxury cars:** The emphasis in this segment is not so much on experience as a driver but rather as a passenger. Most Chinese executives are driven by chauffeurs, so carmakers have rushed to expand backseat legroom and conveniences. Potential buyers often want a vehicle that conveys an impression of prestige without being too flashy in a way that might single out an individual for criticism, especially if the person holds a government office.

- **Compact cars:** Around three-quarters of Chinese car buyers are purchasing their first automobile, most commonly in the compact car segment. Approximately 80 percent of buyers use cash rather than financing.[7] Consumers are highly connected to digital resources: more than 90 percent reportedly use social media to inform themselves about a possible purchase, and they view comments from fellow consumers as being relatively trustworthy; over half interact directly with companies through the web about their products or services.[8] Advertising and Internet descriptions must be tailored to these newbie buyers, and there is ample room for introducing novel marketing and financing practices. Some dealers even organize social clubs with outings such as hiking and rafting trips for youthful customers, publicizing these events in their facilities and on the web to create an inviting sense of community.

- **Sport utility vehicles:** Prospective SUV buyers are often making their second purchase, so they are looking to this next vehicle as a symbol of their climb to a higher social rung. They want to feel they can leave China's crowded, polluted cities to breathe cleaner air on holiday outings or to travel to their hometown. Many SUV buyers— a rapidly growing segment of the market—are looking for a car that will seat seven people: parents, the one child allowed in China unless both parents are from one-child families, and sometimes two sets of grandparents.[9]

Meanwhile, the Chinese government is trying to foster the development of locally based champions, thereby reshaping the competitive environment. For example, given the perpetual grayness in many cities from rampant pollution, the government has been strongly encouraging the development of electric cars by offering financial incentives to consumers who purchase one from a domestic maker. Many cities have also begun to restrict the number of cars that can be purchased each year, with a significant quota reserved for electric vehicles. This supports potentially disruptive Chinese entrants into the industry such as BYD Automobile, which was originally a battery maker; the company's most famous investor is Nebraska billionaire Warren Buffett. BYD has struggled recently, facing accusations of copying and of safety hazards as well as declining sales of its conventional vehicles. In the face of these setbacks, it has announced daring plans to go all-electric, and is currently winning a substantial share of China's still small electric vehicle market.[10] Time will tell whether BYD or another Chinese automaker will be a successful challenger to foreign automakers on its own turf and on a more global basis.

Innovation on a Global Scale

It is easy to underestimate the potential impact of innovation that is occurring outside of more mature markets, even for those who are based in fast-growth markets themselves. Would-be innovators in these newer markets are often characterized as tinkering around the margins with adaptations, incremental improvements, or outright copies that are winked at in countries with loose intellectual property standards, corruption, and large gaps between rich and poor. China's automotive industry provides an outrageously rich set of copycat examples, including domestic cars that appear to be exact copies of foreign models. For example, there is a clunky Hummer lookalike as well as a copy of Audi's A6 that is labeled with a cheeky and ungrammatical name: Refine A6.[11] Some hybrid copies actually mimic the front end of one model and the rear end of another.

Leaders from the developed world may steer away from new market opportunities due to what they perceive as their incremental, bargain-hunting nature—plus ample evidence that the art of copying still abounds. It is common to hear statements such as the following:

- "It would be easiest just to tweak what we've got already and send it to other markets. They're going to copy what we do anyway."
- "We can do a phased rollout that starts in our most mature markets; this will help to protect our intellectual property."
- "We need to focus on our core competencies and our biggest customers at home, as that's where we're making money."
- "The opportunities out there look small. We need to be able to quantify our return on investments in new markets."
- "Let's target just the top tier of the market in Country X, as we know we can be profitable there."

Meanwhile, current and future leaders in fast-growth markets face a mirror set of challenges of their own:

- "I wish we had been involved earlier in the product development effort. Now we have a product that doesn't really fit this market, with too big a footprint, too high a price, and features that local consumers don't need. We're told we can 'tweak' the product, but we really need to completely redesign it."
- "It is frustrating to bring our company's own product to market six months after its initial introduction elsewhere and to find that competitors have already adapted and have come out with a superior product."

- "It is hard to feel like our market is a second or third priority when we're aware of its potential and how fast our competitors are growing."
- "I know the market here is growing rapidly and providing us with a huge opportunity, but it is hard for me to demonstrate this to people at headquarters; they see our current market size as too small to justify a significant investment."
- "Everything in our company moves too slowly. Our local competitors are not slowed down by so many internal processes and systems."
- "We do not have the sales and service networks that our local competitors have. They are better at responding quickly and providing good service in many locations around the country."

BEYOND PRODUCTS

Innovation can be defined as "new ideas plus action or implementation which results in an improvement, gain, or profit."[12] Based on this definition, innovation may take various forms anywhere. However, a key feature of innovation in fast-growth markets is that it extends far beyond hot new products. Many subsidiaries or companies based in fast-growth markets do not possess strong R&D capabilities, receive the latest technologies from headquarters, or even have access to products that are precisely targeted at the needs of local customers. They must learn how to pilot other kinds of innovative measures to create an attractive overall package—for example, a new marketing campaign that fits local tastes while supporting the company's global brand image, a more responsive supply chain, faster and more reliable service, a process for recruiting or retaining new kinds of qualified employees, or improved manufacturing techniques. These may be exactly what they need to fill out a successful business model by providing a competitive edge. Companies can also succeed by identifying and addressing local deficits in institutions or infrastructure.[13]

It is worth considering specific examples of paths that lead to both disappointment and success in fast-growth markets.

Example: iPad's India Launch

Widely regarded as one of the world's most innovative organizations, Apple stumbled badly in India when first introducing its iPad. The company's approach outside of mature markets has been to position itself as a higher-end player and to retain its pricing premium over other market entries. However, as Sanjeev Prashar and his co-authors observe in their account of this rollout, the iPad came to the Indian market nine months later than in the United States, had far fewer applications available, and was handled by a limited number of distribution channels, many with poorly trained retail staff. Archrival Samsung beat Apple to market in India by two months, with aggressive pricing and features that already addressed the original iPad's deficiencies.[14] As a result, Apple's market share in India was less than a quarter of its worldwide iPad market share. Although it has owned about half the global market in this product category, Apple's tablet offering continues to struggle in India. A recent report cites only 7 percent market share, with not only Samsung but also local competitors such as Micromax, iBall, and Datawind holding larger market segments.[15]

Part of the problem may have been strategic choices Apple made regarding the Indian market. Given the rich opportunities in North America and Europe for a hot new product like the iPad, it may have seemed logical at the time to make India a secondary priority, and to assume that a later rollout could still be successful there based on the strength of the Apple brand, even at premium prices. Decision-makers likely underestimated the country's tech-savvy, rapidly evolving market situation, including stiff competition and demanding consumers. The company was overconfident that its globally standard product offering would carry the day and failed to place sufficient emphasis on strengthening and positioning its local functions in India to win for it the success gleaned elsewhere.

The pricing and features of the product itself were only one set of obstacles to winning larger market share (although Samsung quickly exploited the original iPad's lack of a second camera, USB ports, and a Flash multimedia player—especially important in India's entertainment-focused market). A more critical problem was that the overall product offering—including rollout schedule, applications, distributors, and quality of retail staff—was inadequate, reflecting lower prioritization in Apple's system and insufficient capabilities of its local functions such as marketing, sales, and distribution.[16]

In order to be a successful innovator in India—even with a product that did not require extensive local adaptation—Apple clearly needed to rethink its strategy and to increase its local capabilities in a number of functional areas. Figure 7.1 summarizes the reasons other than pricing that the iPad did not do as well as it has in other markets; its attractive features were offset by the shortcomings in the product offering based on limited local adaptation and capabilities.

Example: Haier India Restructures

Haier, the Chinese maker of appliances and electronics, took a different approach after struggling for many years in the Indian

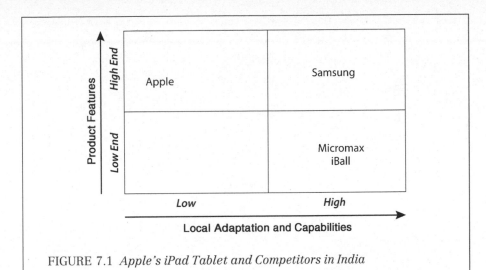

FIGURE 7.1 *Apple's iPad Tablet and Competitors in India*

market. In the face of sluggish sales and strong competition (also Samsung in this case), it revised its retail structure. According to Nikhil Celly's analysis of this subject, Haier added new dealers and retail outlets, provided substantial dealer incentives, and strengthened after-sales support to respond to every customer issue within six hours in all major cities. The company also made its pricing more attractive while preserving its premium image, launched a whole series of new products, upgraded the capacity of local factories, paid for in-store promotions, and advertised aggressively using television advertisements and a Bollywood actor as brand ambassador.[17]

While none of the products in Haier's portfolio had the appeal of an iPad, it nonetheless managed to more than double its sales revenue within a couple of years. Figure 7.2 shows Haier's market position before and after the successful changes; it has both upgraded its product features and added local capabilities that have made its products more accessible and attractive to Indian consumers.

It is easy to equate innovation with a new phone, an electric car, a piece of software, or a blockbuster drug. However, as the iPad example illustrates, bringing an innovative product to a different global market doesn't guarantee success, even when the product has a brilliant design, desirable features, and an impressive track record of sales results elsewhere. Innovation is ultimately judged by buyers in each marketplace, and they naturally weigh what is the best *total package* of product features, price, and related services. Haier, in spite of its humble origins as a bankrupt

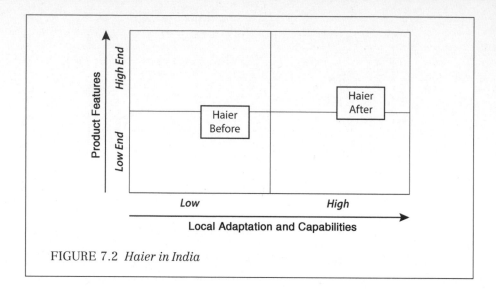

FIGURE 7.2 *Haier in India*

collective enterprise,[18] has grown rapidly in India because the total package of products and services it offers is now seen as desirable. While Apple has garnered far greater global recognition as an innovator, Haier's innovation strategy in India created a value proposition that local consumers perceived more favorably. From this perspective, Haier has been a more successful innovator than Apple in the Indian market to date.

GLOBAL INNOVATION SURVEY: COMMON CHALLENGES

Leaders who recognize the changing innovation landscape and seek to innovate on a global scale now face familiar challenges on a vastly broader and more complex playing field. The following five survey items—from a database that includes responses from employees in more than 20 major companies headquartered in North America, Europe, and Asia-Pacific—received the lowest overall scores in a highly reliable statistical survey:

1. The company is able to introduce new innovations even when they threaten established business lines.
2. Metrics that quantify work results are used to support innovation.
3. Strong connections and alignment between different functions (marketing and sales, R&D, manufacturing, finance, etc.) foster innovation that leads to good business results.

4. Team members are well-linked with other parts of the organization so they can obtain the resources and cooperation that they need.

5. Promising new ideas are given a high priority and rapidly implemented or commercialized.[19]

These findings indicate that the "innovator's dilemma"—that is, "What do we do when innovation threatens our current business?"[20]—is alive and well on a global basis, with even more compelling reasons to address it. There is always a temptation to hold back and defend familiar territory with stalwart champions and a reliable track record, especially when nascent opportunities or competitors are located on the other side of the world. This temptation is frequently melded with the human predilection, cited in previous chapters, to see other people and places as more similar to what we know than they actually are, and to attempt to reproduce our prior success story either at home or in new locations abroad. As Vijay Govindarajan and Chris Trimble point out in their account of Deere & Company's ultimately fruitful efforts to build a tractor suited to farmers in India, "a long track record of success can create a dominant logic." Innovation in fast-growth markets may require us to forget history, or at least some parts of it. Deere's successful creation of the "Krish," or baby Krishna tractor, began with a careful analysis of the needs of Indian farmers and their small agricultural plots, without assuming that they would eventually consolidate into giant Midwestern-style farms.[21]

Organizational goals and metrics must be carefully structured to support innovation and not simply reinforce established business lines. It may be a serious mistake to apply headquarters' metrics to a subsidiary operation experimenting with newer products. Moreover, alignment and teamwork across different functions—already difficult to achieve in a domestic contest—becomes even more critical when employees are also divided by time zones, national cultures, and the needs of different stakeholders. Similarly, it is even more challenging for team members not located at headquarters to gain access to the resources they need to pursue opportunities for innovation. Business leaders need a truly global perspective to ensure that the most promising new ideas are prioritized and implemented rapidly, and that they can create hybrid innovations melding together product, process, and marketing strengths.

The innovator's dilemma is ultimately a challenge to existing mindsets as well as to organizational systems. A company's "dominant logic" can be embedded even in assumptions about who the innovation champions and the go-to people are.

Finding New Champions

Wolfgang is the HR director for a high-end technology company headquartered in Europe. He has a strong global background, and easily slides between English, French, and German—painfully articulate in each. He has been with the firm for eight years, joining from a large multinational. "I came in and found this company with a strongly centralized approach, revolving around a very specific European region. We are a very successful and proud organization. We have achieved a lot, but we are not really ready for a new world or for international success.

"When we were first trying to examine our global future as a company, we did an engagement survey. The change in the company actually has been very interesting. In the first engagement survey, the focus was on leading quality by example—inclusive leadership and a customer-centric organization. In the second survey, which we put out more recently, it was all about innovation. The survey revealed that we are starting to see how innovation is strongly correlated to the way people are managed. Are leaders really open to new ideas? Do they champion them? Do they allow these ideas to come from different corners of the company? We were losing our innovative edge, and we realized that what we needed could not be the same type of innovation that we had relied on before.

"So at that moment, in an effort to restore innovation, we set up a process to get new ideas from around the world, and to encourage sharing between diverse teams. We gave all the participants nicknames so that no one could tell where the ideas were coming from—they could not associate the name with a certain region or country. Our European engineers had a tendency to ignore the ideas of our engineers in India. But these nicknames obliterated the prejudice because the ideas had no nationality. People started working together better after this.

"We have a tradition of working for high-end customers. But now we are looking at mid-range and entry-range products. We will not develop these in Europe; they will come out in China and India, and be designed by and for people living daily in these environments. With this change in approach, we need to move more decision-making power to those teams versus having European teams making the decisions. If you look at compounded growth, it is not happening in Europe but in China and other developing economies. When you don't incorporate people who know the markets in these decisions, then you are missing out on a lot. Engineers who have no contact with customers get out of touch with them. We needed to bring diversity into our product development cycle in order to be relevant. The new process made us see the possibility of innovation through diverse thought in our own organization. It made us listen to one another in new ways, without our normal filters, and it powered a real shift in the organization."

As this example illustrates, many common assumptions about innovation capabilities in less developed markets are no longer valid. In order to overcome the mindset and organizational challenges highlighted by the survey data and to innovate on a global scale, leaders must take a fresh look at several areas: current sources of global innovation, the roles of their subsidiary operations, and how to best build and leverage the evolving capabilities of their colleagues around the world.

GLOBAL INNOVATION TRENDS

Here are four trends that have been reshaping the global innovation playing field:

1. **Incremental modifications to existing technologies can produce disruptive outcomes.**

   After getting their start as copycats with less expensive me-too products, many companies have transitioned to a steady focus on continuous improvement. This has been occurring for decades, particularly in Asia. Japanese, South Korean, and Chinese firms, for example, have all pursued variations of this path and therefore are often dismissed as innovation lightweights. (A common statement in many Western corporations is, "They do the small stuff but we're the ones who make the real breakthroughs.") Because each incremental innovation appears to be minor—a step saved here, a lighter part there—it is easy to underestimate the cumulative impact.

   Western auto manufacturers and many consumers initially dismissed Japanese and later South Korean carmakers as inferior, low-end econoboxes. Yet patient, incremental innovation ultimately produced luxury vehicles such as Toyota's Lexus and Honda's Acura lines that have long since equaled or surpassed the market share and profitability of some Western domestic luxury brands in their home markets.[22] These Asian carmakers have undergone a classic disruptive progression from low-end to high-end market positions. Hyundai, from South Korea, now offers its own luxury Genesis model, and Chinese automakers and other types of manufacturers are laying out plans for the future. A false dichotomy between incremental changes and more radical forms of innovation may provide comfort to those who seek to defend their high-end market niche, but this ignores the evidence that a succession of incremental improvements can lead to disruptive results.

   Companies famous for their continuous improvement practices may also change over time as their capabilities evolve, and some become ready for more radical leaps. For instance, Toyota has transformed itself over the decades from being a laughingstock to one of the world's top carmakers in terms of the total number of vehicles it sells. More recently it has been a pioneer in creating the global market for hybrid gas and electric cars, with plenty of money to invest due to its enormous profitability and a mountain of accumulated cash. Toyota's Prius family of hybrids, praised by many environmentalists for superb fuel economy, has already sold approximately five million vehicles worldwide in spite of skeptical early reviews. The company has also recently introduced a mass-market hydrogen car with a driving range of 300 miles, using no gas whatsoever, in the United States and Europe.[23]

2. **Innovation in fast-growth markets can have disruptive impacts, even in developed markets.**

Developed markets are by no means insulated from innovations from other parts of the world. There are examples of innovation that appear to be clever and valuable, but primarily attractive to rural consumers at the lower part of the global economic pyramid. Water-cooled refrigerators or washing machines that can scour vegetables, for instance, are unlikely to have broad appeal in Shanghai or Mumbai, let alone London or New York. However, an increasing number of products coming from fast-growth markets bear striking similarities to the classic description of a disruptive innovation. This type of innovation is characterized by technologies that initially underperform against established products, but are simpler, smaller, more convenient, and sold at a compellingly lower price point. Often new types of organizational systems and even different customers are needed for the innovation to really take hold.[24]

Starting many decades ago when Japan's economy was in a period of rapid growth, small motorcycles produced by Honda, Yamaha, and Kawasaki that were considered quaint or even ridiculous in North America and Europe gradually moved up the value chain to earn the lion's share of their industry, finding many new customers who had never thought of owning a motorcycle before (a company advertisement at the time declared: "You meet the nicest people on a Honda"). The success of these motorcycle brands helped to spawn a wide set of related product families such as all-terrain vehicles, jet skis, snowmobiles, outboard engines, garden tillers, and lawnmowers, which the same companies still largely control.

Given the growing scale and pace of expansion in fast-growth markets, disruptive technologies can now be invented, tested, and disseminated in newer market environments before they ever reach mature ones. This makes it a strategic imperative for firms in many industries to track and gauge the importance of such developments. In the pharmaceutical industry, for example, generic drugs produced by companies in locations such as India, South Africa, or Israel have not only come to dominate their local markets, but they've also gained a significant foothold in the developed world. India alone is estimated to have 3,500 pharmaceutical manufacturers. In response, many established pharmaceutical companies have built their own generic business units internally or through acquisition in order to compete.

Other aspects of medicine are being reinvented as well in markets with large populations demanding better medical care. These include, for instance, hip replacement surgery, weight loss programs, and dentistry in places like India or Thailand where mobile foreigners also travel in search of decent care at more affordable prices. Related technologies such as low-cost diagnostic instruments will inevitably migrate from these locations to developed markets.

3. **Subsidiaries and companies based in fast-growth markets with limited resources are often strong innovators.**

Subsidiary operations around the world have often proven adept at making the best of their limited resources. Distance from headquarters has advantages as well as disadvantages. While it could mean "out of sight, out of mind," there may also be a freedom to explore new technologies or ways of doing business not available to company employees in close proximity to the corporate center.[25] Headquarters-based staff departments tasked with enforcing corporate policies and priorities sometimes display a vigilance that unintentionally impedes innovation. The ability of subsidiaries to make quick decisions and get immediate feedback from customers can compensate for lack of resources, enabling them to innovate in ways that others might underestimate or overlook—for instance, through product packaging, sales and marketing techniques, concurrent development with other regions, or original inventions based on fresh market intelligence.[26]

The paucity of resources in many global markets may, in fact, stimulate the development of various kinds of creative solutions. Malcolm Gladwell, in his book *David and Goliath: Underdogs, Misfits, and the Art of Battling Giants*, notes that a weakness can become a source of strength if it leads to the cultivation of compensatory skills. David was able to fell Goliath because he chose not to fight on Goliath's terms, close hand-to-hand combat, but rather flung a stone at him using a flexible long-range weapon that required mobility and accuracy. David redefined the terms of the conflict and engaged in a form of asymmetric warfare in a way that proved fatal to the slow-moving giant Goliath.

Companies that are themselves based in fast-growth markets have proved adept at battling global giants through their own forms of asymmetric combat. For example, mighty Walmart has found Grupo Elektra in Mexico to be a formidable competitor.

Many Mexican consumers want to buy consumer durables such as refrigerators or washing machines, but lack the cash for an immediate purchase and have no credit history. Although Grupo Elektra is a retail chain, it has also obtained a banking license and opened branches inside its stores. In addition, the company has established a fleet of more than 5,000 motorcycle-riding loan officers to visit consumer residences and verify credit-worthiness. This approach has enabled Grupo Elektra to compete effectively with Walmart by vastly expanding its base of customers to include more upwardly mobile families. Thanks to its innovations in establishing and extending credit, people with modest incomes can now purchase big-ticket items on affordable installment plans.[27]

The most powerful innovations generate a business model that combines novel products and/or services, innovations in product development or supply chain processes, and innovative marketing (see Figure 7.3). Such a combination requires R&D staff to work seamlessly with other functions such as manufacturing, purchasing, and sales and marketing. This is unlikely to happen automatically, as each of these functional groups often has its own unique subculture and values that do not guarantee the success of such interaction. But when all of these functions work in concert, the net result can be an innovative business model with unique competitive strength. Companies like Samsung, Haier, or Toyota have been successful not just because they built great products, but because they have combined these with global process

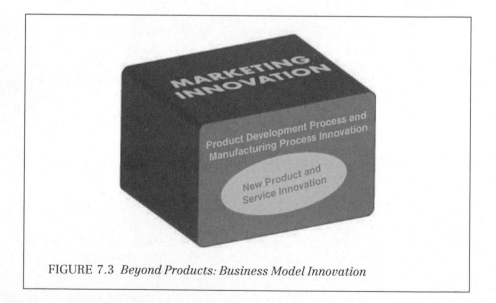

FIGURE 7.3 *Beyond Products: Business Model Innovation*

excellence and marketing skills in a total package that customers find compelling.

An increasing number of national champions from China, India, and elsewhere have gained substantial market share based on the process and marketing strengths they have cultivated. Lenovo has recently passed all its rivals, including Hewlett-Packard and Dell, to become the world's largest personal computer maker, more than doubling its market share since acquiring IBM's PC division. Its products were initially solid but not particularly distinctive; recently it has won greater acclaim as an innovator in terms of product design and function.

However, a more salient reason that Lenovo has gained worldwide market share is that, in contrast to the general computer industry trend to outsource manufacturing operations, it has chosen instead to vertically integrate its operations in-house. Such an approach allows the company to introduce changes and new models more quickly than other firms—a process innovation that has helped to create better products. Lenovo has also leveraged its domestic presence in China by dominating the market there with more than 40,000 partner-owned retail outlets and a growing number of company-owned flagship stores, gaining significant economies of scale.[28] It has also marketed its products more aggressively than its competitors in markets such as India and Russia.[29] Here, too, the formula for successful innovation is attractive products plus strong process infrastructure and superior marketing.

Example: 3M China

3M has long been renowned for its innovative products. While consumers are most familiar with Scotch Tape and Post-it® Notes—product categories that the company invented—3M has literally thousands of products, many with less widely known business or industrial applications. There's the brightness enhancement film that goes on laptop screens, a huge family of nonwoven fiber products such as respirators and floor mats, and abrasives used for everyday carpentry or to polish jet engine turbine blades. The Minnesota-based enterprise, with an international presence for more than 60 years, has become a thoroughly global company, with operations in more than 70 countries and 63 percent of its sales coming from outside of the U.S. home market.[30]

3M China is now the company's largest subsidiary operation, and its share of total revenue is increasing: its 10 to 15 percent annual growth target in China is about twice 3M's global average. After more than 30 years in the country and a billion dollars in investments, 3M has considerable infrastructure in place, including 11 manufacturing plants and one of its four global R&D centers, along with 27 branch offices. The company has been increasing its presence in expanding regions such as the country's west and north. The majority of the leadership roles in China have been localized, and nearly 30 business units in the country are all managed on a local basis to ensure the relevance of their offerings to the China market. There are now more indigenous firms among the company's customers and suppliers, too. For example, 3M once focused on foreign automakers such as Volkswagen and BMW, but now it considers Great Wall Motors, the China-based maker of sports utility vehicles, to be a viable prospect as well.[31]

Bullish 3M China executives have predicted that the subsidiary's revenues will eventually exceed those in the United States;[32] sales for Asia as a whole are already close to the U.S. total.[33] China has sufficient visibility within the 3M world that the company has made Greater China—including mainland China, Hong Kong, and Taiwan—its own region, reporting directly to headquarters. 3M's CEO Inge Thulin points to air pollution, water, and food safety as examples of areas in China where demand is currently strong.[34]

Wayne Xue is 3M's director of corporate strategy and communications for the Greater China area. His title includes an unusual job combination that he explains by saying, "3M has such a broad range of products that it is hard to know about them all. I can respond to questions because I do both strategy and communications."

Wayne comments that 3M has done well in China over time by following the market's path from infrastructure (e.g., traffic signs) to manufacturing (e.g., electronics) and now domestic consumption. "Our strategy here is 'China for China,' and we have been successful at following the megatrends closely and building up our local capabilities. At first, our focus was on infrastructure such as highways and telecommunications. After China's entry into the World Trade Organization in 2001, it became a manufacturer for worldwide consumption; about two-thirds of the world's cell phones and laptops are made in China. Now, however, external demand is slowing to single-digit growth, and the Chinese government is focused on increasing domestic consumption, with the goal of doubling per capita income over the next decade and adding 10 million urban residents from rural areas on an annual basis. There is still plenty of room for growth in areas increasingly important to domestic consumers such as health care or the automotive industry—3M is a major supplier for both."

"We are doing well in water filtration," Wayne adds, referring to 3M China's Residential Water business unit as an example. "The market has been growing by around 20 percent per year, and we are beating that pace. China's market for water filtration is different from the U.S. market in that people in the States usually drink the tap water. We were also comfortable drinking tap water in China two or three decades ago, but this has changed due to concerns about pollution. So the consumer business is actually much larger here than in the United States, where the focus is on water filtration for industry. Growing this business in China requires a lot more than just selling our products. We are investing to build 3M's brand in the market, expanding geographic coverage, and accelerating local new product development. The national 5-Year Plan includes an initiative to 'Promote Innovation Culture,' and the government offers certain kinds of tax incentives. Consumer education is also required. People need to learn about pollution and the benefits of filtration."

When describing the extent to which 3M's product development in water filtration has been localized, Wayne is understandably cautious about providing specifics. "Let's just say that the majority of our products have been or are being locally developed." He explains his hesitation to provide more detail: "This market here is not yet stable, with intense competition. In other markets you know who is who. Here we have both foreign companies and very aggressive local competitors." This is clearly a business that Wayne and others in the company are proud of while being prudent enough to quietly keep the momentum going.

3M's water filtration business in China has won numerous internal company awards and is gaining strong momentum in market competition. The company has been successful as an innovator not only because of its attractive products, but because of the focus it has placed on creating local R&D and manufacturing, building country-wide sales infrastructure and brand awareness, educating consumers, and aligning its strategy with government initiatives. 3M has made China the home of its Residential Water Center of Excellence for the region, and this center is now supporting other regions or countries such as Taiwan, South Korea, and Australia. "China for China" is still the core strategy, but 3M China's capabilities have begun to support business growth beyond China through testing, knowledge transfer, and product development.

4. **Product innovation and social innovation are often linked.**

The world's hottest growth markets in places such as India and China face deeply troubling socioeconomic gaps, appalling environmental problems, and a host of other pressing issues that go beyond traditional "business challenges." Many parts of these societies are still so mired in poverty, corruption, pollution, and social unrest that they haven't even begun to address the most serious problems. However, the future gold standard for innovation is already appearing in locations where companies such as Infosys (notwithstanding the criticism it has received for its role in outsourcing) have integrated world-class product or service innovation with tangible social contributions. In addition to more common types of donations for health care and relief work, for example, Infosys used its IT expertise to develop a flood relief management system that consolidates data regarding flood victims and monitors reconstruction progress.[35] Wipro, its Indian IT service industry rival, touts its smart grid solutions for more than 15 utility companies along with its green data centers.[36]

Leaders who can understand the scope and severity of the broader societal challenges in the markets they serve—and who can integrate their product expertise with social and environmental innovation—are the most likely to attract customers, talented employees, and a well-deserved reputation for global citizenship that will enhance their future prospects in world markets. In an age of ever more alarming human and environmental crises, the task of growing ideas increasingly means that companies must address universal human issues at the same time that they furnish products or services that customers are ready to buy.

NEW SUBSIDIARY ROLES

Based on the trends described above, many subsidiaries and their employees are ready to play new roles. Fortunately, there are success stories that illustrate potential opportunities within changing circumstances. The example of 7-Eleven in Taiwan shows how a fully grown subsidiary with a strong partner can take on a leadership role within a global system.

7-Eleven Taiwan: When the Child Outgrows the Parent

7-Eleven Taiwan would be a baffling place for a store employee from Dallas, Texas, where the familiar chain of stores was born. Aihwa Chang and Shih-Fen Chen, who have written a fascinating case study on this topic, note that 7-Eleven customers in Taiwan typically arrive on foot rather than by car. Some may even live upstairs in the same building, as many homes in this small and densely populated island off the coast of China are located in high-rise buildings with retail establishments on the lower floors. A variety of Chinese foods await customers in the store: tea eggs, breakfast buns, simmered vegetables, and rice wrapped in seaweed with meat or fish inside.

Beyond the sight and smell of such unfamiliar foods, other activities in the store would seem out of place. One customer is picking up books and dropping off laundry; another is purchasing tickets for an upcoming concert and a train trip and paying her personal taxes and electricity bill. A third customer is leaving an item he just sold on an auction site for delivery to the buyer at another store and receiving the Valentine's Day chocolate he had preordered on his cell phone the previous week. Other customers, particularly elderly ones, are sitting at the store's coffee counter, known as City Café, having a drink and chatting with other seniors; one of them, a disabled individual who is ready to leave, asks the store clerk to call him a cab. Meanwhile, children who have finished school are sitting and doing their homework, waiting for their parents to pick them up on the way home from work.[37]

At first glance, the Dallas visitor to 7-Eleven Taiwan might regard this plethora of products and services as an odd jumble—a bit like 7-Eleven, Amazon, Ticketmaster, eBay, Starbucks, a laundromat, a senior center, a taxi service, and a daycare center all rolled into one. The visitor might wonder what 7-Eleven Taiwan executives could possibly be thinking to try to compete in so many different areas at the same time. On the other hand, the store is full of people of all ages, and seems to be doing a brisk business.

7-Eleven is an example of a company whose overseas subsidiary children have literally outgrown the original parent. Afflicted by financial woes after a management buyout provoked by a corporate takeover threat, in 1991 the bankrupt firm sold a controlling share to its largest franchisee—the Japanese company Ito-Yokado—which later rescued it from bankruptcy. Japan now has nearly 16,000 outlets, almost double the approximately 8,000 stores in the United States. Tiny Taiwan, which is the size of South Carolina and less than half as big as Ireland, now holds close to 5,000 7-Eleven stores.

As the revitalized 7-Eleven under Japanese ownership targets major growth markets in other countries, innovations from 7-Eleven Taiwan appear to be more relevant in many locations than the U.S. store formula, which still prominently features low-tech products such as pizzas, sodas, and Spicy Wing Zings. (An informal inquiry by one of the authors at his local 7-Eleven about the store's best-selling items elicited the laconic reply, "sandwiches.") 7-Eleven Taiwan is, in fact, taking the lead on expansion to nearby Shanghai, which has a similar urban population density and set of consumer tastes. One of the most successful elements of Indonesia's relatively new 7-Eleven franchise seems to be its Internet café seating. As in Taiwan, Indonesia's 7-Eleven provides what many consumers consider to be affordable luxury, serving inexpensive local foods in a clean, well-lit facility that both offers the favorite menu items of local street vendors and surpasses them in terms of hygiene and air-conditioning.[38]

It is likely that a different physical environment and competitive landscape render some of the products and services invented in Taiwan or elsewhere in Asia unfeasible for introduction into North America. 7-Eleven Taiwan is run by a local conglomerate that has access to significant information technology, warehousing, and delivery capabilities, providing it with unique infrastructure strengths as well. In spite of these differences, however, surely the U.S.-based former parent has as much to learn from its erstwhile children these days as vice versa. The U.S. operation of 7-Eleven has been focused in recent years on upgrading dingy stores and introducing private-label 7-Select brand products. It could certainly benefit from the image of a convivial, safe, social gathering spot that has been created in Taiwan and Indonesia; stores in Jakarta are such popular places for young people to gather that they have even hosted live bands.[39] The U.S. stores also now offer prepaid cell phones, electronics, gaming, and financial services, so Taiwan's experience with online services and e-commerce should hold considerable interest.

In their classic work, *Managing Across Borders: The Transnational Solution*, Christopher Bartlett and Sumantra Ghoshal described four possible roles for subsidiary operations, depending upon the strengths of the subsidiary and the strategic significance of their market:

- Implementer (low capability, low market importance)
- Contributor (high capability, low market importance)
- Black Hole (low capability, high market importance)
- Regional Leader (high capability, high market importance)[40]

Some 7-Eleven subsidiaries have clearly outgrown all four of these categories. In the case of Taiwan, it has become a global innovation leader, while 7-Eleven Japan has become the new parent.

The 7-Eleven example suggests wider roles that subsidiaries can fulfill, in contrast to previous eras when headquarters drove innovation and subsidiaries were supporting cast members. These newer roles—shown in Figure 7.4—may undergo a radical metamorphosis as a subsidiary matures.

- **Market Observer:** A subsidiary in a rapidly evolving market that seeks out and transmits to other global locations new ideas and

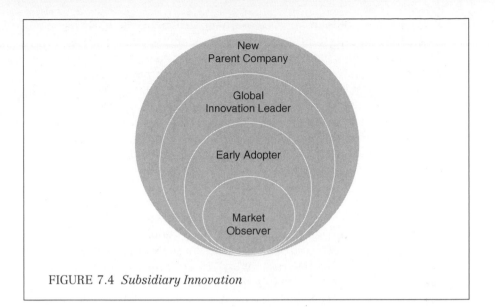

FIGURE 7.4 *Subsidiary Innovation*

applications of products or services occurring in this market for the first time.

- **Early Adopter:** A subsidiary that experiments with new technologies, products, or services not currently in use at headquarters, sharing the results with the rest of the company's global network.

- **Global Innovation Leader:** A subsidiary that takes on the role of generating new solutions and transmitting them to other locations in the world based on its acknowledged areas of world-class expertise.

- **New Parent Company:** A subsidiary that outgrows the parent, acquires greater market and financial momentum, and becomes the new owner and driver of the global innovation process. Some companies also have implemented a dual headquarters strategy, placing a second headquarters in a location where the local and/or regional market opportunities are the greatest.

As subsidiaries' capabilities and resources grow, they may become able to do much more than extend the core strengths of headquarters—they can gauge fresh threats and even create new markets. There is often a fundamental tension between two popular approaches to business strategy, known by the labels "core competencies" and "blue ocean." Core competencies are by definition limited, and the general advice to leaders is to find out what their organizations are really skilled at and then stick to their knitting. Blue Ocean Strategy, on the other hand, offers the enticing prospect that there are adjacent businesses which, with a targeted expansion beyond the organization's current business model, could offer major new market opportunities without the bloody competition found in waters closer to well-traveled shores.[41] Subsidiaries are frequently better positioned to explore possible blue oceans, as they are less tied to the parent's core competencies and the market environment in which they were originally developed.

For example, the underlying company principle of customer convenience at 7-Eleven Taiwan has been expanded to e-commerce and community services for which customers are willing to pay. Such services have helped to create a virtuous cycle of increased consumer footfalls and collateral purchases, contributing to a growing, profitable country operation with the highest density of 7-Eleven stores anywhere in the world, even double that in Japan. Has 7-Eleven Taiwan strayed beyond the original parent's core competencies of making reasonably priced goods available in a uniform set of locations on a 24-hour basis? It has, but by drawing upon additional core infrastructure competencies of its Taiwanese parent, it appears to have hit upon complementary and profitable forms of customer convenience, appreciated by consumers elsewhere in Asia's fast-growth markets, opening up a new ocean of possibilities.

From Fast Follower to Innovation Leader

Andrea Robbins was at her desk shortly after sunrise, sipping her first cup of coffee. One of her favorite practices was to arrive at the office early and spend an hour planning and reflecting before the first of her scheduled meetings. She looked over yet another very full day on her calendar. Ever since she had taken over leadership of the business unit, each day seemed to bring with it more responsibility and more complex problems, especially with her company's ongoing expansion in global markets. She was grateful just to have a few quiet moments to reflect, as early and late conference calls with colleagues in different time zones had made it increasingly difficult to find time for this.

Today Andrea had a series of one-on-one meetings scheduled: the first was with the head of R&D for her business unit. Taking out a fresh pad of paper, Andrea wrote a bullet point heading for each meeting and began to take a few notes. She was lost in thought as Sanjay, the R&D head, knocked on her door.

Sanjay: Good morning. I hope I'm not too early!

Andrea: No, you're right on time, as usual. It's good to see you. How are you?

Sanjay: Fine, thank you. I just got back from another trip to India, so am still feeling a bit jet-lagged.

(Continued)

(Continued)

Andrea: I know the feeling. How was the trip? I'm very interested to hear what you saw this time. I know you had some key meetings with technical people on the client side and that you were also going to take a look at new competitive products.

Sanjay: Yes, we had a number of good meetings, and our clients seem to be pretty pleased with our products, although they always want a better price and more service. I'm also happy to see the continuing development of our staff members there. Their capabilities are really growing.

Andrea: That's good to hear. Anything else?

Sanjay: Something I noticed did concern me. A local competitor has introduced a replacement for one of our core products. At first I thought it was just a cheap copy, but the quality is not bad, there are no flagrant violations of our intellectual property, and the functionality is adequate for many purposes. Locally based customers in India who are very price-sensitive are finding it to be an attractive alternative to our product, particularly because they have been promised a one-day turnaround on any service issues. And it appears that our competitor has also found new customers in small and medium-sized enterprises that never purchased from us before. Our current version has more bells and whistles, but it is 50 percent more expensive and our service network is lagging behind.

Andrea: I suppose we could introduce a stripped down product at a lower price, but that would undermine our profit position in the Indian market and possibly in Europe and the United States longer-term if clients find it does the job. I'd hate to do anything that might compromise our quality as well. We don't want to build something like that Tata Nano that caught on fire. . . .

Sanjay: Yes, this could become a real dilemma for us, and the Nano was a disaster — even Tata has abandoned it. Shall we start looking into building a less expensive but adequate version in terms of quality in order to stay competitive? We can also continue to offer more advanced functionality and premium service to those who are willing to pay higher prices.

Andrea: Maybe it's best to be a fast follower on this cheaper version and respond as the need arises, while maintaining our profit margin so we can meet our current targets. It's fine to begin looking at the feasibility of a cheaper version, but let's wait to introduce it until we see if this new competitor gains momentum.

Andrea's choice to react to a locally based rival in India with a fast-follower strategy could lead to significant risks and missed opportunities. Indeed, Sanjay's description of the product introduced by a local competitor includes several signs of disruptive innovation, referred to earlier in this chapter: adequate functionality, significantly lower price point, interest from new types of customers. What if this product succeeds not only in India but in other markets beyond the region and Andrea's business unit does not have an effective response? Is there a large new market that her company might be missing? She would probably be better off with a different approach that gauges the extent of the competitive threat and experiments with new possibilities.

There are a number of specific steps Andrea, Sanjay, and others in their organization might take to ensure that their company is enhancing its position as a market innovator and that they themselves are serving as effective global leaders:

- Assign a cross-functional team of high-potential employees with the necessary expertise—including representatives from the local subsidiary and from headquarters—to take a closer look at the competitor's product and evaluate its market potential, both in India and beyond.

- Learn more about customer perceptions of the business unit's current product, with a focus on whether it is vulnerable to an alternative product offering with disruptive characteristics or ancillary benefits; find out about the needs of those new customers who are snapping up the competitor's product.

- Consider the potential for a more comprehensive product package that would be superior to the local Indian competitor's in terms of process infrastructure and marketing along with product features.

- Take full advantage of the company's worldwide network and presence in other markets to look for new ideas, economies of scale, and opportunities for regional or global collaboration.

- Be ready to accelerate the prioritization or pace of new product development and commercialization if necessary; examine how to support the product development process with metrics that are suitable to the current stage of innovation.

- Enforce bottom line standards for quality and safety to uphold the company's brand and avert disasters, while avoiding overly bureaucratic, risk-averse, or overengineered processes.

- Plan a trip, possibly with other members of the leadership team, to view the market firsthand in order to better understand customer needs and to gauge its potential as a launch point for global innovations.

- Carefully examine the strengths and weaknesses of the functions and product offerings in the India subsidiary with an eye toward determining the right global/local balance for each; augment the areas that need to be strengthened.

- Seek opportunities to make social contributions tied to the business unit's products and services that would embody the company's values and enhance its brand image as a good corporate citizen in the local market.

WHAT YOU CAN DO

- Be prepared to recognize innovation from anywhere, actively requesting ideas from your global colleagues and responding to nascent competitive threats.

- Spread innovation from one global location to another by seeking and sharing new information — cultivate a network of colleagues around the world who will keep you abreast of fresh developments.

- Recognize that what is considered to be an attractive innovation in one country may not be perceived the same way in another location.

- Strive not only to create innovative products or services, but also to create a total innovation package that is compelling to local customers.

- Build alignment across internal functions — product development, manufacturing, supply chain, marketing, sales, and so on — to support innovation.

- Look for new roles that subsidiary operations can play in creating, testing, and growing innovative business concepts.

Global Ethics: Beyond Integrity

Conscious Choices to Ensure a Sustainable Future

JOINING THE MIDDLE CLASS

Ethical conduct in a business context is commonly defined in terms of "integrity." Corporate employees usually interpret this to mean observing each country's laws faithfully and not engaging in illicit practices such as fraud, bribery, or other forms of corruption. But as vital as these kinds of ethics are to build civil societies around the world and a fair playing field for competition among private enterprises, they are no longer sufficient. The sheer scale of the current global economic shift requires much broader ethical engagement from companies and their employees as previous patterns of production and consumption are transformed.

Mr. and Mrs. Feng Buy a Car

It is a warm, rainy Saturday morning in the month of May in Chongqing, a city in southwestern China. Mr. Feng, in his early 30s, is dressed casually in a sports shirt and jeans. He sits in the driver's seat of a shiny new car, a compact sedan. There is a red ribbon tied on the side mirror, and another on the front hood—red symbolizes happiness and good fortune. Mr. Feng smiles shyly as the dealer sitting next to him, dressed more formally in his white, short-sleeved shirt and tie, points to dashboard lights and cruise control. Mrs. Feng leans forward from the back seat, watching with sharp eyes; she wants to see and learn as well.

After absorbing a detailed review of the car's features, both under the hood and inside the vehicle, Mr. and Mrs. Feng step out of the car and stand to one side. Other employees from the dealership gather, including the branch manager. Two young men pull the chords on confetti poppers, there are loud bangs, and brightly colored pieces of paper fall slowly to the ground, catching the light coming through the showroom window. Mr. and Mrs. Feng pose for many pictures, and there are congratulatory handshakes with the branch manager, the salesman, and other members of the dealership staff.

Although they often look down modestly at the floor during the short ceremony marking their purchase, this is a proud and exciting day for Mr. and Mrs. Feng. They are the first members of their extended family to own a car, the first in hundreds of generations of Fengs in their nearby hometown. They have borrowed some of the money from other family members, and have paid in cash more than a full year's salary for many white-collar workers in their part of the country. But cars are faster than walking or taking the bus and safer than putting the family on a motorcycle. When he moved from his parents' farm to the city, Mr. Feng had long since decided that an office job would be better than rising before sunrise to feed the animals, plowing behind an ox, and worrying about how to make a living from a small plot of land. Soon the couple drives away in their new car as the dealership employees smile and wave.

This memorable morning for Mr. and Mrs. Feng is repeated in various ways throughout many parts of Asia, Africa, and Latin America each day. As the ranks of the urban middle class grow, new entrants also want housing, appliances, and transportation. Those in the developed world who always assumed they would own a car, may find it difficult to appreciate the Feng's determination to better their lives and their joy at achieving each milestone.

POPULATION × CONSUMPTION/PERSON = IMPACT

The earth's population is on its way to quadrupling between 1950 and 2050, from 2.5 billion to 10 billion, with the total already well over 7 billion. We are in the process of adding approximately 7.5 billion more people on our planet in the course of a single incredible century, a rise in population unprecedented in human history. Nearly all of these new citizens are outside of the developed countries, with billions already born and billions still coming. Each of these people needs food, water, and a place to live. Most of them would like to have cars, cell phones, and refrigerators as well.

Thanks in part to global trade, new technologies, and higher agricultural productivity, hundreds of millions of people in places like China and India who were once poor have lifted themselves out of poverty to join a giant new middle class larger than Europe's. Teeming urban areas continue to expand, featuring both luxury high-rises and vast slums as well as a concrete forest of middle-income apartment towers. Hundreds of new cities are under construction as the world's poorest citizens have been moving in vast numbers from farms to the city.

So here we are all living together on one planet—sawing, hammering, eating, drinking, driving, twittering, storing photos, trying to stay warm, buying new appliances, and taking out our garbage—with appetites that would tax the resources of three planets or more. The basic equation is simple: population multiplied by consumption per person equals impact. Population and consumption are both still increasing at breakneck speed.

The human dilemma of our era is that if 10 billion people all continue to think and act in the same way, the future of the planet and of our grandchildren is likely to be bleak. There are just too many of us with not enough resources to go around—even with technological ingenuity that has produced miraculous results like the agricultural "green revolution" and its vastly increased crop yields, or new methods to drill deeper and more efficiently for oil or natural gas. The net impact of vast increases in agricultural productivity and energy supplies over the past 50 years has been a swollen population that demands and consumes even more. Even officials in oil-rich Saudi Arabia, for example, have expressed concern about how to handle their own citizens' demand for oil; according to some estimates, domestic demand could exceed their country's massive domestic production and make the country a net oil importer within a couple of decades. And the Saudis are not alone in terms of rising consumption; one recent estimate projects a 37 percent increase in global energy consumption by 2040.[1]

Aside from predictable human struggles over resources—for instance, riots over access to drinking water, or armed conflict due to rivers being diverted upstream from thirsty populations—a further direct impact of humankind's insatiable appetite is on the other species that share our planet. Humans are monopolizing and fouling the planet's air, water, and plant life. On any given day, we hear alarming news about disappearing populations—not only of large mammals such as tigers or elephants, but also fish, birds, insects, and other flora and fauna, many too small to see or as yet undiscovered.

Even familiar species like honeybees and butterflies are not immune.[2] The storybook animals whose names parents pronounce to teach their children the alphabet are rapidly receding into memory and fantasy, slaughtered for food, pelts, or aphrodisiacs, or wiped out as collateral damage of industrial-scale agriculture and destruction of forest habitat.

Dismal Science

Economics is often called the dismal science. However, a stronger claim for this title could be made by the environmental sciences these days. The most sober researchers sound like alarmists when citing their grave findings. Here is a partial summary of the new reality humans are facing:

- Global climate patterns are changing rapidly due to massive burning of fossil fuels, leading to warmer average temperatures, melting polar ice caps, and shifting weather patterns that appear to be linked with disasters of enormous scale: Hurricane Katrina in New Orleans or Typhoon Haiyan in the Philippines.
- Many of the earth's species of plants and animals are being wiped out, with current rates estimated at 1,000 times or more of the natural background level. As many as 30 to 50 percent are expected to vanish within this century.[3]
- Rain forests, often called "the earth's lungs" because of their ability to convert carbon dioxide into the oxygen that humans need, are being destroyed at a rapid rate.
- Competition among and within nations for scarce resources such as water, cropland, or strategic minerals is intensifying.
- Approximately 2 billion people on the planet are still living at subsistence levels and are often most vulnerable to environmental degradation and natural disasters.

A Global Tragedy of the Commons

There are too many sheep grazing in almost every global pasture. A "tragedy of the commons" is said to occur when individuals overuse public space for their own benefit, thereby damaging a shared resource. The accelerating destruction of the earth's resources, driven by ravenous human consumption, is now occurring on a scale that threatens human life as well: fish stocks that are crashing due to overfishing currently feed one-third of the world's population; 70 percent of farm crops require pollination from honeybees afflicted by spreading colony collapse; the destruction of rainforest biodiversity precludes the discovery of new antibiotics to stem the tide of resistant bacteria. In many cases, humans may never know or fully understand what has been wiped out, and risk further unforeseen consequences of the destruction we have perpetrated.

BUSINESS ETHICS FOR A CROWDED PLANET

In the face of this slow- and sometimes fast-moving global catastrophe, socioeconomic concepts such as government regulation of "externalities" and the focus on "shareholder value" that anchored corporate ethics in previous decades now seem hopelessly narrow. The sharp-tongued economist Milton Friedman once wrote, "There is one and only one social responsibility of business—to use its resources and engage in activities designed to increase its profits so long as it stays within the rules of the game, which is to say, engages in open and free competition without deception or fraud."[4] While this mindset supports integrity in that it encourages us to follow a common set of rules and to avoid corporate malfeasance, it is a recipe for disaster in today's world.

Friedman mistakenly assumes that governments will cope effectively with the wider impacts of business activities by establishing and enforcing legal and regulatory frameworks to mitigate possible negative consequences. Yet governments at all levels have utterly failed to stem the onrushing tide of environmental damage. Singapore chokes on the smoke from fires due to illegal logging in Indonesia; Brazil still converts millions of acres of precious rainforest every year for grazing and soybean cultivation; Japanese and South Korean officials condone massive overfishing on the open ocean by their commercial fleets; China plugs in a new coal-fired power plant each week, sending pollution across the Pacific; until quite recently Filipino government officials discouraged the use of contraceptives, fueling the country's population boom; and the U.S. Congress is gridlocked by zealot ideologues who challenge the overwhelming scientific consensus regarding climate change. All the while, international bodies such as the United Nations or the International Monetary Fund are frequently hamstrung by dithering and dissention among member states, or are actually funding the wrong kinds of projects, such as highways into forests that encourage illegal logging.

Governmental bodies are making fitful progress in some areas, but it is regularly too little and too late. There are many reasons that public officials have been unable to stem the rising planetary tide of environmental destruction: lack of resources, widespread poverty, corruption, greed, ignorance, short-term thinking, powerful special interest lobbies, outdated ideas. Environmental issues are also inconveniently transnational. Country borders—even those with high walls and vigilant guards—mean nothing to fish, birds, and butterflies that live and migrate within their own biozones; this makes it even more difficult for national entities to respond to their plight.

Perhaps the most critical indictment of the collective governmental failure to act in a meaningful way is the steady, unabated growth in the level of carbon dioxide in the earth's atmosphere. This indicator has risen on a steep curve throughout the modern industrial era, and recently exceeded 400 parts per million—a level 25 percent above just a century ago, and perhaps last reached in the Pliocene Epoch 3 million years ago when the Earth's oceans were 30 feet higher.[5] Elevated levels of carbon dioxide are associated with global warming and the melting of polar ice. According to NASA, average global temperatures have already increased by 1.4 degrees since 1880, and two-thirds of this warming has occurred since 1975.[6] Antarctica has lost ice every year for the past 20 years, and the rate of ice loss in Greenland has increased by nearly five times since the mid-1990s.[7] The drastic speed of these changes and their implications still only seem to gain brief recognition during catastrophic events—after which most governments go back to business as usual. Atmospheric carbon dioxide continues to rise in the face of feeble countermeasures, and this trend appears to be accelerating.

Companies large and small cannot expect governments to adequately address the dire challenges of a bustling, warming planet where nearly every natural treasure is under assault. In many cases, commercial enterprises and their employees have more and better information, the resources to act, and a global footprint. And in spite of Friedman's profit-centered imperative, it is important for their immediate and future position in the marketplace to proactively tackle wider social and environmental issues. Their reputation can suffer almost immediately by association with environmental damage or the exploitation of poor workers. National governments often single out infractions by foreign capital companies to make an example of them and tilt the playing field toward local champions. First-rate employees are most likely to remain in a company whose practices they admire. Affluent consumers are also increasingly inclined to select the products they purchase based on a definition of integrity that goes beyond following traditional rules of fair marketplace conduct to include the ways in which goods are produced. The term "ethical brand" has been coined to distinguish firms that seek to address social and environmental problems through their business.[8]

Example: Nike's Transformation

In the late 1990s, Nike was a poster child for abusive labor practices. The company had been accused of paying slave wages and was the target of public protests over this and additional issues regarding working conditions, overtime requirements, and damage to the environment. The reputational risk to the company was so severe that its legendary co-founder and then CEO Phil Knight made the decision to publicly acknowledge the issue and to launch his organization on a different course.[9]

For Nike to take sustainability seriously was no small task; in addition to the company's approximately 50,000 regular employees, it has more than 900 factories and a million associated contract workers located in countries around the world. Like other firms facing this situation, Nike first established a Corporate Responsibility team to oversee the implementation of better labor practices. Over time, however, this function has evolved into a far more strategic and comprehensive part of the organization and has broadened its mission to encompass social and environmental issues as well. Instead of merely policing and controlling labor abuses and products at the end of the pipeline, it has been relabeled as the Sustainable Business & Innovation team, and tied into all phases of Nike's product development cycle and supply chain. This includes both upstream—how products are designed—and downstream, or how they are produced in the factories. A detailed set of six different sustainability indices has been put in place to measure everything from the environmental impact of materials to factory labor practices, with the ultimate goal of making sustainability an integral part of the company's business model.[10]

Debra Schifrin, Glen Carroll, and David Brady portray the remarkable path that Nike has since followed in transforming its giant enterprise. They comment, "Originating in labor, the scope of sustainability was broadened to include the roles of all the environmental and social impact areas across the whole value chain. The company regarded sustainability as a way to address global trends that would impact its business."[11]

Despite overall production increases, Nike has made tremendous, measurable strides versus earlier baselines. These include the use of recycled and organic materials as well as reductions in water use, carbon emissions, petroleum-derived solvents, energy consumption, and solid waste sent to landfills. They've been able to achieve results in part because the company pairs measurements with rewards and sanctions: top-rated factories are targeted to receive more business, while Nike drops from their supply chain those that are consistently rated poorly. Product designers, too, receive scores based on their choices of materials, with higher ratings going to designs incorporating recycled fabrics or more sustainable materials such as rubber or cotton.[12]

Nike executives now see sustainability as both an organizational responsibility and an opportunity to innovate. Mike Parker, the current CEO, is a prominent corporate champion of sustainable thinking.

He explicitly cites exploding populations, the power of emerging markets, and the vital importance of sustainability. The company's upgraded practices have fostered the creation of green products, and Nike employees now recognize sustainability's power as a source of innovation. For example, the Nike Flyknit running shoe, worn by many Olympic athletes, uses a special yarn for the upper section of the shoe that is lighter and leads to less waste; its break-through design was achieved through careful, metrics-driven scru-tiny of the materials that go into shoe production. This product is now used as a platform for other types of shoes. Parker touts the virtues of knitting technology in creating sustainable footwear that does not require the wasteful cutting and stitching of traditional manufacturing processes.[13]

Much has changed for Nike since it first became a punching bag for social activists. It is now more often viewed with respect by both activists and industry peers as a pioneer of improved practices, and has received additional kudos for partnering with competitors and smaller firms to improve the performance of its industry as a whole. The company and its employees continue to push forward their sustainability initiatives even beyond what consumers demand— most consumers are still not aware of the company's transformation or willing to pay a premium for sustainable products. According to Nike CEO Parker, "consumer awareness will become a bigger factor over time, and customers will begin to expect sustainability." He adds that sustainable practices "improve our business and our ability to grow in a resource-constrained world [. . . and] to actually influence and inspire others at a corporate level around the world."[14]

Examples: Unilever and the B-Corp Movement

While Nike's turnabout is remarkable, it is not unique or exclusive to the shoe-making and apparel industries. Nike is part of a growing movement of companies across a range of industries—food and drink, consumer products, heavy manufacturing, and so on—that have been broadening their ethical stance to include a range of social and environmental impacts and incorporate the concept of sustainability. Some of these efforts appear to be more talk than action, with weak certification programs that are open to charges of greenwashing— that is, co-opting the language of sustainability for marketing pur-poses or to deflect public criticism while continuing harmful practices. "Clean coal" initiatives have provided some of the most egregious examples of brightly packaged resistance to change. But other ini-tiatives are ambitious, far-reaching, and significant for workers, consumers, and the environment.

Rebecca Henderson and Frederik Nellemann describe how consumer products giant Unilever has embarked on a new "Sustainable Living Plan" that sets company goals for addressing consumer health, mitigating its environmental impacts, and sourcing all of its raw materials sustainably within the next five years. For a multinational enterprise that has 167,000 employees, 2 billion consumers using its products each day, and commodities sourced from 50 different crops, this represents a mind-boggling commitment with enormous potential impact worldwide. Unilever's CEO Paul Polman is responding to the same global crisis just described and trying to position his company for the future: "When you look at the interdependent challenges that we face on food security; poverty reduction; sustainability of resources; climate change and social, economic, environmental development, [you realize that] these challenges have never been greater. And . . . these pressures will only increase as 2 billion more people enter this world and many aspire to increase their living standards."[15]

Unilever has partnered with the Rainforest Alliance to certify farms growing its famous tea brands, including the venerable Lipton Tea, based on environmental and social criteria. It began with farms the company itself owned in Kenya and Tanzania and with larger private landholders; now it has moved on to certifying tens of thousands of smaller farmers, working through intermediaries such as a Kenyan farmer's cooperative. Unilever's sustainability initiatives have reportedly led to higher market share for its tea products in some countries, while the results elsewhere have been neutral or inconclusive. Discriminating consumers increasingly expect sustainable practices as a minimum standard and may reward the maker with higher market share, but only a small minority is inclined to pay premium prices for such products.[16]

Although Nike and Unilever's sustainability movements have been driven from the top by the companies' CEOs, employees from many other functions are involved: supply chain, marketing, brand management, manufacturing, design, and staff functions such as human resources, training and development, quality, and finance. The engagement and enthusiasm of people working at factories and farms throughout their vast sourcing operations, reaching far beyond the ranks of company employees, has been and will continue to be critical as well.

There has also been a groundswell among smaller firms that seek to address environmental and social issues as part of their mission; many have explicitly committed to considering the interest of a broader set of stakeholders. Certified B Corps, for instance, now include a wider set of stakeholders and broader social goals in their organizational charters. Patagonia, Ben & Jerry's, and Seventh Generation were early pioneers in a movement that now encompasses more than 1,000 companies in 60 industries and in 30-plus countries.

Jay Coen Gilbert is one of the co-founders of B Lab, the nonprofit that since 2006 has certified B Corps based on standards of social and environmental performance, accountability, and transparency. He is attempting to address the same basic dilemma perceived by Mike Parker of Nike and Paul Polman of Unilever, which is that there are critical global challenges that government or traditional nonprofits cannot solve by themselves. As Gilbert comments, "We're at this very early stage of one of the most important movements of what I think will be our lifetimes: . . . a growing consensus among entrepreneurs, consumers, investors, and policymakers to look at the latent potential to use market forces to solve social and environmental problems. . . . We think about success in generational terms."[17] One of B Lab's mottos is therefore to shift the goal of organizations from being "best *in* the world" to "best *for* the world." Its founders want to change the face of capitalism by using business to address social and environmental problems and are creating institutional mechanisms that will help to make this possible.[18] A growing number of other profit and nonprofit ventures are pursuing similar goals. Several that have already been active for many years include the Social Venture Network, Business for Social Responsibility, and Root Capital.

ETHICS FOR A NEW ERA

So what is the best ethical stance for leaders at all levels who are working in a shifting global context? Corporate integrity starts with what Milton Friedman called the "rules of the game," but needs to go further. In the face of increasingly dire environmental and social equity challenges on a planet that is becoming "hot, flat, and crowded,"[19] companies need a more comprehensive definition of integrity that extends far beyond the way that it has traditionally been defined. Here is a more comprehensive and multi-layered definition, with key principles in ascending order of novelty and challenge.

Baseline Integrity

"Follow the law" may sound obvious and straightforward—but even this is not a simple matter in global settings where laws and standards differ country by country, enforcement is spotty or nonexistent, judicial systems are subject to outside pressures, and a mixed bag of competitors play by rules of their own making. There are locations where tax evasion is common, officials are corrupt, and competitors either collude illegally or seek to crush each other by nefarious means. The legal framework and actual practices in many countries are also likely to be wholly inadequate to address larger issues of climate change and social equity, even when governments and businesses pay lip service to them.

Nonetheless, adhering both to local laws and to the laws of one's headquarters country comprises an essential baseline form of integrity. This may sometimes create a short-term competitive disadvantage when others win contracts by paying bribes to government officials or ply them with lavish and even illegal forms of entertainment, and it could possibly preclude doing business in certain countries. Yet there are significant advantages. Following the law is a better policy for:

- *The company:* Refusing to pay a bribe may lead to the loss of a sale or delays in permit approval; however, companies that cut corners are vulnerable to selective enforcement of laws and severe sanctions applied by governments that prefer to penalize foreign firms rather than local champions.

- *Company employees:* Motivated and capable workers in many countries dislike corruption, nepotism, and rigged markets. They want to work for a firm that contributes to their communities in a positive way and promotes employees based upon merit. Law-abiding enterprises are more likely to attract and retain high-quality employees.

- *The economy:* The rule of law creates a more level playing field for competitors and enables market forces to function rather than allowing entrenched insiders to have a prohibitive advantage.

- *Individual consumers:* Buyers get a better product at lower prices, and members of the public are less subject to arbitrary discrimination by petty bureaucrats in positions of power.

- *Society as a whole:* When companies compete by illegal means or shirk their responsibilities to pay taxes, it weakens the social fabric—including vital services such as the educational system from which employers draw their workforce.

Another powerful argument for following the law is that it gives companies the standing and credibility to argue for better labor and environmental laws, regulations, and enforcement throughout their industries.[20]

Violations of baseline integrity come in many forms, and no country is exempt. Corporate scandals occur everywhere, particularly at the nexus between business and government. Washington, D.C., for example, has been compared with notoriously corrupt Jakarta, the exception being that corruption in the United States is more often legitimized in the form of payments to lobbyists, candidates, and political action committees. Company leaders who regard bribes paid to traffic police or inspectors in other countries as wrong and distasteful should keep in mind that large cash contributions made to opaque political organizations on behalf of doubtful causes may appear to some as a crime of far greater proportions. The United States is ranked 17th on the Corruption Perceptions Index, tied with Hong Kong, Ireland, and Barbados, and just above Uruguay—hardly qualifying it as the world's exemplar.[21]

Any society's ethical basis can ultimately be judged at least in part by its fruits, and every major economy has experienced a balance of positive and negative results. China's admirable success at bringing hundreds of millions of people out of poverty is tarnished by polluted waterways, toxic air, and restricted freedom of expression. The dark side of America's free-wheeling economy and material abundance includes tremendous waste and overconsumption. And India's vibrant democracy and burgeoning information technology industry have failed to stem graft or to build sufficient infrastructure to keep the power on all day in many major cities.

Ethical Outreach

Deliberately or by default, global leaders inevitably make ethical choices. They regularly must decide whether to observe or to ignore laws; they can also make the decision to set a higher standard for themselves and their enterprise or to settle for the status quo. This decision is often best made with the perspective of global counterparts in mind.

Supply Chain Complaint

Fabian is a mechanical engineer who works as a manager in supply chain operations. Part of his job is contracting with suppliers, and he has logged many miles traveling to factory locations around the world—an airline stewardess recently greeted him by name, which he regarded as a dubious distinction. Fabian's division was recently contacted with a complaint that has been referred to him because it involves one of the suppliers he handles. The charges come from an NGO activist group called Global Vision 2050. After looking them up online, Fabian notes, based on their organizational description, that they seem energetic as well as somewhat strident and unfriendly to business.

The NGO claims that an Asia-based manufacturer with whom Fabian's firm has done contract work is forcing employees in Vietnam to toil under foreign supervisors who demand excessive overtime work. His company does not have explicit global standards for contractors in this area as long as the workers are paid for their labor. The NGO's complaint also mentions that the factory is

(Continued)

(Continued)

emitting waste chemicals and other effluent into the nearby river at night. Local government officials concerned about keeping factory jobs typically look the other way and ignore this kind of discharge, although Fabian knows that there are towns downstream that use the river for drinking water, and small-scale businesses that catch and sell fish from the river for food.

Fabian immediately contacts his company's legal counsel, who advises that they are covered in terms of any direct legal culpability. Vietnam's labor and environmental laws are weak and seldom enforced due to cronyism and a revolving door between government ministry positions and managers of state-owned enterprises. His supplier has also signed agreements promising that it will abide by the company's labor and environmental standards set by Fabian's company.

The supplier has been a good partner in many respects, as it typically provides components that meet high quality standards at very competitive prices. It has taken a long time for Fabian to build this partnership with them, and it would be very time-consuming to find another supplier, which may not be any better. To be thorough, Fabian forwarded the NGO letter to his counterparts in the supplier's organization. They have advised him not to worry and that they have handled the problem.

What should Fabian do now? There is no clear violation of company standards or national laws, and there are short-term business reasons to not upset the relationship with a valued supplier. Should he invoke a higher standard, and, if so, on what basis? A relativistic perspective that regards a given culture's ethics as being just as good as those of any other would suggest that Fabian need not act. It also does not provide answers for how to curb labor abuses or deal with the looming global environmental crisis.

Fabian ultimately needs to weigh the importance of possible labor and environmental issues against more immediate concerns such as profit, convenience, and supplier relations. He can probably make the best decision if he consults not only his own ethical North Star and the spirit as well as the letter of his company's standards, but also the perspective of employees and community members in the factory location. Ethical views in one environment may be shaped by a different set of considerations than in another, and it is important to be able to reach out and accurately understand why other people regard something as right or wrong. The blend of factors that either consciously or unconsciously shapes ethical decisions throughout the world usually includes a combination of the following elements:

- **Legal code:** "Follow the law." This is the basis for civil society and fair competition.
- **Family and friends:** "Do what's right for your family." "What are friends for?"

- **Social responsibility:** "We have an obligation to contribute to the good of the whole and to help those who are less fortunate."
- **Patriotism:** "Duty, honor, country." How can I protect my country's citizens and make their lives better?
- **Lifestyle:** "Do you live to work or work to live?" Is it more important to "do" or to "be"? Does your life include grace and beauty?
- **Gift exchange:** "I must repay the gifts I have received." Gift-giving builds reciprocal ties, raises the status of the giver, and shares wealth more broadly.

Following are two representations of how different blends of these priorities can shape ethical choices. One, Figure 8.1, is reflective of Northern Europe and the United States, where corporate leaders commonly first ask: "Is it legal?" The other, Figure 8.2, is more relationship-based, reflective of many countries in Asia, Africa, and Latin America, where the first question is often, "How will this affect the people who are closest to us?"

Ethical outreach requires putting yourself in the position of counterparts in a particular location, asking what is important to them as well as to you, and building support based on this knowledge. In a country like Vietnam where the second scenario predominates, Fabian might find that any assurances he makes regarding legal compliance actually provoke workers' outrage because they and people they know are directly affected (family and friends). This counts for far more than abstract standards set in a faraway capitol or corporate headquarters.

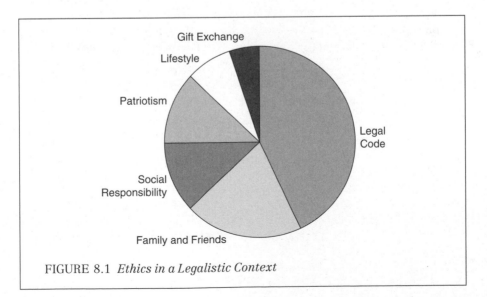

FIGURE 8.1 *Ethics in a Legalistic Context*

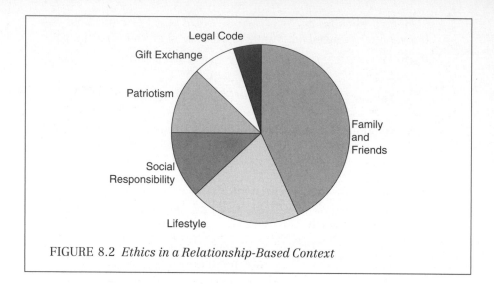

FIGURE 8.2 *Ethics in a Relationship-Based Context*

Conversely, based on a real understanding of local perspectives, Fabian could build support for higher ethical standards on the grounds that better labor and environmental practices will be good for workers and their families (family and friends), the downstream community and businesses will benefit (social responsibility), and a local waterway of deep historical significance will be preserved (patriotism). Fabian's supplier, local officials, and community members can all reap benefits. Short-term costs to investigate and address issues that the NGO has identified could be recouped through stronger governmental ties, better worker engagement and employee retention, and goodwill in the local community. Fabian would also be heading off potential damage to his company's brand through negative publicity gone viral in a digital age.

Integrity for a Small Planet

The term "triple bottom line" was coined in the mid-90s to highlight the importance of *people* and *planet* as well as bottom-line *profit*. This notion has proved difficult to implement on a mass scale, however, as the planet side of the equation still involves only a miniscule percentage of overall corporate efforts, and social and environmental impacts are often less tangible and more difficult to quantify than last year's profitability. As *The Economist* notes, it is difficult to fully measure the cost of an oil tanker run aground, the destruction of an ancient forest, or the cost of child labor.[22]

Over the decades since the triple bottom line idea was introduced, it has become manifestly clear that the planetary impacts of climate change, in particular, threaten to explode this neat trilogy, with lethal threats to both people and profits. For an increasing number of companies, the planet side of the equation has grown from a catchy but difficult to quantify "nice to have" to a moral imperative.

Integrity in a world of melting polar ice caps and rapidly vanishing species must be redefined in three ways:

1. **Ecological ethics:** Life in all forms is precious, and wiping out life on a mass scale is unethical, whether the perpetrator is a company or a government. It is not just humans that matter, whether one takes a practical perspective or draws upon teachings from one of the world's religious traditions.[23] Human existence depends on the web of life that people rely upon for food, warmth, and materials. Continually removing strands from this web is bad policy.

2. **Product life cycle ethics:** Companies are increasingly using terms like "cradle to grave" to refer to their responsibilities for the product cycle. Offering a shiny new widget at a neat profit is not ethical if the costs of pollution, unsafe working conditions, and disposal of hazardous wastes are offshored to another location. Poor people desperate for any jobs and government officials fueled by greed and callous attitudes toward their own environment may accept these negative impacts for the time being, but the widget producer is still accountable. NGOs and savvy consumers are increasingly willing to track each phase of this cycle and single out issues that companies formerly ignored or swept under the rug—such as workers in a small town in China disassembling our discarded laptops to salvage valuable metals while breathing toxic fumes and dumping waste in their own backyards.

3. **Generational ethics:** Each generation has the duty to hand down a world that is better than the one it inherited. But in our time, the reverse is happening to the natural world. Since 1950, approximately 60 percent of the world's rainforests—the earth's best antidote to rising rates of atmospheric carbon dioxide—have been cut down. This destruction continues at a rapid rate and could even be augmented by global warming, as droughts may weaken trees and create conditions conducive to forest fires.[24] It will take hundreds of years for these forests to be restored, if ever. The planetary resources we leave to our grandchildren will unquestionably be diminished in these and many other ways. One firm, Seventh Generation, has literally incorporated into its name the ethical obligation to hand over a world to our children that retains its vital resources and natural beauty.

Never in the existence of humankind has the need for wise, ethical leadership in all walks of life been more pervasive or more urgent. Our ethical choices often reflect the tension between what we must do to survive and our hopes for a better future. Both the rules for survival and the future possibilities open to humankind are undergoing a fundamental shift that requires a more comprehensive definition of organizational ethics. This new ethical perspective must be embedded throughout each company's business model and in each employee's daily actions.

WHAT YOU CAN DO

- Choose to work for — or *be* — an employer with a broad definition of integrity.
- Set a personal example in your own daily actions through using and advocating for sustainable actions (purchase carbon offsets for air travel, use mass transit, drive a hybrid, put solar panels on your home).
- Create a sustainability index for your business:
  - Consider ecological, product life cycle, and generational impacts.
  - Measure your carbon footprint and contributions to worker and community health and well-being; set and track progress toward goals for improvement.
- Build partnerships to promote sustainable practices in your industry:
  - Supply chain partners.
  - Industry peers.
  - Government at national, regional, and local levels.
  - Local communities: connect with history and points of local pride; help to achieve local goals or to define new aspirations and standards.

Leading from Your Own Center

Integrating Your Own Heritage, Present Awareness, and a Vision for the Future

THE NEXT LEVEL: WHAT'S MISSING?

If we forge ahead in this new global century—as organizations or as individuals—with the intent to maintain existing power structures, then we will probably fare poorly. The shifting economic center requires all of us to shift fundamentally with it, toward a reality we still need to define. A new generation of leaders is beginning to wield greater influence in global organizations and will eventually influence the nature of global leadership itself. The critical shift most companies need to make at this juncture involves determining how to position these future leaders in a way that enables them to define leadership on their own terms and thereby to transform the organization.

A Catch-22

Steven Chen leans across his broad desk on the 33rd floor of a glossy office building in Shanghai's Lujiazui financial district. Outside his window, construction on the Shanghai Tower is about three-quarters of the way completed, with crews working 24-hour days to finish Asia's latest mega tower, second in height only to the Burj in Dubai. Steven is originally from Guangdong, and his fluent English—complete with well-chosen slang expressions—still holds a hint of his native Cantonese dialect not erased by his graduate school years in the U.K. Having proven himself on the shop floors of factories in Guangzhou and Shenzhen, he now heads Learning and Development for the Asia Pacific (APAC) region of an iconic U.S. company, working out of its regional headquarters in Shanghai.

"We basically have a leadership crisis here when we start to hit the director level. This is our ceiling. And we are finding this across the region. At present, we are completely run on an expat model from the director level up," Steven says. His speech is animated with gestures and his eyes spark with intelligence. He has stories of confronting the American old boys' club during the journey to his current position. "We still have a lot of leaders who don't see what the issue is. They say, 'There are no local leaders at the top levels in the region? So what?' But if this company wants to invest over a billion dollars in the China market alone and triple production over the next three years, then it's actually a huge issue.

"And it's interesting what we are seeing. There are all the normal issues that we talk about with leadership development in Asia-Pacific—the gaps that people struggle with when they start moving out of local roles into more global responsibility. But when we look at our high-potentials, we see a group of individuals who have gotten to where they are based on their ability to adapt to this very American corporate environment. This next stage—the role change into the director level—is where the ceiling is holding fast. It is really a transition from management into leadership. You have to be someone that others want to follow when you hit this level."

Steven puts his arms on the desk and leans forward. "But by this stage, these leaders have adapted so much that the people they need to lead regard them as inauthentic—and they actually experience themselves as inauthentic as well. This makes it almost impossible for them to really identify with being a leader because they have somehow lost themselves along the way up this American corporate ladder. This is what we are doing to our talent. They are in a Catch-22—and no one is really talking about it."

The Conference Board, a U.S.-based corporate research organization, recently held a series of three "un-Conferences" across Asia: in Bangalore, Shanghai, and Bangkok. Each event was based on a crowd-sourcing model. Facilitators sourced ideas from a hand-picked group of high-profile attendees and enlisted panelists instead of keynote speakers to discuss pointed questions. The topic for the series was leadership, and the breakout sessions focused attendees' creative energy on the question that is on the minds of every business leader in the region: How will tomorrow's generation of leaders from India,

China, and Southeast Asia define leadership? How will this differ from common definitions of leadership during the past century of Western corporate economic dominance?

In Bangalore, the participants sit on the floor and begin to draw pictures of a new leadership model rooted in core Indian values. Small groups of consultants and corporate darlings of Western multinational corporations gradually drop their professional reserve. They sit cross-legged and their faces light up as discussions turn to the classic tales in the Mahabharata, stories of Arjuna, the shining warrior prince and friend of Krishna, and a leadership heritage that goes back thousands of years. The mood shifts dramatically as participants begin to speak from a place they know, rather than from their acquired MBA school personas. Their voices deepen and become more emphatic, displaying a rising confidence. A new leadership image emerges from the participants, depicted as a thousand-petaled lotus, rooted in the very core of Indian philosophy.

Throughout the two-day conference in Bangalore, the participants speak about India's transition to the global stage and their move into leadership roles in global companies. When asked what is needed to make this transition, the resounding refrain is a need for leadership borne out of Indian core values—for Indian leaders to lead from their own center.

There is more of a disconnect at the Shanghai session of the un-Conference. There is no consensus around what Chinese leadership will look like—only a growing clarity that the leadership model that Western multinationals have offered over the past 20 years is not a good fit. The head of a new regional Leadership Academy for a global pharmaceutical company says softly, "It seems like we are constantly being evaluated with a foreign standard and we never measure up. Maybe the standard itself is what is wrong."

When asked what leadership in China will look like as the country assumes a larger role on the global economic and political stage, a seasoned Shanghainese consultant answers that "we will know how Chinese will lead when they are in the role." True to a Chinese hierarchical approach and contrary to Western management expectations, one shouldn't be seen to display the traits of a leadership position before one actually enters the role. Given that many current Chinese corporate leadership models are relatively top-down and autocratic, and younger Chinese themselves are groping for a different way forward, there may also be a reluctance to broadcast this dilemma too openly. However, they have an increasingly diverse array of successful indigenous role models to consider: Ren Zhengfei, CEO of Huawei, has run his company in a command and control style, although now he is experimenting with rotating CEOs; Zhang Ruimin, CEO of Haier, has been decentralizing his company into self-organizing units; Yang Yuanqing, Lenovo's CEO, works with dual headquarters in Beijing and North Carolina and an executive team with members representing six different nationalities.[1]

On an executive panel during the last day of the Shanghai un-Conference session, another veteran Chinese business leader turns to the participants and says, "What we are actually missing here in China is value-led leadership. Many of us don't know what our values are anymore. This is why we are facing a glass ceiling in multinational organizations . . . and why our local companies are often full of corruption. We actually don't know what we believe in. We are just working hard and making money, but if we actually want to lead, we need to know *why* we are working hard and what we are making money *for*."

SYSTEMIC CHANGES

There are a number of systemic adjustments most companies can make that will better prompt new talent to emerge. Organizations that strive to be globally relevant need a leadership talent pool that is effective within multiple disparate contexts. Rather than creating clones of the organization's dominant Western culture, the developmental model needs to be truly global: recognizing the value of a broad range of approaches while rewarding flexibility and adaptation in different cultural environments.

For many companies, the shift to an advanced stage of globalization has come very rapidly, through mergers and acquisitions or aggressive growth strategies. Often they have not yet established the organizational strategy, talent management practices, support structures, and cultural shift needed to ensure consistent growth. Evaluating an organization's overall talent structures in a comprehensive way can provide a strategic path toward getting the talent equation right.[2]

Here are several examples of pivotal, make or break areas for creating an organization able to harness the potential of a new generation of global leaders.

Leadership Competencies

Defining truly global leadership competencies, as opposed to just steamrolling one leadership style across all markets, will create a more globally agile organization. Making these leadership expectations explicit will also allow organizations to assess what competencies are necessary for global success rather than falling back on culturally embedded expectations of leadership springing from their own cultural experience.

Reviewing existing leadership competency models for cultural bias and global relevance is a good place for organizations to start. First, they should seek out leadership models and behaviors based on truly global research and use this as a benchmark for their review. Second, it is a good idea to involve stakeholders who represent the company's diverse global presence in order to conduct this review with an intercultural filter. Reviewers can focus on the following questions:

- Which of our current leadership competencies are essential for operating in a global environment?
- Which competencies are relevant for our new growth markets? Are these reflected in our leadership model?
- Are there other competencies necessary for success in a global market or individual growth markets that we aren't measuring or rewarding?
- Which competencies are primarily relevant in a particular culture?
- How do different cultures and markets interpret these competencies differently?
- Are there competencies the organizational environment needs now but will be less relevant later?
- Are there competencies critical to the organization's future global presence that should be built now?

Figure 9.1 lists some examples of common generic leadership competencies coined by multinational organizations and additional considerations for applying them in a global context.

Company Brand

As an organization's revenue footprint begins to shift outside its home market, the organizational identity will need to be reassessed for its relevance to a global platform. Does the company's brand resonate with its new target consumers? Does its mission attract the best talent in the markets where it wants to grow? Do its values inspire commitment from the employees it wants to retain?

In Tokyo, a group of handpicked high-potentials from across the APAC region gather for a global leadership development program. They work for one of the world's most iconic beverage companies, and it is clear that they are proud to be a part of this global brand. But as the discussion turns to their core values as leaders, a Vietnamese marketing director raises his hand and asks, "What happens when my core values conflict with the values of the company?"

How can companies keep the aspects of the brand that makes them recognizable and appealing to consumers in new markets while also

Leadership Competency	Additional Global Considerations
Driving Outcomes • Delegating • Influence and Negotiation • Developing Direct Reports and Others	Exercises leadership across multiple functions to accomplish objectives; serves as a corporate "ambassador," or the face of the company; finds solutions when local resources are limited
	Identifies and champions high-potential individuals, regardless of country of origin, who can provide the future impetus to growth in key global markets
Decision Making • Seasoned Judgment • Conflict Management	Knows when to adapt to local practices and when to assert a different perspective as a constructive change agent, when to learn and when to teach
Results Orientation	Leads through relationships rather than immediate task focus when necessary; cognizant of dependency on others to get things done in a foreign setting, and able to build ties with a cultural guide when needed
Inspiring Others • Managing Vision and Purpose	Able to shift communication style, leadership methods, and strategy to fit different contexts; can move skillfully back and forth between different business environments, even when they call for very different approaches
	Leads through relationships rather than immediate task focus when necessary; cognizant of dependency on others to get things done in a foreign setting, and able to build ties with a cultural guide when needed
Executing Strategy • Strategic Agility	Leads in development of unique solutions by articulating own expectations, drawing out perspectives of important participants not normally included in decision making, "bridging" different views to create best solution for organization and its customers

FIGURE 9.1 *Globalizing Leadership Competencies*

changing aspects of the corporate personality to give global talent a stronger sense of ownership? French fashion companies, retail chains, makers of consumer goods, pharmaceutical firms, and others are grappling with this question in different ways. Here are more specific points to take into account:

- Does the organization have an attractive employee value proposition that can be leveraged across diverse talent in different geographies?
- Does the organizational brand (mission, vision, values) serve to unify globally diverse talent?
- Does the brand enhance the organization's ability to recruit and retain talent in all key global locations?
- Do the organization's values actively promote a globally inclusive environment?
- Does the organization have a clear business case linking global talent to its strategic goals?

Branding and Motivation

Jim talks quickly over the telephone line, dialing in from his office in São Paulo. He heads the Brazilian operations for a U.S. heavy equipment company, and he speaks in the cadence of someone used to balancing thoughtfulness with speedy results.

"At the end of the day, we are a very American brand with these Midwestern American values and extremely capitalistic drivers. I have found that there is a much broader range here in Brazil in terms of what motivates people: they may like feeling part of team; they may come to work for us because they like our industry . . . the interests are more diverse. The whole idea of earning money as a mission is less valued in Brazil and in France, where I was based previously. They are both more socialist cultures, so this whole capitalist value proposition of working hard to make money for the shareholders doesn't have any traction here.

"We really had to rethink some of the core aspects of our brand in order to connect in our growth markets. If you don't do this, you will lose people. You will not get the best out of them because they won't be committed. Both the customers and the employees need to see themselves in the brand. They need to own what it means."

Companies can address this challenge in a number of ways. A medical equipment company engaged its Indian employees in a rebranding exercise where it asked them to redefine the mission, vision, and values to better align with and motivate Indian employees. A global pharma giant tasked its Beijing research and development team with creating a vision for how China would engage with and transform the global organization. A European consumer goods company in Bangalore reevaluated its employee value proposition in order to gain an advantage in the city's fierce talent market. After mapping out the local values as well as key employee pain points, the company launched a campaign based on a "best work-life balance" employer brand. The company's practices in India were completely countercultural in comparison with the prevailing work model in the city that often involved a great deal of overtime and required employees to work hours suited to U.S. or European schedules. However, this campaign tapped into the budding aspiration among many overworked professionals for a healthier and more appealing lifestyle. The bold move not only attracted and retained top talent, but it also boosted the brand's local performance among consumers who associated its goods with its respectful practices.

One of the world's largest energy companies engages global employees in defining the company's values in their own words—and then has them identify local values that the company will exhibit when working in that specific location. For example, the joint Iraqi and foreign team added values related to investing in people and community relationships to existing values of safety and quality, underlining how they should operate within the Iraqi environment. The company created Arabic videos of executives speaking about what these values mean and how they guide employees' everyday behavior. They then began to assess how well they were measuring up to these values through an extensive organizational health survey conducted annually. Local employees can now see values that they have chosen in action, driving how the organization operates on a daily basis.

International Assignments

As organizations move through the stages of globalization, from domestic to mature global, the frequency of international assignments should also move from rare to essential for senior leadership roles and from stop-gap to strategic. Key questions should include:

- Are global assignments (both short and long term) integral to the organization's talent development strategy?
- How is global mobility positioned in the organization? Does it report into talent strategy?
- Do global rotation programs account for local motivations and incentives or disincentives?

In most organizations, mobility operates as a logistics arm of HR or is linked to compensation and benefits instead of being a strategic tool for global leadership development. Assignments are focused on fulfilling particular business needs, and candidates are selected by business units primarily based on technical skills. At many companies, the retention rate for international assignees after their return is appallingly low. Turnover is usually linked to the lack of a reentry plan or a suitable position. Returned assignees frequently report that they miss having broad responsibilities and the chance to learn new things every day, and they regret that their global skills are not being leveraged back home.

The Former Expat

Frank is a serial expat for a major consumer goods company. From his first assignment in Thailand, he moved on to Mexico and India before returning to headquarters on the East Coast of the United States.

"I came back and was basically going out of my mind. It is really hard to go back to a job that makes you feel limited in bandwidth. You need to do things in the company that leverage all the things you learned on assignment. People at headquarters have no way to relate, and it sometimes seems that they don't care. The perspective is just not there, and so the company doesn't give their assignees the opportunity to feel like what they experienced is valuable to the organization. The organization needs to put senior people in the room and have the returnees talk about their markets and the business there. People want to feel that their experience is utilized."

Frank elaborates, "Most of the benefits of global assignments—things like improved communication and listening skills, increased ability to work across functional silos—are long-term. People on assignment are usually working in a much smaller entity than headquarters. They work outside their function, experience an increased breadth of communication, and learn to work with people from all parts of the organization. They're better able to quickly establish trusting and productive relationships, are creative at solving problems, and have a broader global business perspective. They enhance their ability to adapt their leadership style to different circumstances, are more patient in dealing with others' differences, and have greater self-awareness, appetite for risk taking, cultural sensitivity, and open-mindedness. These are all the things that we need from our leadership if our company is going to be viable in a global environment. But no one is tracking this."

Organizations looking to globalize should first address the structural elements, aligning the mobility reporting structure with strategic talent development. Once this structure is in place, global assignments and rotations can be leveraged as strategic development opportunities and used deliberately to cultivate key global leadership competencies. A company can track high-potentials through this process, and successful global assignments will eventually help create a globally savvy set of executives driving key decisions.

When a German family-owned business decided to focus its growth strategy on its global markets, it hired a CEO who had worked in six different countries. After taking over, the new CEO began to restructure the organization along functional lines. He required all of the functional leaders and anyone holding an executive level role to have spent at least four years working outside their home market. The global HR director backs up the re-org: "If the company wants to go global, it has to start with the leadership. We have to be global first in order to shift the mindset."

Assignments from Asia

Assignments for individuals from fast-growth markets bring with them their own set of challenges. The global HR VP for a consumer goods company shares what he has learned through tough experience:

"Assignments out of Asia are critical, but you have to set it up right. We have to recruit people here young, because too many family factors come into play later. Once [employees] get to the senior levels, they are not willing to go on assignment because they need to take care of aging parents or have children who have gotten into highly competitive secondary schools. They are also afraid of failure and of leaving a market that is growing so fast. There are some that worry they will lose their competitive advantage if they stay out of the country too long.

"To make these assignments work, we keep them short, and it is critical that they are positioned well. They must also be well outlined and well-structured: What are the goals, what is the reporting structure, what are the expectations?

"We ensure that there is a leader in place to oversee the entire assignment program and designate a sponsor and a mentor for each assignee. They can contact any of these individuals at any moment to discuss issues. We also set up a complementary program where they have meetings with global VPs. The program arranges for site visits; they go to sales offices and spend a full day with the local teams. We have them attend virtual meetings with different business units or functions where these guys introduce their main priorities and strategies. It is like a mini organizational discovery trip. They attend one of these web-based meetings per month for different business units. One day per quarter provides a full agenda of training and skills; they have consistent contact with sponsors; and we provide them with a platform to share documents and chat on the intranet about their experience with others on the program. This has been working really well. Not having these structures in place can actually lead to disaster."

Executive Representation

It is very difficult for an organization to successfully transition to a mature global model if those leading that transition are not globally minded themselves. As organizations move through the various stages of globalization, leaders around the world must increasingly make organizational strategy and resource decisions that affect multiple regions and countries.. It is worth asking:

- Are all major fast-growth markets represented in the decision-making process?
- Are employees from the organization's key growth markets represented on the senior leadership team and the board?

The Belgian Team

A Belgian technology company is globalizing rapidly through a combination of aggressive growth strategies in global markets and a series of acquisitions. But all decisions are still made out of Belgium by a nearly all-Flemish executive team. Petrit is a Kosovar sales director for the organization. He currently works out of Prague but travels frequently to China and South America to work with project teams there.

"Our board is also entirely Belgian except for one person, and there is only one woman. At the central leadership team, there is one person from the United States — but no one from China, which is a huge market for us. "The Belgian team makes decisions around things that affect the entire company. They just go ahead without any involvement from the regions. To not have input and feedback around those decisions is mind-boggling.

"And no matter how well I perform, I am sure that I do not have a shot at becoming the CEO because of the simple fact that I am not Belgian. Someone like me has limited upward mobility in the company. There is starting to be a level of awareness around this. But at the end of the day, the central leadership team is still very Belgium-centric. Some foreigners have come in, but they have left again. It is hard to succeed on that team if you are not Belgian — and when I say Belgium, I mean Flemish. If you are South American or Asian, it is very challenging to bring value and be a part of that leadership meeting. As an outsider, sitting there and brainstorming with seven Belgians is a challenge and a stretch."

Petrit is young, in his mid-30s, and he is clearly energized by the possibility he sees for the organization to globalize:

"There is a limited pool of talented people for my teams. If you exclude part of them explicitly or implicitly, then you have lost this talent as an organization — and this is dangerous for us as a business. You need to have people grow and enter management instead of leaving. A diverse pipeline is important to make this possible. Any brainstorm is better off with as much diversity as possible; to be successful in strategy and execution, we need a diverse management team. We can't get this without having a diverse company. It is easy to build a team out of 40-year-old white men, but it won't give us long-term success.

"Where it doesn't work is when you have a group of white dogs and a black dog who enters is bitten to death. We had some really great regional leaders who were growing into top management roles, but then they got bitten and fell out."

In order to change the old guard, organizations must be purposeful and work systemically. Some level of discomfort should be expected as power shifts from its traditional haunts to new faces and locales. Equipping current leadership with the business case, gathering a strong cadre of champions for change at the top, and removing structural barriers to executive diversity are all critical.

Talent Flow

The flow of talent should increase as an organization globalizes, eventually becoming multidirectional. When companies begin to build an international presence, the talent flow is usually to and from headquarters, with expats being sent out to transfer knowledge or take on leadership roles in other locales. Global talent from key markets is also sent to headquarters in order to better understand the business, gain access to resources, and connect with decision-makers. As the capabilities of regional operations around the world grow, the organization's talent should flow in a variety of directions. Intraregional or cross-regional assignments become more common, and flow to and from headquarters becomes less significant. The purpose of talent flow becomes less focused on one-directional knowledge transfer and more about creating and disseminating global organizational knowledge.

As organizations try to structure their talent flow on a more global model, they should assess whether it is multidirectional and used to spread global organizational knowledge across all key markets. Locating key business units within critical markets can be useful in making multilateral talent flow possible.

Global HR in Shanghai

A French electronics company recently began an aggressive structural reorganization focused on stepping up its global talent flow. Ignasi is the company's Global VP of human resources, based in Shanghai. He is from Spain and moved into the position in China from his previous base in Barcelona. He identifies himself as Catalonian. "Previously, everything in the world came from and went back to France. No leadership existed outside of France and no decisions were made that did not take place in France.

"When I was in Barcelona, I used to travel to France two or three times a month for meetings. But that has all changed now. This has been a shock for some of our French colleagues, but it is the right course to take because of where we are going as an organization.

"We have been doing a lot with global leadership development, sending our high-potentials on intensive leadership weeks in Brazil, Russia, China, and India; but the structural change was the

(Continued)

(Continued)

big signal that we were committing to a global identity. Several years ago, we moved our global human resources—the entire function—to Shanghai. It makes sense actually, if you look at the numbers, since we are hiring the most people here. So, now, if I want to stay in my HR role, I need to do that out of Shanghai—not out of Barcelona, which is attached to the French umbilical cord.

"And from here, we are getting really aggressive about increasing talent flow. We have ramped up our short-term assignment program. Before, we had maybe eight cases a year; now we have moved that to 35 for just our Chinese talent. Most of them are in their 30s, and this is their second rotation outside China. We are generating new jobs regularly. The goal is global exposure and a global perspective on the organization. We are growing quickly and working in a complex matrix. We need our leaders to be on the ground in the places where we operate and to bring that level of knowledge to the business decisions.

"This is all driven by the business needs, not some nice idea around travel opportunities for our top talent. For example, we have big problems with capacity in our factories. There is an issue with our sales forecasting—an activity that has a huge impact on our planning with suppliers and others. So we are trying to develop a group of experts to create processes that work well on a global basis. Because our Chinese factory supplies 10 different countries, we had someone in our Shanghai office who started working with salespeople in various locations to understand how the sales team makes the forecasts. We then sent him to Hungary, which receives goods from the Chinese factory, so that he can understand how their requests impact Chinese supply chain planning. The goal is to bring this guy back to the central team in China to serve as one of the experts on planning production. Hopefully, after gaining exposure to different realities, he will come back to plan supply chain capacity for factories in China, and he will then have the networking exposure and relationships in place to make some big improvements.

"In my entity here in China, the executive VP is French, the finance director is from Serbia, and the China country director is Chinese. Right now, we are still heavy on the expats here at the executive level, but things are changing fast, and we are reducing the number of expats. A few years ago, this would have been driven by costs. But we just hired a Chinese finance director at an annual salary, which is more expensive than any expat. We are transforming our expat system to more of a talent flow model, using expats to build capacity, leverage global resources, and increase their own exposure to key markets. Now the movement of talent is really about knowledge sharing."

PERSONAL TRANSFORMATION: CONNECTING PAST, PRESENT, AND FUTURE

Indigenous corporate leadership styles are still a work in progress in this era of "emerged" powers. It's likely that individuals will find their own ways to connect past, present, and future to forge a new identity.

Each country has its own unique set of circumstances influenced by its cultural history, colonialism, ideology, and institutional structures. India's boisterous democracy and wide range of educational institutions—along with the everyday presence of religion and spirituality in myriad forms throughout the country—provide plenty of access to its ancient traditions for people who are interested. China's Cultural Revolution of the 1960s, during which cultural treasures of previous eras were methodically eradicated in the name of rooting out class-based privilege, has made it harder for many individuals in that country to feel or to even find connections with the past, except through their own families and hometown ties. Many countries, such as Indonesia and Malaysia, have multicultural histories with several contemporary threads that leaders must learn to integrate.

Truly centered global leaders are rare. They must have a keen understanding of their own cultural identity as well as their personal core values or guiding principles, strong business acumen, awareness of how people from different cultural backgrounds respond to them at any given moment, and the ability to inspire people across levels, functions, markets, and nationalities. This level of mastery requires years of experience and a healthy balance of self-confidence and humility.

Western Roots

Dave Schoch has been with Ford Motor Company for several decades, and has held roles at world headquarters in the United States as well as in Brazil, South Africa, Europe, and Asia-Pacific. He is currently the president of Asia-Pacific based in Shanghai. One of his favorite methods for communicating his philosophy about leadership is through telling stories about his experiences in various roles around the world. Here is one example.

> *When I arrived in South Africa as the chief financial officer for our business there, the organization was in the process of rebuilding following the end of apartheid. Virtually the entire management of the business and our manufacturing operations were still white—both local Afrikaaners and some expatriates like me from the U.S. and Europe. During my first week in the office, located at our assembly plant site in Pretoria, I stopped to say hello to everyone I encountered, from janitors to clerks to senior-level managers. I noticed a middle-aged black South African woman mopping the hallway and decided to stop and introduce myself to her. When I approached her and said 'hello,' she stopped mopping but would not raise her eyes and look at me. I stepped in closer and extended my hand, introduced myself and asked her name. She slowly and nervously looked up at me and finally offered her hand for a brief touch. I told her I was very happy to meet her and thanked her for her service to the company.*

I made a point of always greeting her by name any time our paths crossed. After a few days, she began to look up when I approached. She would look me directly in the eye and say hello. She seemed to stand up taller while she worked. This became our pattern during my tenure. What I didn't realize at the time was that the report of my reaching out to this one woman would quickly spread throughout the organization. This story formed an important aspect of my leadership "brand" to the local employees.[3]

Dave Schoch is culturally very American, yet is widely regarded throughout the diverse markets and organizations within Asia-Pacific as a good listener, approachable, empathetic, and also an astute business general manager. He is known by his given name throughout the employee community for which he is responsible, which numbers in the tens of thousands. Dave possesses a rare combination of global wisdom, sensitivity, calmness, and professional competence. He is a champion of leadership development for the local national employee population throughout Asia-Pacific and beyond, and insists that his senior leadership team members also devote time and energy to the development of non-Western talent.

Dave's conduct appears to be grounded in his own convictions, as a person who grew up in the United States, regarding the fundamental dignity and worth of each individual—"all men are created equal and are endowed by their Creator with certain unalienable rights." He is so effective, in part, because he has joined these values with the needs of the present, such as overcoming the legacy of apartheid and supporting his employees' aspirations for the future: believing in and making every effort to grow talent across the Asia-Pacific region, regardless of an individual's personal background. Dave's leadership image among people in his organization has come to include his belief in human possibility and his deep commitment to developing it.

Eastern Roots

An India-based leader describes his personal leadership journey in ways that are equally moving and relevant to many counterparts in the region.

I used to be insensitive to the needs of others and also deeply racist. My family was forced to leave what is now Pakistan during the Partition era. Many of my relatives died at the hands of Pakistanis, and most lost nearly everything they had during the migration into India. My parents worked very hard to rebuild a life for my family and achieved modest success. I was able to gain a solid education and get a good job. We had several servants in India, and I had little interest in their lives or welfare. Several years ago I took an international assignment in Melbourne, Australia, and had an experience that changed my core values completely.

We arrived in Melbourne in the middle of the night and took a taxi to our temporary flat. We had a lot of luggage, and I carried my sleeping three-year-old daughter in my arms. My wife was seven months pregnant with our second child. When we arrived at the building, there was no one at the front desk. A note with my name on it said, "Welcome to Australia! Your flat is on the seventh floor. Unfortunately the lift is out of order until later this week. We apologize for the inconvenience." I stood looking at the empty lobby area. It was about 1:00 A.M. on a Sunday morning. We tried to climb the stairs, but my wife suddenly sat down with pains in her abdomen. We returned to the lobby realizing it was too dangerous to try to get her up to the seventh floor. I decided we needed to find a hotel for the night with a working lift, and went outside and looked up and down the deserted street. I was desperately worried about my wife and did not know what to do. I was in a strange country where I had no friends or family.

After a couple of minutes, a lone taxi drove slowly down the street. I waved it down. The driver immediately pulled up to the curb, got out of the car, and came to me asking if he could help. He was Pakistani.

I stood there for a few seconds considering all of my lifelong hatred for his country, looked at my wife who was exhausted and in pain, and said, "Please, we need help." He helped my wife into his car where she could lie down, put all of our luggage in the trunk, and drove us to a nearby hotel.

But this Pakistani man did not stop there. He came into the hotel with us, insisted on helping us with our luggage to our room, and finally refused to take any money from me—no fare, no tip, nothing. I did not know what to say to this man. He handed me his card and said, "Tomorrow, after you have rested, I would like to invite you and your family to my home for a meal. You can repay me by accepting my offer."

This Pakistani man and his family became very close friends with me and my family during our stay in Australia. After getting to know me better, he told me that when he first came to Australia, his child became very ill during the night. He was unable to find anyone who could take him to the hospital, and his child died of a high fever. Because of this tragedy, every night after he finishes his official workday driving his cab, he drives around for one more hour trying to find someone in need *of help in the hope that he might save a life. He never takes any money during this hour. This is what he was doing when he found my family.*

The kindness that this man showed to me and my family fundamentally changed my core values. It has forced me to become more accepting of differences, much slower to anger, and much better able to give others the benefit of the doubt. It has also positively changed the way I lead others.

This leader has also linked past, present, and future. His story ties South Asia's bitter history of religious, ethnic, and caste-based strife to the present by noting the bias lurking in his own attitudes—something that doubtlessly resonates with listeners from almost any background. He also offers a vision of the future with a style of leadership that is open-minded and willing to reach beyond old prejudices.

Leadership from a New Center

Companies and industries differ depending upon the nature of their customers, their technologies, and marketplace dynamics. Some—like Apple, Samsung, and Huawei—have performed quite well using a more centralized structure; others, including Unilever, Lenovo, and 7-Eleven, have benefited from decentralization. All, however, are being impacted by the global shift in economic power, with supply chains and markets that span the globe.

Organizations that are able to nimbly navigate the complexity of a world where the markets are giving voice to myriad new economic players are the ones that will survive this borderless century. Firms with growth plans that depend on winning customers in distant places must have the leadership talent to attain their objectives. Leadership for a shifting center requires companies to create pathways for development that hold relevance and resonance across multiple markets and conflicting value systems. A variety of personalities and values can be effective in a global business context; however, those that are chauvinistic, narrow-minded, or mistrustful of people who are different are unlikely to succeed over the long term. Leaders' ability to change and adapt without losing their own center becomes the critical personal balancing act.

In an interview with Errol Morris, director of MIT's Media Lab, Joi Ito points to the implications of open source business models at companies like Mozilla, Lennox, and Wikipedia for traditional forms of leadership: "You look at open source projects [and see that] people participate because they want to. . . . When you try to lead a group like that, you lead them in a completely different way."[4] While the open source movement itself is still too young and limited to certain kinds of applications to judge its long-term significance, it is clear that global talent itself is mobile and therefore, to some degree, voluntary. Leaders must be able to attract people to their cause and to develop leaders in new markets in order to drive growth.

It is unsettling to groom others for leadership roles, especially when the center is no longer defined by old borders and static identities. Leaders who are clear about their own personal core values—knowing both what they stand for and where they are willing to be flexible—are best suited to handle shifting economic realities and to identify and cultivate fresh talent. Taking on new responsibilities requires a leap of faith on the part of those who accept them as well. Yet leaders who have found their own center can also be trusted to shape the future.

WHAT YOU CAN DO

- Work to build globalized systems in your organization, especially in key areas such as:
  - Leadership competencies
  - Company brand
  - International assignments
  - Executive representation
  - Talent flow
- Clearly define your own core values—the critical few principles that you find inspirational and/or essential and are willing to stand for under any circumstances. Keep in mind that most effective values are likely to be deeply rooted in your past, applicable in the present, and relevant for your own future and that of your organization. Sources of values could include your civic, religious, artistic, and family background as well as your prior work experience; they may also draw upon lessons from human history's darker chapters as well as ways that people have overcome them. Here are examples of values and possible sources:
  - Equity, respect: "All men are created equal, that they are endowed by their Creator with certain unalienable rights . . ." (United States Declaration of Independence).
  - Compassion, empathy: "I am a Muslim, and a Hindu, and a Christian, and a Jew, and so are all of you" (Mahatma Gandhi).
  - Environmental integrity: The smallness of humanity in comparison with nature, and the imperative to live in harmony with it (Taoism, Chinese landscape painting).
  - Responsibility to future generations: Leaving a viable world for our children and grandchildren (family values, environmental science).
- Compare your definition of your own values with the way that others perceive you. How would they express what you stand for? Have they observed you enacting the values you describe?
- Demonstrate these values to others through the personal example that you set in your daily leadership activities and through sharing stories about your experiences.

Team Launch: Foundations

Paying attention to how a team is positioned within a matrix organizational structure can do much to make a team leader's tasks more feasible. There are other steps team leaders can take to build the foundations for effective teamwork. Each of the five steps recommended here corresponds with a high-priority item from the GlobeSmart Teaming Assessment^{SM} survey data on global teams cited in Chapter 4; these steps have been reordered slightly to provide team leaders with a logical sequence for action.

While many team leaders may find these topics familiar and easily checked off their long list of tasks, the evidence from more than 2,000 global teams suggests that they should take a closer look, dig deeper, and ensure that their own team's foundations are set on firm bedrock. Global teams live in earthquake country where structural weaknesses can be fatal and higher building standards are required!

Global Team Leader Checklist (II): Team Foundations

1. Assess stakeholders
2. Establish shared goals
3. Build trust among team members
4. Clarify roles and responsibilities
5. Use rewards to support alignment

STEP ONE: ASSESS STAKEHOLDERS

Priority survey item: The team receives the resources and cooperation it needs from other parts of the company.

Team leaders should kick off the interactions between team members with a thorough stakeholder analysis. Participants on a matrix team may or may not be aware of all the stakeholders their team is serving. By hearing from all team members about the contacts they regard as being their most important ones outside of the team, it becomes easier to understand and appreciate their priorities.

Team leaders can build greater mutual awareness through a stakeholder mapping exercise that graphically displays each team member

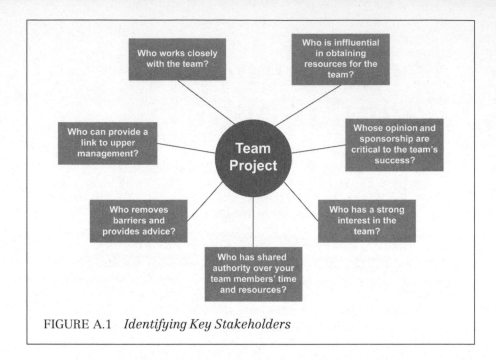

FIGURE A.1 *Identifying Key Stakeholders*

electronically or on a wall chart and asks them to add their key stake-holders along with requirements or outcomes these stakeholders might expect from the team. Once all of the stakeholder relationships are listed, it will probably be necessary for the team leader to carry out a prioritization exercise in order to identify possible conflicting interests and determine which of these are most crucial and how best to balance the team's efforts. Sometimes team members find it difficult to identify and articulate the needs of all their stakeholders. The questions in the diagram shown in Figure A.1 may be helpful in such situations.

A predictable outcome of stakeholder mapping efforts is the need to deepen team members' collective knowledge about high-priority stakeholders who are still relatively unfamiliar to key team members. This can be accomplished in part through various forms of people exchange:

- **Team leader visits:** One of the best first steps a team leader can take is to visit each site where team members are located, get together with them face to face, and arrange to meet important stakeholders together. Most team leaders have a clear project plan and are skilled at driving for results. The team leader should have a network strategy as well as a project plan, because personal connections with team members and stakeholders may turn out to be equally vital for getting things done.

- **Face-to-face meeting:** For many reasons it is best for teams to meet in person during the kickoff phase of their efforts. This builds personal bonds and further creates shared context for understanding one another as well as a mutual sense of commitment. It can be very effective to invite key stakeholders to such a meeting as well so that their perspectives are heard directly by all team members and they have the chance to meet people on the team.

- **Window person:** Having a person in each key location who knows the other sites and team members is useful in providing contacts and background information. As one member of a global team testified, "A best practice is to . . . place liaisons or representation with the parent team and in other key locations to help bridge the communication, logistical, and geographic gaps."

- **People exchange:** Systematic people exchange between team members from different locations can also serve to more readily convey stakeholder needs while enhancing skills development, mutual learning, and knowledge transfer.

- **Tag teams:** These are close partnerships between individuals, sometimes occurring naturally with people who have an affinity for each other. As one such team member noted, "My tag team partner helps me to plug into the headquarters decision-making process, and I help her to get direct input from clients in our local market."

Step Two: Establish Shared Goals

Priority survey item: All members of the team support and understand the team's goals.

Every team, global or not, needs a shared sense of direction. Team members who are focused on what they can achieve together are more likely to succeed than those who are more focused on their personal priorities. The unifying impact of common goals is especially vital for matrix teams whose members represent different parts of the organization and disparate interests. Depending on the type of team, its vision, goals, and/or objectives may be predetermined, or the leader of the team and its members might have more latitude in setting them. Here are several recommendations offered by experienced global team leaders:

- Set a clear vision and goals: "You need to establish the team's vision/mission plus high-level roles and responsibilities before or soon after you launch the team, or team members will already be lost. I try to have these worked out before the team starts to keep people focused and give them the opportunity for input without being overwhelmed."

- Provide a big picture introduction: "Ensure that each team member, including new entries, has a structured orientation to the team's goals and their links with corporate strategy."
- Use a service level agreement to specify sub-team objectives: "One of our best practices is establishing a clear service level agreement [SLA] for fielding and responding to issues that arise between sub-teams. The SLA specifies the obligations of each unit to the team as a whole."

STEP THREE: BUILD TRUST AMONG TEAM MEMBERS

Priority survey item: There is a high level of trust among team members.

Trust is an enormous topic that has generated its own army of consultants. One common observation about human nature is that people tend to demonstrate greater trust toward members of their own "in-group," while harboring suspicion and mistrust towards outsiders. This was probably a sensible attitude in traditional societies where social mobility was uncommon, nation states were rare, and the people living in the next town or valley could be hostile. In a contemporary organizational setting, however, matrix teams, by their very definition, require people to work together who are to at least some degree outsiders to one another, even if they belong to the same company.

Team members from the marketing department may be required to collaborate closely with people from information technology or manufacturing. Likewise, headquarters employees representing a business unit have to coordinate their activities with various regions, and countries within regions need to work with each other. Each organizational unit is likely to have a distinctive set of goals, values, norms, and assumptions that are not unlike those found in traditional societies or insular tribes still sought out by anthropologists, yet they must find ways to constitute a new in-group—perhaps even a temporary one—and work successfully together.

A superficial approach to trust-building in a global team setting is to set aside an hour or two for it as part of a busy agenda, engage in a few facilitated activities, or a social occasion, and then declare that "trust has been established!" Team leaders who move on to other concerns at this point do so at their peril, as trust issues will likely resurface along the way. It is far better to regard trust as an ongoing part of teamwork that requires constant attention and cultivation. Trust is difficult to establish in the first place and even more challenging to maintain and increase over time; it is also easily damaged. There is a Japanese saying, *It takes three years to build a castle and three days to burn it down.*

Global team leaders are well advised to consider their own assumptions about trust and to learn about personal and cultural factors that shape the assumptions of their team members. For example, trust may be based upon any or all of the factors described in Figure A.2. The emphasis that a particular team member might place on each of these factors is often shaped by culture. Another lens through which to view trust is the set of cultural dimensions presented in Chapter 3. Cultural perspectives influence what behaviors or characteristics are regarded as trustworthy. Depending on the cultural orientation of each person, it could be advisable for a team leader to go about building trust with them in different ways (see Figure A.3).

Matrix team leaders can most immediately cultivate trust among team members by taking the kinds of measures listed below during the start-up phase. These steps may be modified to accommodate different cultural perspectives on the team, as indicated by sample references to each of the cultural dimensions:

Qualifications

- Post resumes and pictures on a team site.
- Provide background as to why team members were chosen for this team.
- Highlight the way that different team members can contribute to accomplishing the team's tasks.
  - *Direct orientation:* Encourage direct communicators on the team to draw out the prior experience and expertise of others when they are speaking one-on-one.
  - *Indirect orientation:* Position less direct communicators on the team with others by noting credentials and expertise that they are not likely to mention themselves.

Relationships

- Kick off the team effort with a face-to-face meeting and dedicate time to building personal relationships; create informal settings in which team members are comfortable sharing their personal stories.
- Make short-term site visits at an early stage to build an understanding of the business and organizational context in other locations.
- Hold periodic face-to-face meetings if possible.
- Build time in meeting agendas for mutual check-ins.
- Create ways for remote team members to have a more visible presence (through instant messaging, use of video cam functionality during calls, and regular one-on-one meetings).

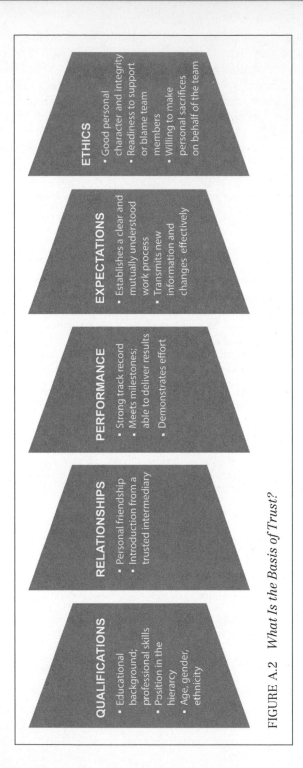

FIGURE A.2   *What Is the Basis of Trust?*

Establishing Trust: Cultural Contrasts

Independent • Demonstrates ability to handle tasks on his/her own	**Interdependent** • Consults with others in a careful and timely way when problems come up
Egalitarianism • Willing to consider others' ideas regardless of age or rank	**Status** • Holds a position of authority or is introduced by a high-status third party
Risk • Willing to take calculated risks to achieve team objectives	**Certainty** • Close attention to detail, data, and process to ensure high quality
Direct • Communicates openly in a clear and timely manner	**Indirect** • Is discreet about sharing information; respects confidentiality
Task • Jumps quickly into the work at hand and gets things done	**Relationship** • Starts by building strong & positive relationships among team members

FIGURE A.3   *Culture and Trust*

- Take virtual coffee breaks.
- Use instant messaging, texting, or chat to expand modes of communication.
  - *Task orientation:* Focus on building stronger and more trusting relationships through accomplishing tasks together.
  - *Relationship orientation:* Express concern for the well-being of other team members; check in periodically with team members, even when there is no immediate problem to solve.

Performance

- Carefully assess the skill sets of team members at different sites and delegate tasks that are suited to these skills; build in a level of stretch that fits existing skills as well as team member aspirations.
- Begin with closely spaced milestones to create a mutual sense that performance goals will be met.

- Hold periodic celebrations to mark the achievement of significant milestones.
  - *Risk orientation:* Encourage team members who value risk-taking and creativity to tap the expertise of individuals who are more focused on data analysis and quality control.
  - *Certainty orientation:* Encourage team members who value careful data analysis and quality control to tap the skills and ideas of individuals who are willing to take calculated risks.

Expectations

- Set up a regular and routine meeting flow to help team members understand and participate.
- Establish ground rules for team meetings that encourage participation by all, especially remote participants.
- Establish frequent check-ins.
- Follow up on meetings verbally and in writing to clarify understanding and ensure real agreement.
- Inform all team members about changes in a timely manner.
- Develop well-defined guidelines for streamlining handoffs between team members.
- Clarify the team's decision-making process, including who is consulted for what, and how final decisions will be made.
  - *Egalitarianism orientation:* Emphasize frequent consultation with team members.
  - *Status orientation:* Combine consultation and information-gathering with authoritative decisions by the team leader.

Ethics

- Set a tone of seeking first to understand and making judgments based on a balanced set of information when ethical issues arise.
- Be clear about bottom-line rules for team members with respect to potentially controversial topics such as confidentiality, handling of intellectual property, supplier relations, escalation of issues beyond the team, and so on.
- When apparent problems arise, avoid being overly dependent on e-mail (which can cause conflicts to escalate), and use higher-context forms of communication such as phone, video-conference, or in-person meetings.

- Address perceived ethical breaches immediately; determine whether they are based on real violations of team or company rules or on cultural misunderstandings.
  - *Independent:* Encourage more independently minded team members to share information and consult with others before moving ahead.
  - *Interdependent:* Encourage more interdependent team members to take individual initiative when circumstances require a quick response, and clarify when information-sharing is or is not appropriate with people beyond the team.

STEP FOUR: CLARIFY ROLES AND RESPONSIBILITIES

Priority survey item: Members of the team are clear on their roles and responsibilities.

When team members with disparate backgrounds come together, there are frequently misunderstandings about who is responsible for what. Job titles do not necessarily translate easily from one location, function, or language to another, and the same term can have different meanings. Job responsibilities may overlap, or important tasks are neglected because everyone assumes that they will be completed by somebody else. It is advisable for global team leaders to devote extra time at the outset to this topic, carefully discussing with team members their own responsibilities as well as their level of clarity about the jobs of others. Figure A.4 contains an exercise that can be used with the whole team, either face-to-face or in a virtual format, and even repeated at intervals when the team's charter changes or new team members join. Although the exercise seems to be relatively straightforward, it is remarkable how many potentially dangerous alignment issues it can surface.

For far-flung global teams, it is prudent to limit dependencies between the roles and responsibilities of team members or sub-units. If a team member needs to interact multiple times a day with remote colleagues, the chances for misunderstandings and dropped handoffs increase. Well-structured, less frequent handoffs are easier to manage and to execute.

STEP FIVE: USE REWARDS TO SUPPORT ALIGNMENT

Priority survey item: The team's reward system encourages cooperation and shared effort among team members.

Team leaders may or may not be able to determine the way that their team members are rewarded. Ideally, the performance evaluation of

A. Have team members define their roles, including the activities they will carry out and their target objectives (on a piece of flip chart paper if face-to-face, or a shared electronic document if the format is virtual), and make these visible to the whole team.

B. Give everyone time to read what their teammates have written.

C. Ask team members to make short presentations on what they wrote.

D. Ask team members to write their comments on Post-it Notes or on the shared electronic document, including:
   - Activites that are valuable;
   - Activities that overlap and require further discussion;
   - Activities that may not be worth doing.

E. Create a separate document as a parking lot for notes regarding items that need to be addressed but nobody is currently handling.

F. Give team members a chance to review the notes they have received and to create a revised description of their roles in response to this input; provide all team members with a second brief opportunity to describe their revised role for the rest of the team as well as any follow-up conversations they need to have for better clarity or collaboration.

G. Write up and disseminate to the whole team a summary of the new roles and responsibilities.

FIGURE A.4   *Clarifying Roles and Responsibilities*

- Opportunities for travel
- Relationships with global colleagues
- Creative challenges in new markets
- Global knowledge & experience
- Meaningful tasks; broad impact
- Wider cross-border network
- Being part of a "winning" team
- Satisfaction with a job well done
- Enjoyment of team activities
- Sense of belonging
- Career growth
- Variety and change
- Coaching and/or mentorship
- Personal autonomy
- Pride in the team's mission
- Close ties with the team leader
- Work/life balance
- Respect & recognition; visibility

FIGURE A.5   *Potential Motivators for Global Team Members*

team members is based at least in part on the accomplishment of team goals, and the team leader has a voice in the assessment process, even for matrix team members whose direct reporting relationships are elsewhere. Shared commitments of team members that are tied to employee performance measurements and incentives go a long way to enhancing alignment among participants.

In the absence of a link between team objectives and team member assessment, team leaders can still seek to discover what motivates each participant and to distribute team activities in a way that fits the needs and aspirations of individual team members. Figure A.5 contains a list of common motivators, with an emphasis on intrinsic rewards rather than the more obvious extrinsic ones such as compensation or bonuses.

Assessments from Aperian Global

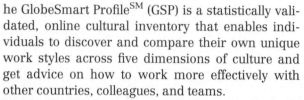he GlobeSmart Profile^SM (GSP) is a statistically validated, online cultural inventory that enables individuals to discover and compare their own unique work styles across five dimensions of culture and get advice on how to work more effectively with other countries, colleagues, and teams.

As a benefit of reading this book, you can obtain free, temporary access to the GlobeSmart Profile by typing the following URL into your web browser:

http://learning.aperianglobal.com/go/profile

Aperian Global also offers other assessments:

GlobeSmart Teaming Assessment^SM (GTA) offers a fast and powerful way for teams to gauge their effectiveness and gather feedback to improve their performance.

GlobeSmart Leadership Assessment^SM (GLA) examines global leadership strengths and areas for improvement based on 10 behaviors that define great global leaders.

GlobeSmart Innovation Assessment^SM (GIA) measures eight dimensions of individual, team, and organizational innovation, providing a means to accurately focus innovation efforts.

Intercultural Effectiveness Scale (IES), offered in collaboration with the Kozai Group, evaluates competencies critical for effective interaction with people from different cultures.

Global Competencies Inventory (GCI), also offered in collaboration with the Kozai Group, assesses beliefs, values, and practices in 16 different areas related to leading and working effectively with people from different cultures.

You can learn more about these assessments at:
www.aperianglobal.com/learning-solutions/assessments-surveys/

Recommended Case Studies

CROSS-BORDER MERGERS AND ACQUISITIONS

Bharti Airtel

Palepu, Krishna, and Tanya Bijlani."Bharti Airtel in Africa." Case Study, Harvard Business School (April 10, 2012).

Renault-Nissan

Ramaswamy, Kannan."Renault-Nissan: The Challenge of Sustaining Strategic Change." Case Study, Thunderbird School of Global Management (January 5, 2009).

Yoshino, Michael, and Perry Fagan."The Renault-Nissan Alliance." Case Study, Harvard Business School (May 9, 2003).

GLOBAL INNOVATION

iPad in India

Prashar, Sanjeev, B. Adeshwar Raja, V. S. Parasaran, and Vijay Kumar Venna. "Apple iPad in India: Was There a Way Out?" Case Study, Richard Ivey School of Business Foundation (2012).

Haier in India

Celly, Nikhil."Haier in India: Building Presence in a Mass Market Beyond China." Case Study, Asia Case Research Center, University of Hong Kong (2012).

7-Eleven Taiwan

Chang, Aihwa, and Shih-Fen Chen."7-Eleven in Taiwan: Adaptation of Convenience Stores to New Market Environments." Case Study, National Chengchi University and Richard Ivey School of Business Foundation (2012).

GLOBAL ETHICS

Nike

Schifrin, Debra, Glenn Carroll, and David Brady. "Nike: Sustainability and Labor Practices 1998–2013." Case Study, Stanford Graduate School of Business (2013).

Unilever

Henderson, Rebecca, and Frederik Nellemann. "Sustainable Tea at Unilever." Case Study, Harvard Business School (November 21, 2012).

Chapter 1 The Shifting Center: Emerging Markets Have Emerged

1. John Hawksworth and Danny Chan, "The World in 2050: The BRICs and Beyond; Prospects, Challenges and Opportunities," PricewaterhouseCoopers, 2013, www.pwc.com/gx/en/world-2050/assets/pwc-world-in-2050-report-january-2013.pdf; "The World in 2050: Will the Shift in Global Economic Power Continue?," PricewaterhouseCoopers, 2015, www.pwc.com/gx/en/issues/the-economy/assets/world-in-2050-february-2015.pdf. See also "Global Trends 2030: Citizens in an Interconnected and Polycentric World," European Union Institute for Security Studies, March 2012, http://europa.eu/espas/pdf/espas_report_ii_01_en.pdf.

2. "The World in 2050: The BRICs and Beyond," PricewaterhouseCoopers.

3. China's population in 2012 was estimated at 1,377,065,000. See *World Statistics Pocketbook, 2014 edition* (New York: United Nations, 2014), 43; Matt Schiavenza, "A Surprising Map of the World's Population Shows Just How Big China's Population Is," *The Atlantic*, August 14, 2013, www.theatlantic.com/china/archive/2013/08/a-surprising-map-of-the-world-shows-just-how-big-chinas-population-is/278691/.

4. Adam Minter, "China's Runaway Steel Industry," BloombergView, September 2, 2014, www.bloombergview.com/articles/2014-09-02/china-s-runaway-steel-industry; Lydia DePillis, "U.S. Steel plants are on a layoff spree. Here's why," *Washington Post*, March 16, 2015, www.washingtonpost.com/blogs/wonkblog/wp/2015/03/16/u-s-steel-plants-are-on-a-layoff-spree-heres-why/

5. USGS Cement Statistics 1900–2012; USGS, Mineral Industry of China 1990–2013, quoted in Bill Gates, gatesnotes, June 25, 2014, www.gatesnotes.com/About-Bill-Gates/Concrete-in-China. An estimated 45 percent of China's cement is low-grade, however, and its industry is beginning to consolidate. See also, Russell Flannery, "As the Market Hardens," *Forbes Asia*, July 2015, 64.

6. Richard Dobbs, James Manyika, and Jonathan Woetzel, "The Four Global Forces Breaking All the Trends," book excerpt from forthcoming publication, *No Ordinary Disruption*, McKinsey Global Institute, April 2015, www.mckinsey.com/insights/strategy/The_four_global_forces_breaking_all_the_trends?cid=other-eml-alt-mgi-mck-oth-1504.

7. Howard French, *China's Second Continent: How a Million Migrants Are Building a New Empire in Africa* (New York: Knopf, 2014).

8. Jason Chow, "China Is Now the World's Biggest Consumer of Red Wine," *Wall Street Journal*, January 29, 2014, http://blogs.wsj.com/scene/2014/01/29/china-is-now-worlds-biggest-consumer-of-red-wine/.

9. "China Produces and Consumes Almost as Much Coal as the Rest of the World Combined," U.S. Energy Information Administration, May 14, 2014, www.eia.gov/todayinenergy/detail.cfm?id=16271.

10. United Nations, Department of Economic and Social Affairs, *World Population Prospects: 2012 Revision*, June 2013, http://esa.un.org/unpd/wpp/index.htm, 43.

11. "An Indian Summary," *The Economist*, www.economist.com/content/indian-summary.

12. "Wasting Time," *The Economist*, May 11, 2013, www.economist.com/news/briefing/21577373-india-will-soon-have-fifth-worlds-working-age-population-it-urgently-needs-provide.

13. "India Overview," *World Bank*, www.worldbank.org/en/country/india/overview.

14. U.S. Energy Information Administration.

15. Hawksworth and Chan, "The World in 2050. 2.

16. Chrystia Freeland, "Globalization Bites Back," *The Atlantic*, May 2015, 83.

17. Danny Quah, "The Global Economy's Shifting Centre of Gravity," *Global Policy* 2, no. 1 (January 2011), 3–9.

18. Carlos Ghosn, interview at Stanford Graduate School of Business, "Carlos Ghosn of Nissan/Renault: Look Ahead, Don't Stand Still," February 4, 2010, www.youtube.com/watch?v=yChtop17sd8.

19. Jim O'Neill, "Who Defines the Next Economic Giants?," *New York Times*, December 4, 2014, www.nytimes.com/2014/12/04/opinion/jim-oneill-who-defines-the-next-economic-giants.html?_r=0.

20. See David Jin et al., "Winning in Emerging-Market Cities: A Guide to the World's Largest Growth Opportunity," Boston Consulting Group,

September 2010, 5–6. According to this report, "By 2030, the number of emerging market urban dwellers will increase by another 1.3 billion," and this will drive 67 percent of world GDP growth by 2015.

21. "Five Megatrends and Possible Implications," PricewaterhouseCoopers, April 2014, Directors edition, www.pwc.com/en_US/us/corporate-governance/publications/assets/pwc-corporate-goverance-directors-megatrends.pdf; "Asia will represent 66% of the global middle-class population and 59% of middle-class consumption by 2030, up from 28% and 23%, respectively, in 2009."

22. Dobbs, et al., "The Four Global Forces Breaking All the Trends."

23. Jeffrey Passel and D'Vera Cohn, "U.S. Population Projections: 2005–2050," Pew Research Center, February 11, 2008, www.pewhispanic .org/2008/02/11/us-population-projections-2005-2050/.

24. Rand Corporation, "Foreign-Educated Health Workers Play Vital Role in the U.S. Health System," *ScienceDaily*, November 4, 2013, www .sciencedaily.com/releases/2013/11/131104162708.htm.

25. "The Global Leader," Corporate Leadership Council (CLC) Human Resources, Corporate Executive Board, Executive Briefing, February 2012.

Chapter 2 Global Talent: Beyond Outsourcing

1. Martin Dewhurst, Jonathan Harris, and Suzanne Heywood, "The Global Company's Challenge," *McKinsey Quarterly*, June 2012.

2. "15th Annual Global CEO Survey 2012: Delivering Results, Growth and Value in a Volatile World," PricewaterhouseCoopers, 2012.

3. Shirley Daniel and Ben L. Kedia, "US Business Needs for Employees with International Expertise" (paper presented at the Conference on Global Challenges and US Higher Education at Duke University, Durham, North Carolina, January 23–25, 2003), cited in Pankaj Ghemawat, "Developing Global Leaders: Companies Must Cultivate Leaders for Global Markets," *McKinsey Quarterly*, June 2012.

4. "15th Annual Global CEO Survey 2012," 8.

5. *Developing the Global Leader of Tomorrow*, a joint project of Ashridge Business School as part of the European Academy of Business in Society (EABIS) and the United Nations Global Compact Principles for Responsible Management Education (PRME), based on a survey conducted in 2008, cited in Ghemawat, "Developing Global Leaders."

6. Todd Guild, "Think Regionally, Act Locally: Four Steps to Reaching the Asian Consumer," *McKinsey Quarterly*, September 2009.

7. See Ernest Gundling, Terry Hogan, and Karen Cvitkovich, *What Is Global Leadership? 10 Key Behaviors That Define Great Global Leaders* (Boston & London: Nicholas Brealey, 2011).

8. Winnie Ng and Kate Vernon, "Adopting an Asian Lens to Talent Development," *Community Business* (Hong Kong), March 2012, 21.

Chapter 3 Global Mindset: Beyond Culture

1. Geert Hofstede, *Culture's Consequences: Comparing Values, Behaviors, Institutions and Organizations Across Nations* (Thousand Oaks, CA: Sage Publications, 2001).

2. These five dimensions and related survey questions were originally established with Dr. David Matsumoto of San Francisco State University. Dr. Matsumoto exchanged data with Geert Hofstede, Ronald Inglehart, and Shalom Schwartz in creating the initial country profiles. Dr. William Doherty has done further analysis and upgrading of the *GlobeSmart Profile*[SM] questions and country profiles, incorporating data from users of the tool. The most recent round of data analysis included input from more than 60,000 users.

3. The authors are indebted to their former colleague David Eaton, founder of Eaton Consulting Group, for the "why behind the behavior" phrase; Brad Bungum, another colleague, coined the term "box over our heads."

4. Tarun Khanna, "Contextual Intelligence," *Harvard Business Review* (September 2014), 59–68; Herminia Ibarra, "The Authenticity Paradox," *Harvard Business Review* (January–February 2015), 52–59. Ibarra comments: "Authenticity . . . has, ironically, come to mean something much more limiting and culturally specific. A closer look hellip2;reveals a model that is, in fact, very American, based on ideals such as self-disclosure, humility, and individualistic triumph over adversity."

5. Mary Yoko Brannen and David C. Thomas, "Bicultural Individuals in Organizations: Implications and Opportunity," *International Journal of Cross Cultural Management*, 10 (2010), 5.

6. China has also traditionally been highly communitarian and group-oriented, with these interdependent ideals further reinforced by many decades of communism; however, its one-child policy has created a younger generation of "Little Emperors." These newer members of Chinese society have never had to compete and compromise with siblings, and may have been pampered by one set of parents and two sets of grandparents for whom they are the only heir; they are often described as selfish individualists who are less inclined to be good team players.

7. "The Global Leader," Corporate Leadership Council (CLC) Human Resources, Corporate Executive Board, Executive Briefing, February 2012.

8. The very presumption that culture and business can somehow be separated, like work and life or church and state, is itself the product of the particular Western, Protestant phenomenon of sociocultural

differentiation. There are countervailing forces in every society—for example, fundamentalist movements within Christianity, Islam, or Hinduism—that push in exactly the opposite direction, seeking to infuse their preferred brand of culture into all aspects of human life, including business and government. Many ideal visions such as those of a Promised Land, the return to a Golden Age, or a Caliphate that governs according to Sharia law all presume that religious norms will be universally embraced and/or enforced.

9. *GlobeSmart Profile*^{SM} Data Analysis, Dr. William Doherty; excerpts available on request.

10. "The Global Leader," Corporate Leadership Council (CLC) Human Resources.

11. Ernest Gundling, Terry Hogan, and Karen Cvitkovich, *What Is Global Leadership? 10 Key Behaviors That Define Great Global Leaders* (Boston & London: Nicholas Brealey, 2011), Chapter 6.

Chapter 4 Global Teams: Beyond Facilitation

1. The *Global Teaming Assessment*, a 42-item survey used to collect this data, has shown strong psychometric properties based on several statistical analyses. For more information see: www.aperianglobal .com/learning-solutions/assessments-surveys/.

Chapter 5 Global Inclusion: Beyond Race and Gender

1. Caitlin Dewey, "Map: More Than Half of Humanity Lives within This Circle," *Washington Post*, May 7, 2013, www.washingtonpost.com/ blogs/worldviews/wp/2013/05/07/map-more-than-half-of-humanity-lives-within-this-circle/.

2. Ernest Gundling and Anita Zanchettin, *Global Diversity: Winning Customers and Engaging Employees Within World Markets* (Boston & London: Nicholas Brealey, 2007).

3. "Youth in Developing Countries: A Generation Looking for Work," European Development Days, November 18, 2013.

4. Vivian Hunt, Dennis Layton, and Sara Prince, "Why Diversity Matters," McKinsey & Company, January 2015, 10.

5. Michael Landel, "Gender Balance and the Link to Performance," *McKinsey Quarterly*, February 2015, 2; Claudia Sussmuth-Dyckerhoff, Jin Wang, and Josephine Chen, "Women Matter: An Asian Perspective," McKinsey & Company, June 2012, 6.

6. Hunt, "Why Diversity Matters," 3.

7. *GlobeSmart Profile*^{SM} data. Each of the 20 countries for which data was analyzed had in excess of 500 respondents.

8. "The Millennial Myth," Corporate Leadership Council (CLC), 2014.

9. David Hole, Le Zhong, and Jeff Schwartz. "Talking About Whose Generation: Why Western Models Can't Account for a Global Workforce," *Deloitte Review*, 2010, 4.

10. *GlobeSmart Profile*^{SM} data. Each of the 20 countries for which data was analyzed had in excess of 500 respondents.

11. Jeff Bercovici, "Facebook's Maxine Williams on Why Sensitivity and Diversity Don't Mix," *Forbes*, November 5, 2014, www.forbes.com/sites/jeffbercovici/2014/11/05/facebooks-maxine-williams-on-why-sensitivity-and-diversity-dont-mix/.

12. M. E. Heilman, "The Impact of Situational Factors on Personnel Decisions Concerning Women: Varying the Sex Composition of the Applicant Pool," *Organizational Behavior and Human Performance* 26 (1980): 286–295.

13. Steve Dennings, "Why Is Diversity Vital for Innovation?," *Forbes*, January 16, 2012, www.forbes.com/sites/stevedenning/2012/01/16/why-is-diversity-vital-for-innovation/.

14. David Rock, *Your Brain at Work: Strategies for Overcoming Distraction, Regaining Focus, and Working Smarter All Day Long* (New York: Harper Business, 2009).

15. S. Plous, "UnderstandingPrejudice.org: Implicit Association Test," Social Psychology Network, January 2002.

16. Nancy Adler, *International Dimensions of Organizational Behavior*, 4th ed. (Cincinnati, OH: South-Western, 2002), 143.

17. Dorothy Leonard, Susan Straus, "Putting Your Company's Whole Brain to Work," *Harvard Business Review* (July–August 1997), 119.

18. Jonamay Lambert and Selma Myers, "50 Activities for Diversity Training," (Amherst, MA: HRD Press, 1994).

Chapter 6 Global Mergers and Acquisitions: Beyond Diligence

1. "Perspectives on Merger Integration," McKinsey & Company, June 2010.

2. Niccolo Machiavelli, *The Prince*, trans. Peter Bondanella and Mark Musa (New York: Oxford University Press, 1979), 50.

3. Krishna Palepu and Tanya Bijlani, "Bharti Airtel in Africa," Case Study, Harvard Business School (April 10, 2012). See also, "Bharti Closes $10.7-bn Zain Africa Ops Deal," *Mail Today (India)* via *Acquire Media NewsEdge*, June 9, 2010, Interactive Intelligence, http://callcenterinfo.tmcnet.com/news/2010/06/09/4835232.htm.
For more information on Bharti Airtel's strategy, see Surajeet Das Gupta and Mansi Taneja, "Bharti Airtel's African Safari: Telco Using Tried and Tested India Strategy," *Business Standard*, June 10, 2011, www.business-standard.com/article/technology/bharti-airtel-s-african-safari-111061000093_1.html.

4. Palepu and Bijlani, "Barti Airtel in Africa."

5. David Herbling, "Corporate India Struggles to Crack Kenyan Market," *Business Daily Africa*, March 13, 2014, www.businessdailyafrica .com/Corporate-News/Corporate-India-struggles-to-crack-Kenyan-market/-/539550/2243168/-/3n3hw2/-/index.html.

6. Palepu and Bijlani, "Bharti Airtel in Africa." The authors have described in rich detail the challenges that Bharti Airtel encountered in a new continent. For more on protests in Nigeria in response to outsourcing, see: Emele Onu, "Airtel Nigeria Closes Call Centres After Ex-Workers Make Threats," *Bloomberg Business*, October 4, 2011, www.bloomberg.com/news/articles/2011-10-04/airtel-nigeria-closes-call-centres-after-ex-workers-make-threats; Dupe Olaoye-Osinkolu and Adline Atili, "NLC Protests Sack of Airtel's 4000 Workers," *The Nation*, October 5, 2011, www.thenationonlineng.net/ 2011/index.php/mobile/business/21833-nlc-protests-sack-of-airtel %E2%80%99s-4000-workers.html; Ekow Quandzie, "Airtel Denies Media Reports on Dismissals, Salary Reductions," *Ghana Business News*, October 4, 2011, www.ghanabusinessnews.com/2011/10/04/ airtel-denies-media-reports-on-dismissal-salary-reduction/.

7. Sounak Mitra, "Bharti Airtel's Overseas Operations Continue to Struggle," *Business Standard*, November 5, 2014, www.business-standard.com/article/companies/bangladesh-goes-africa-way-for-bharti-airtel-114110400936_1.html.

8. Anandita Singh Mankotia, "Bharti Airtel Recasts Unprofitable Africa Operations," *Economic Times*, January 30, 2014, http://articles .economictimes.indiatimes.com/2014-01-30/news/46828270_1_ african-operations-airtel-africa-christian-de-faria.

9. Nancy Adler, *International Dimensions of Organizational Behavior*, 4th ed. (Cincinnati, OH: South-Western, 2002), 89.

10. The Intercultural Development Inventory, created by Milton Bennett and Mitchell Hammer, defines five stages: Defense, Polarization, Minimization, Acceptance, and Adaptation. For information on the Intercultural Development Inventory, see https://idiinventory.com/; the predominance of Minimization in corporate groups was shared in a certification session conducted by Dr. Hammer.

11. Adler, *International Dimensions of Organizational Behavior*, 147.

12. David Olive, "Auto Comebacks Without Borders," *Toronto Star*, January 16, 2015, www.thestar.com/business/2015/01/16/auto-comebacks-without-borders-olive.html#.

13. Kannan Ramaswamy, "Renault-Nissan: The Challenge of Sustaining Strategic Change," Case Study, Thunderbird School of Global Management (January 5, 2009), 5. This is one of several good case studies on this topic as well as writings and recordings from Ghosn himself.

14. Ibid., 4.

15. Michael Yoshino and Perry Fagan, "The Renault-Nissan Alliance," Case Study, Harvard Business School (May 9, 2003), 3.

16. Ramaswamy, "Renault-Nissan," 6.

17. "Carlos Ghosn of Nissan/Renault: Look Ahead, Don't Stand Still," Stanford Graduate School of Business, February 4, 2010, www.youtube.com/watch?v=yChtop17sd8.

18. Carlos Ghosn, "Saving the Business Without Losing the Company," Case Study, *Harvard Business Review* (January 2002), 11.

19. Ramaswamy, "Renault-Nissan," 8–12.

20. Ibid.

21. Yoshino and Fagan, "The Renault-Nissan Alliance," 14.

22. Olive, "Auto Comebacks without Borders."

23. Yoshino and Fagan, "The Renault-Nissan Alliance," 8, 11.

24. "Carlos Ghosn of Nissan/Renault: Look Ahead, Don't Stand Still."

25. Ghosn, "Saving the Business," 11.

26. Yoshino and Fagan, "The Renault-Nissan Alliance," 13–14.

27. Rik Kirkland, "Leading in the 21st century: An Interview with Carlos Ghosn," McKinsey & Company, September 2012, www.mckinsey.com/insights/leading_in_the_21st_century/an_interview_with_carlos_ghosn.

28. Brian Dumaine, "Renault-Nissan: Can Anyone Succeed Carlos Ghosn?," *Fortune*, December 29, 2014, http://fortune.com/2014/12/29/renault-nissan-carlos-ghosn/.

Chapter 7 Global Innovation: Beyond Products

1. Colum Murphy, "China's Automobile Sales to Slow Further in 2015," *Wall Street Journal*, January 12, 2015, www.wsj.com/articles/chinas-automobile-sales-slow-in-2014-1421046195. For more general information on the shifting global profit picture, see also Detlev Mohr et al., "The Road to 2020 and Beyond: What's Driving the Global Automotive Industry?," *McKinsey & Company*, August 2013, 7–13. "What is most striking about the recent past is how profoundly the source of profits has shifted. In 2007, the BRICs and RoW accounted for 30 percent of global profits (or EUR 12 billion). In 2012, that share rose to nearly 60 percent (EUR 31 billion), as sales in these regions rose 65 percent and outpaced growth in Europe, North America, Japan, and South Korea. More than half of this growth came from China (EUR 18 billion). . . . The automotive industry's economic center of gravity will continue to shift, as sales volumes and market share keep moving toward emerging markets."

2. Tim Dunne, "The Changing Landscape of the Global Automotive Industry," J.D. Power and Associates, McGraw-Hill Financial, October 2013, www.jdpower.com/sites/default/files/2013_White Paper_ChangingLandscape_GlobalAuto.pdf; "2015 Auto Industry Trends," PricewaterhouseCoopers, www.strategyand.pwc.com/perspectives/2015-auto-trends; Paul Gao, Russell Hensley, and

Andreas Zielke, "A Roadmap to the Future for the Auto Industry," *McKinsey Quarterly*, October 2014, www.mckinsey.com/insights/manufacturing/a_road_map_to_the_future_for_the_auto_industry.

3. "Too Many Car Factories in China?," *Bloomberg News*, February 12, 2015, www.bloomberg.com/news/articles/2015-02-12/china-s-car-factory-binge-risks-hurting-automakers-margins.

4. General Motors, "Buick's Road to Success in China," *Insight: The Voice of the American Chamber of Commerce in Shanghai*, February 5, 2015, http://insight.amcham-shanghai.org/buicks-road-success-china/.

5. Abbie VanSickle, "Not Just Your Grandma's Car, Buicks Shine in Chinese Luxury Market," *Seattle Globalist*, May 19, 2014, www.seattleglobalist.com/2014/05/19/not-just-your-grandmas-car-buicks-shine-in-chinese-luxury-market/25116#sthash.2aABan82.dpuf.

6. Alex Davies, "Why Chinese Buyers Are Obsessed with Buick," *Business Insider*, April 23, 2013, www.businessinsider.com/why-chinese-buyers-love-buick-2013-4.

7. "Auto Makers Introduce China to the Car Loan: Young Car Buyers Are Open to Financing Where Cash Has Traditionally Ruled," *Wall Street Journal*, July 9, 2014, www.wsj.com/articles/foreign-auto-makers-introduce-china-to-the-car-loan-1404908023; "China: The Emergence of Auto Finance," *Autofacts*, PricewaterhouseCoopers, December 2014, www.pwc.com/en_GX/GX/automotive/autofacts/analyst-notes/pdf/pwc-analyst-note-china-auto-finance-dec14.pdf; Jim Henry, "In China, Most Car Buyers Still Pay Cash, but Financing Is Slowly Catching On," *Forbes*, September 20, 2014, www.forbes.com/sites/jimhenry/2014/09/30/in-china-most-car-buyers-still-pay-cash-but-financing-is-slowly-catching-on/.

8. "China's Automotive Market: How to Merge into the Fast Lane with Consumer and Digital Marketing Insights," Accenture, 2013, www.accenture.com/sitecollectiondocuments/pdf/chinas-automotive-market-cosumer-digital-marketing-insights.pdf, 9.

9. Two children are permitted for couples that both come from one-child families, although many forgo this option for financial reasons.

10. Stephen Edelstein, "China Adds Even More Electric-Car Incentives—Mostly for Local Brands," *Green Car Reports*, September 3, 2014, www.greencarreports.com/news/1094174_china-adds-even-more-electric-car-incentives--mostly-for-local-brands.

11. "Chinese Automaker Copies Audi A6 Styling and Name," *World Car Fans*, www.worldcarfans.com/114112885112/chinese-automaker-copies-audi-a6-styling-and-name.

12. Ernest Gundling, *The 3M Way to Innovation: Balancing People and Profit* (New York: Kodansha International, 2000), 23.

13. Tarun Khanna and Krishna Palepu, *Winning in Emerging Markets: A Roadmap for Strategy and Execution* (Boston, MA: Harvard Business School Press, 2010).

14. Sanjeev Prashar, B. Adeshwar Raja, V. S. Parasaran, and Vijay Kumar Venna, "Apple iPad in India: Was There a Way Out?," Case Study, Richard Ivey School of Business Foundation (2012).

15. "Samsung Tops Indian Tablet Market Share, Followed by Micromax, iBall," Trak.in, November 28, 2014, http://trak.in/tags/business/2014/11/28/indian-tablet-market-share-growth/.

16. Prashar et al, "Apple iPad in India: Was There a Way Out?"

17. Nikhil Celly, "Haier in India: Building Presence in a Mass Market Beyond China," Case Study, Asia Case Research Center, University of Hong Kong (2012).

18. Haier started as a collective enterprise (集体企业) partly owned by the city of Qingdao; see Art Kleiner, "China's Philosopher-CEO Zhang Ruimin," *Strategy + Business*, November 10, 2014, www.strategy-business.com/article/00296?gko=8155b&cid=TL20141113&utm_campaign=TL20141113.

19. The data cited is from the GlobeSmart Innovation Assessment[SM] created by Aperian Global. Each company surveyed conducts business on a global basis. Respondents included nearly 1,000 individuals representing more than 10 nationalities; most were team leader or project leader level and above, and a significant percentage of the total were working in a subsidiary operation at the time they were surveyed.

20. Clayton Christensen, *The Innovator's Dilemma: The Revolutionary Book That Will Change the Way You Do Business* (Boston, MA: Harvard Business School Publishing, 1997).

21. Vijay Govindarajan and Chris Trimble, *Reverse Innovation: Create Far from Home, Win Everywhere* (Boston, MA: Harvard Business School Publishing, 2012), 109–126.

22. For example, Toyota's Lexus brand vehicles have about double the U.S. market share of Cadillac, while Honda Acura sales are roughly equal. See "U.S. Luxury Car Market Share in 2014, by Brand," *The Statistics Portal*, www.statista.com/statistics/287620/luxury-vehicles-united-states-premium-vehicle-market-share/.

23. Shuan Sim, "Is US Ready for Hydrogen Cars? After Toyota Frees Hydrogen Cell Patents, Market Could Be Slow to Act," *International Business Times*, January 6, 2015, www.ibtimes.com/us-ready-hydrogen-cars-after-toyota-frees-hydrogen-cell-patents-market-could-be-slow-1775082.

24. Christensen, *The Innovator's Dilemma*, xviii.

25. See, for example, Julia Birkinshaw and Neil Hood, "Unleash Innovation in Foreign Subsidiaries," *Harvard Business Review* (March 2001), 131–137.

26. Gundling, *The 3M Way to Innovation*, 122–134.

27. Arindam Battacharya and David C. Michael, "How Local Companies Keep Multinationals at Bay," *Harvard Business Review* (March 2008). See also Erin Carlye, "Mexican (Legit) Loan Shark Is Making Billions the Old-Fashioned Way," *Forbes*, April 18, 2012, www.forbes.com/forbes/2012/0507/global-2000-12-americas-grupo-elektra-ricardo-salinas-pliego-mexico-credit-card.html.

28. "Lenovo Plans to Open About 7 More Flagship Stores Across China," *Bloomberg News*, August 7, 2013, www.bloomberg.com/news/articles/2013-08-07/lenovo-plans-to-open-about-7-more-flagship-stores-across-china.

29. Loretta Chao, "As Rivals Outsource, Lenovo Keeps Production In-House," *Wall Street Journal*, July 9, 2012, http://online.wsj.com/news/articles/SB10001424052702303302504577325522699291362.

30. 3M Company website, http://solutions.3m.com/wps/portal/3M/en_US/3MCompany/Information/AboutUs/WhoWeAre/.

31. Neelima Mahajan, "3M Company: In China for China," *CKGSB Knowledge*, February 13, 2014, http://knowledge.ckgsb.edu.cn/2014/02/13/china/3m-company-china-china/.

32. Jie Liu, "3M's China Sales 'to Exceed Those in US in 10 Years,'" *China Daily*, October 31, 2012, http://usa.chinadaily.com.cn/business/2012-10-31/content_15859665.htm.

33. Michelle Caruso-Cabrera, "3M CEO: Research Is 'Driving This Company'; *CNBC*, June 10, 2013, www.cnbc.com/id/100801531.

34. Gregory Turk, "3M Sees China's Sales Growth Triple Global Pace, CEO Says," *Bloomberg Business*, March 17, 2014; www.bloomberg.com/news/articles/2014-03-18/3m-sees-china-s-sales-growth-triple-global-pace-ceo-says-1-.

35. See www.infosys.com/infosys-foundation/initiatives/karnataka-flood-relief.asp.

36. See www.wipro.org/Wipro-sustainability-initiatives-brochure/index.html#/16/. Wipro notes that it is ranked #5 on the Greenpeace Cool IT Leaderboard.

37. Aihwa Chang and Shih-Fen Chen, "7-Eleven in Taiwan: Adaptation of Convenience Stores to New Market Environments," Case Study, College of Commerce National Chengchi University and Richard Ivey School of Business Foundation (2012).

38. Sara Shonhardt, "7-Eleven Finds a Niche by Adapting to Indonesian Ways," *New York Times*, May 28, 2012, www.nytimes.com/2012/05/29/business/global/29iht-stores29.html?pagewanted=1&_r=0.

39. Ibid.

40. Christopher Bartlett and Sumantra Ghoshal, *Managing Across Borders: The Transnational Solution* (Boston, MA: Harvard Business School Press, 1989).

41. W. Chan Kim and Renée Mauborgne, *Blue Ocean Strategy: How to Create Uncontested Market Space and Make the Competition Irrelevant* (Boston, MA: Harvard Business School Press, 2005).

Chapter 8 Global Ethics: Beyond Integrity

1. Sara Hamdan, "Demand Booms Among Saudis," *New York Times*, June 17, 2014, www.nytimes.com/2014/06/18/business/energy-environment/18iht-ren-saudi18.html; "World Energy Outlook 2014," International Energy Agency, 2014, https://www.iea.org/publications/freepublications/publication/WEO_2014_ES_English_WEB.pdf.

2. Elizabeth Grossman, "Declining Bee Populations Pose a Threat to Global Agriculture," *Yale Environment 360*, April 30, 2013, http://e360.yale.edu/feature/declining_bee_populations_pose_a_threat_to_global_agriculture/2645/; Darryl Fears, "The Monarch Massacre: Nearly a Billion Butterflies Have Vanished," *Washington Post*, February 9, 2015, www.washingtonpost.com/news/energy-environment/wp/2015/02/09/the-monarch-massacre-nearly-a-billion-butterflies-have-vanished/?tid=pm_pop.

3. "The Extinction Crisis," *Center for Biological Diversity*, www.biologicaldiversity.org/programs/biodiversity/elements_of_biodiversity/extinction_crisis/; Elizabeth Kolbert, *The Sixth Extinction: An Unnatural History* (New York: Henry Holt & Company, 2014), 167.

4. "A Friedman Doctrine--; The Social Responsibility of Business Is to Increase Its Profits," *New York Times*, September 13, 1970.

5. Robert Kunzig, "Climate Milestone: Earth's CO_2 Level Passes 400 ppm," *National Geographic News*, May 12, 2013, http://news.nationalgeographic.com/news/energy/2013/05/130510-earth-co2-milestone-400-ppm/. "The last time the concentration of CO_2 was as high as 400 ppm was probably in the Pliocene Epoch, between 2.6 and 5.3 million years ago. Until the 20th century, it certainly hadn't exceeded 300 ppm, let alone 400 ppm, for at least 800,000 years."

6. Michael Carlowicz, "Global Temperatures," *NASA Earth Observatory*, http://earthobservatory.nasa.gov/Features/WorldOfChange/decadaltemp.php.

7. Irene Quaile, "Polar Ice Sheets Melting Faster than Ever," *Deutsche Welle*, April 2, 2013, www.dw.de/polar-ice-sheets-melting-faster-than-ever/a-16432199.

8. See, for example, Sarah Morrison, "Which Is the Fairest Firm of All?," *The Independent*, September 1, 2013, www.independent.co.uk/news/business/news/which-is-the-fairest-firm-of-all-8793024.html.

9. John Cushman Jr., "Nike Pledges to End Child Labor and Apply U.S. Rules Abroad," *New York Times*, May 13, 1998, www.nytimes.com/1998/05/13/business/international-business-nike-pledges-to-end-child-labor-and-apply-us-rules-abroad.html.

10. Debra Schifrin, Glenn Carroll, and David Brady, "Nike: Sustainability and Labor Practices 1998–2013," Case Study, Stanford Graduate School of Business (2013).

11. Ibid., 2.

12. Ibid., 9–11.

13. Ellen McGirt, "How Nike's CEO Shook Up the Shoe Industry," *Fast Company*, September 2010, www.fastcompany.com/1676902/how-nikes-ceo-shook-shoe-industry.

14. Glenn Carroll, Debra Schifrin, and David Brady, "Nike: Sustainability and Labor Practices 1998–2013." Case Study, Stanford Graduate School of Business (2013), 12–13.

15. Rebecca Henderson and Frederik Nellemann, "Sustainable Tea at Unilever," Case Study, Harvard Business School, (November 21, 2012).

16. Ibid.

17. "In Their Own Words: Jay Coen Gilbert, 2011 Finalist," John McNulty Prize, YouTube, May 17, 2012, www.youtube.com/watch?v=2-msUrbFvQ0&noredirect=1.

18. Please see the B Lab website, www.bcorporation.net/what-are-b-corps.

19. See Thomas L. Friedman, *Hot, Flat, & Crowded: Why We Need a Green Revolution—and How It Can Renew America* (New York: Farrar, Straus and Giroux, 2008).

20. Transparency International is an organization that has helped many firms to mitigate the effects of corruption in countries where they do business, and to band together with other corporations, governmental agencies, and NGOs in the process. See www.transparency.org/.

21. See the Corruption Perceptions Index, www.transparency.org/cpi2014/results.

22. "Triple Bottom Line," *The Economist*, online extra, November 17, 2009, www.economist.com/node/14301663.

23. For example, in Genesis 1:28, humankind is instructed to "rule over the fish of the sea and over the birds of the sky and over every living thing that moves on the earth." It is a miserable ruler who wipes out his or her kingdom's subjects, and ultimately that ruler will have none left to serve.

24. J. R. McNeill and Erin Stewart Mauldin, *A Companion to Global Environmental History* (Malden, MA: Blackwell, 2012), 274.

Chapter 9 Leading from Your Own Center

1. "Huawei Founder Ren Splits CEO Role with Rotating Panel," *Bloomberg Business*, April 23, 2012, www.bloomberg.com/news/articles/2012-04-23/huawei-founder-ren-splits-ceo-role-with-rotating-panel; Christina Larson, "China's Jack Welch Rethinks Management Strategies,"

Bloomberg Business, October 11, 2013, www.bloomberg.com/bw/articles/2013-10-11/china-s-jack-welch-rethinks-management-strategies; Christina Larson, "Yang Yuanqing: The *HBR* Interview," *Harvard Business Review*, June 2014, https://hbr.org/2014/06/yang-yuanqing-the-hbr-interview/.

2. The authors' firm has identified 10 talent practices that merit regular scrutiny and updating to reflect global benchmarks. Here we highlight several of these that are most crucial to leadership development. Aperian's *Global Talent Scorecard* is a methodology that rates the health of an organization's global talent management strategy against its revenue and growth rate targets. It provides a snapshot of the organization's current phase of global growth and explores strategies to move from one phase to the next. The scorecard distinguishes "best in class" talent strategy components for success at each stage of global growth, and clearly measures current organizational performance in global talent strategy.

3. This anecdote is used with permission from Dave Schoch.

4. At IBM's THINK Forum in New York City, Errol Morris interviewed Joi Ito, Director at MIT Media Lab, on how leadership is being redefined. "Joi Ito Discusses the Changing Meaning of Leadership with Errol Morris," *IBM THINK* video, 1:11, September 21, 2011, www.youtube.com/watch?v=ukNFAEbXkoE.

BOOKS

Adler, Nancy. *International Dimensions of Organizational Behavior.* 4th ed. Cincinnati, OH: South-Western, 2002.

Bartlett, Christopher, and Sumantra Ghoshal. *Managing Across Borders: The Transnational Solution.* Boston, MA: Harvard Business School Press, 1989.

Christensen, Clayton. *The Innovator's Dilemma: The Revolutionary Book That Will Change the Way You Do Business.* Boston, MA: Harvard Business Review Press, 1997.

———. *Seeing What's Next: Using Theories of Innovation to Predict Industry Change.* Boston, MA: Harvard Business School Publishing Corporation, 2004.

Conger, Jay. *The Charismatic Leader: Behind the Myth of Exceptional Leadership.* San Francisco, CA: Jossey-Bass, 1989.

Conger, Jay, and Ronald Riggio. *The Practice of Leadership: Developing the Next Generation of Leaders.* Hoboken, NJ: John Wiley & Sons, 2007.

Covey, Stephen. *The Speed of Trust: The One Thing That Changes Everything.* New York: Simon & Schuster, 2006.

Deal, Terrence E., and Allan A. Kennedy. *Corporate Cultures: The Rites and Rituals of Corporate Life.* New York: Perseus Books Publishing, 2000.

French, Howard. *China's Second Continent: How a Million Migrants Are Building a New Empire in Africa.* New York: Knopf, 2014.

Friedman, Thomas L. *Hot, Flat, and Crowded: Why We Need a Green Revolution—and How It Can Renew America.* New York: Farrar, Straus and Giroux, 2008.

Govindarajan, Vijay, and Chris Trimble. *Reverse Innovation: Create Far from Home, Win Everywhere*. Boston, MA: Harvard Business School Publishing, 2012.

Gundling, Ernest, and Anita Zanchettin. *Global Diversity: Winning Customers and Engaging Employees Within World Markets*. Boston & London: Nicholas Brealey, 2007.

Gundling, Ernest, Terry Hogan, and Karen Cvitkovich. *What Is Global Leadership? 10 Key Behaviors That Define Great Global Leaders*. Boston & London: Nicholas Brealey, 2011.

Gundling, Ernest. *The 3M Way to Innovation: Balancing People and Profit*. New York: Kodansha International, 2000.

————. *Working GlobeSmart: 12 People Skills for Doing Business Across Borders*. Mountain View, CA: Davies-Black Publishing, 2003.

Gupta, Anil, Vijay Govindarajan, and Haiyan Wang. *The Quest for Global Dominance: Transforming Global Presence into Global Competitive Advantage*. San Francisco, CA: Jossey-Bass, 2008.

Hofstede, Geert. *Culture's Consequences: Comparing Values, Behaviors, Institutions and Organizations Across Nations*. Thousand Oaks, CA: Sage Publications, 2001.

————. *Culture and Organizations: Software of the Mind*. New York: McGraw-Hill, 1997.

Kelly, Eamonn. *Powerful Times: Rising to the Challenge of Our Uncertain World*. Upper Saddle River, NJ: Pearson Education, 2006.

Khanna, Tarun, and Krishna Palepu. *Winning in Emerging Markets: A Roadmap for Strategy and Execution*. Boston, MA: Harvard Business School Press, 2010.

Kim, W. Chan, and Renée Mauborgne. *Blue Ocean Strategy: How to Create Uncontested Market Space and Make the Competition Irrelevant*. Boston, MA: Harvard Business School Press, 2005.

Kolbert, Elizabeth. *The Sixth Extinction: An Unnatural History*. New York: Henry Holt & Company, 2014.

Kotter, John. *What Leaders Really Do*. Boston, MA: Harvard Business Review Book, 1999.

————. *Leading Change*. Boston, MA: Harvard Business School Press, 1996.

Kouzes, James, and Barry Posner. *The Leadership Challenge: How to Keep Getting Extraordinary Things Done in Organizations*. San Francisco, CA: Jossey-Bass, 1995.

Livermore, David. *Leading with Cultural Intelligence: The New Secret to Success*. New York: American Management Association, 2010.

Machiavelli, Niccolo. *The Prince*. Translated and edited by Peter Bondanella and Mark Musa. New York: Oxford University Press, 1979.

McCall, Morgan, and George Hollenbeck. *Developing Global Executives*. Boston, MA: Harvard Business School Press, 2002.

McNeill, J. R., and Erin Stewart Mauldin. *A Companion to Global Environmental History*. Malden, MA: Blackwell, 2012.

Mendenhall, Mark, Joyce Osland, Allan Bird, Gary Oddou, and Martha Maznevski. *Global Leadership: Research, Practice and Development*. New York: Routledge, 2008.

Naisbitt, John. *Megatrends Asia: Eight Asian Megatrends That Are Reshaping Our World*. New York: Simon & Schuster, 1996.

Osland, Joyce. *Advances in Global Leadership (Book 8)*. Bingley, UK: Emerald Group Publishing Limited, 2014.

Pucik, Vladimir, Noel Tichy, and Carole Barnett, eds. *Globalizing Management: Creating and Leading the Competitive Organization*. New York: John Wiley & Sons, 1992.

Rock, David. *Your Brain at Work: Strategies for Overcoming Distraction, Regaining Focus, and Working Smarter All Day Long*. New York: HarperBusiness, 2009.

Schaetti, Barbara, Sheila Ramsey, and Gordon Watanabe. *Personal Leadership: A Methodology of Two Principles and Six Practices*. Seattle, WA: FlyingKite Publications, 2008.

Schein, Edgar. *Organizational Culture and Leadership*. San Francisco, CA: Jossey-Bass, 1991.

Senge, Peter. *The Fifth Discipline: The Art and Practice of the Learning Organization*. New York: Currency Doubleday, 1990.

Tichy, Noel. *The Leadership Engine: How Winning Companies Build Leaders at Every Level*. New York: HarperBusiness, 1997.

Trompenaars, Fons, and Charles Hampden-Turner. *Riding the Waves of Culture: Understanding Diversity in Global Business*. New York: McGraw-Hill, 1998.

World Statistics Pocketbook, 2014 edition. New York: United Nations, 2014.

ARTICLES

"15th Annual Global CEO Survey 2012: Delivering Results, Growth and Value in a Volatile World." PricewaterhouseCoopers, 2012.

"2015 Auto Industry Trends." PricewaterhouseCoopers. www.strategyand .pwc.com/perspectives/2015-auto-trends.

"Auto Makers Introduce China to the Car Loan: Young Car Buyers Are Open to Financing Where Cash Has Traditionally Ruled." *Wall Street Journal*, July 9, 2014. www.wsj.com/articles/foreign-auto-makers-introduce-china-to-the-car-loan-1404908023.

Battacharya, Arindam, and David C. Michael. "How Local Companies Keep Multinationals at Bay." *Harvard Business Review* (March 2008).

Bercovici, Jeff. "Facebook's Maxine Williams on Why Sensitivity and Diversity Don't Mix." *Forbes*, November 5, 2014. www.forbes.com/ sites/jeffbercovici/2014/11/05/facebooks-maxine-williams-on-why-sensitivity-and-diversity-dont-mix/.

"Bharti Closes $10.7-bn Zain Africa Ops Deal." *Mail Today (India)* via *Acquire Media NewsEdge*, June 9, 2010. Interactive Intelligence. http://callcenterinfo.tmcnet.com/news/2010/06/09/4835232.htm.

Birkinshaw, Julia, and Neil Hood. "Unleash Innovation in Foreign Subsidiaries." *Harvard Business Review* (March 2001): 131–137.

Brannen, Mary Yoko, and David C. Thomas. "Bicultural Individuals in Organizations: Implications and Opportunity." *International Journal of Cross Cultural Management*, 10 (2010): 5–16.

Caldwell, Christie. "Tomorrow's Global Leaders." *HR People & Strategy*, 36, no. 3 (2013): 48–53.

Carlye, Erin. "Mexican (Legit) Loan Shark Is Making Billions the Old-Fashioned Way." *Forbes*, April 18, 2012. www.forbes.com/forbes/2012/0507/global-2000-12-americas-grupo-elektra-ricardo-salinas-pliego-mexico-credit-card.html.

Caruso-Cabrera, Michelle. "3M CEO: Research Is 'Driving This Company.'" CNBC, June 10, 2013. www.cnbc.com/id/100801531.

Celly, Nikhil. "Haier in India: Building Presence in a Mass Market Beyond China." Case Study, Asia Case Research Center, University of Hong Kong (2012).

Chang, Aihwa, and Shih-Fen Chen. "7-Eleven in Taiwan: Adaptation of Convenience Stores to New Market Environments." Case Study, National Chengchi University and Richard Ivey School of Business Foundation (2012).

Chao, Loretta. "As Rivals Outsource, Lenovo Keeps Production In-House." *Wall Street Journal*, July 9, 2012. http://online.wsj.com/news/articles/SB10001424052702303302504577322552269929 1362.

"China Produces and Consumes Almost as Much Coal as the Rest of the World Combined." *U.S. Energy Information Administration*, May 14, 2014. www.eia.gov/todayinenergy/detail.cfm?id=16271.

China: The Emergence of Auto Finance. *Autofacts*, PricewaterhouseCoopers, December 2014. www.pwc.com/en_GX/GX/automotive/autofacts/analyst-notes/pdf/pwc-analyst-note-china-auto-finance-dec14.pdf.

"China's Automotive Market: How to Merge into the Fast Lane with Consumer and Digital Marketing Insights." Accenture, 2013. www.accenture.com/sitecollectiondocuments/pdf/chinas-automotive-market-cosumer-digital-marketing-insights.pdf.

"Chinese Automaker Copies Audi A6 Styling and Name." *World Car Fans*. www.worldcarfans.com/114112885112/chinese-automaker-copies-audi-a6-styling-and-name.

Chow, Jason. "China Is Now the World's Biggest Consumer of Red Wine." *Wall Street Journal*, January 29, 2014. http://blogs.wsj.com/scene/2014/01/29/china-is-now-worlds-biggest-consumer-of-red-wine/.

Cushman, John, Jr. "Nike Pledges to End Child Labor and Apply U.S. Rules Abroad." *New York Times*, May 13, 1998. www.nytimes.com/1998/05/13/business/international-business-nike-pledges-to-end-child-labor-and-apply-us-rules-abroad.html.

Daniel, Shirley, and Ben L. Kedia. "U.S. Business Needs for Employees with International Expertise." Paper presented at the Conference on Global Challenges and U.S. Higher Education at Duke University, Durham, North Carolina, January 23–25, 2003. Cited in Pankaj Ghemawat. "Developing Global Leaders: Companies Must Cultivate Leaders for Global Markets." *McKinsey Quarterly* (June 2012).

Davies, Alex. "Why Chinese Buyers Are Obsessed with Buick." *Business Insider*, April 23, 2013. www.businessinsider.com/why-chinese-buyers-love-buick-2013-4.

DePillis, Lydia. "U.S. Steel plants are on a layoff spree. Here's why." Washington Post, March 16, 2015. www.washingtonpost.com/blogs/

wonkblog/wp/2015/03/16/u-s-steel-plants-are-on-a-layoff-spree-heres-why/.

Dennings, Steve. "Why Is Diversity Vital for Innovation?," *Forbes*, January 16, 2012. www.forbes.com/sites/stevedenning/2012/01/16/why-is-diversity-vital-for-innovation/.

Dewey, Caitlin. "Map: More Than Half of Humanity Lives Within This Circle." *Washington Post*, May 7, 2013. www.washingtonpost.com/blogs/worldviews/wp/2013/05/07/map-more-than-half-of-humanity-lives-within-this-circle/.

Dewhurst, Martin, Jonathan Harris, and Suzanne Heywood. "The Global Company's Challenge." *McKinsey Quarterly* (June 2012).

Dobbs, Richard, James Manyika, and Jonathan Woetzel. "The Four Global Forces Breaking All the Trends." In *No Ordinary Disruption* (forthcoming). *McKinsey Global Institute*, April 2015. www.mckinsey.com/insights/strategy/The_four_global_forces_breaking_all_the_trends?cid=other-eml-alt-mgi-mck-oth-1504.

Dumaine, Brian. "Renault-Nissan: Can Anyone Succeed Carlos Ghosn?," *Fortune*, December 29, 2014. http://fortune.com/2014/12/29/renault-nissan-carlos-ghosn/.

Dunne, Tim. "The Changing Landscape of the Global Automotive Industry." J.D. Power and Associates, McGraw-Hill Financial, October 2013. www.jdpower.com/sites/default/files/2013_WhitePaper_Changing Landscape_GlobalAuto.pdf.

Edelstein, Stephen. "China Adds Even More Electric-Car Incentives—Mostly for Local Brands." *Green Car Reports*, September 3, 2014. www.greencarreports.com/news/1094174_china-adds-even-more-electric-car-incentives–mostly-for-local-brands.

Fears, Darryl. "The Monarch Massacre: Nearly a Billion Butterflies Have Vanished." *Washington Post*, February 9, 2015. www.washingtonpost.com/news/energy-environment/wp/2015/02/09/the-monarch-massacre-nearly-a-billion-butterflies-have-vanished/?tid=pm_pop.

"Five Megatrends and Possible Implications." PricewaterhouseCoopers, April 2014. Directors edition. www.pwc.com/en_US/us/corporate-governance/publications/assets/pwc-corporate-goverance-directors-megatrends.pdf.

Flannery, Russell. "As the Market Hardens." *Forbes Asia*, July 2015.

Freeland, Chrystia. "Globalization Bites Back." *The Atlantic*, May 2015.

Friedman, Milton. "A Friedman Doctrine--; The Social Responsibility of Business Is to Increase Its Profits." *New York Times*, September 13, 1970.

Gao, Paul, Russell Hensley, and Andreas Zielke. "A Roadmap to the Future for the Auto Industry." *McKinsey Quarterly* (October 2014). www.mckinsey.com/insights/manufacturing/a_road_map_to_the_future_for_the_auto_industry.

General Motors. "Buick's Road to Success in China." *Insight: The Voice of the American Chamber of Commerce in Shanghai*, February 5, 2015. http://insight.amcham-shanghai.org/buicks-road-success-china/.

Ghemawat, Pankaj. "Developing Global Leaders: Companies Must Cultivate Leaders for Global Markets." *McKinsey Quarterly* (June 2012).

Ghosn, Carlos. "Saving the Business Without Losing the Company." *Harvard Business Review*, January 2002.

"The Global Leader." Corporate Leadership Council (CLC) Human Resources, Corporate Executive Board, Executive Briefing (February 2012).

"Global Trends 2030: Citizens in an Interconnected and Polycentric World." European Union Institute for Security Studies, March 2012. http://europa.eu/espas/pdf/espas_report_ii_01_en.pdf.

Grossman, Elizabeth. "Declining Bee Populations Pose a Threat to Global Agriculture." *Yale Environment 360*, April 30, 2013. http://e360.yale.edu/feature/declining_bee_populations_pose_a_threat_to_global_agriculture/2645/.

Guild, Todd. "Think Regionally, Act Locally: Four Steps to Reaching the Asian Consumer." *McKinsey Quarterly* (September 2009).

Gupta, Surajeet Das, and Mansi Taneja. "Bharti Airtel's African Safari: Telco Using Tried and Tested India Strategy." *Business Standard*, June 10, 2011. www.business-standard.com/article/technology/bharti-airtel-s-african-safari-111061000093_1.html.

Hamdan, Sara. "Demand Booms Among Saudis." *New York Times*, June 17, 2014. www.nytimes.com/2014/06/18/business/energy-environment/18iht-ren-saudi18.html.

Hawksworth, John, and Danny Chan. "World in 2050; The BRICs and Beyond: Prospects, Challenges and Opportunities." PricewaterhouseCoopers, January 2013. www.pwc.com/gx/en/world-2050/assets/pwc-world-in-2050-report-january-2013.pdf.

Heilman, M.E. "The Impact of Situational Factors on Personnel Decisions Concerning Women: Varying the Sex Composition of the Applicant Pool." *Organizational Behavior and Human Performance* 26 (1980): 286–295.

Henderson, Rebecca, and Frederik Nellemann. "Sustainable Tea at Unilever." Case Study, Harvard Business School (November 21, 2012).

Henry, Jim. "In China, Most Car Buyers Still Pay Cash, but Financing Is Slowly Catching On." *Forbes*, September 20, 2014. www.forbes.com/sites/jimhenry/2014/09/30/in-china-most-car-buyers-still-pay-cash-but-financing-is-slowly-catching-on/.

Herbling, David. "Corporate India Struggles to Crack Kenyan Market." *Business Daily Africa*, March 13, 2014. www.businessdailyafrica.com/Corporate-News/Corporate-India-struggles-to-crack-Kenyan-market/-/539550/2243168/-/3n3hw2/-/index.html.

Hole, David, Le Zhong, and Jeff Schwartz. "Talking About Whose Generation: Why Western Models Can't Account for a Global Workforce." *Deloitte Review* (2010): 84–97.

"Huawei Founder Ren Splits CEO Role with Rotating Panel." *Bloomberg Business*, April 23, 2012. www.bloomberg.com/news/articles/2012-04-23/huawei-founder-ren-splits-ceo-role-with-rotating-panel.

Hunt, Vivian, Dennis Layton, and Sara Prince. "Why Diversity Matters." McKinsey & Company, February 2015.

Ibarra, Herminia. "The Authenticity Paradox." *Harvard Business Review* (January–February 2015): 52–59.

Jin, David, David C. Michael, Paul Poo, Jose Guevara, Ignacio Pena, Andrew Tratz, and Sharad Verma. "Winning in Emerging-Market Cities: A Guide to the World's Largest Growth Opportunity." Boston Consulting Group, September 2010.

Khanna, Tarun. "Contextual Intelligence." *Harvard Business Review* (September 2014): 59–65.

Kirkland, Rik. "Leading in the 21st Century: An Interview with Carlos Ghosn." McKinsey & Company, September 2012. www.mckinsey.com/insights/leading_in_the_21st_century/an_interview_with_carlos_ghosn.

Kleiner, Art. "China's Philosopher-CEO Zhang Ruimin." *Strategy + Business*, November 10, 2014. www.strategy-business.com/article/00296?gko=8155b&cid=TL20141113&utm_campaign=TL20141113.

Kunzig, Robert. "Climate Milestone: Earth's CO_2 Level Passes 400 ppm." *National Geographic News*, May 12, 2013. http://news.nationalgeographic.com/news/energy/2013/05/130510-earth-co2-milestone-400-ppm/.

Lambert, Jonamay, and Selma Myers. "50 Activities for Diversity Training." Amherst, MA: HRD Press, 1994.

Landel, Michael. "Gender Balance and the Link to Performance." *McKinsey Quarterly* (February 2015): 1–3.

Larson, Christina. "China's Jack Welch Rethinks Management Strategies." *Bloomberg Business*, October 11, 2013. www.bloomberg.com/bw/articles/2013-10-11/china-s-jack-welch-rethinks-management-strategies.

———. "Yang Yuanqing: The *HBR* Interview." *Harvard Business Review* (June 2014). https://hbr.org/2014/06/yang-yuanqing-the-hbr-interview/.

"Lenovo Plans to Open About 7 More Flagship Stores Across China." *Bloomberg Business*, August 7, 2013. www.bloomberg.com/news/articles/2013-08-07/lenovo-plans-to-open-about-7-more-flagship-stores-across-china.

Leonard, Dorothy, and Susan Straus. "Putting Your Company's Whole Brain to Work." *Harvard Business Review* (July–August 1997). https://hbr.org/1997/07/putting-your-companys-whole-brain-to-work#.

Liu, Jie. "3M's China Sales 'to Exceed Those in U.S. in 10 Years.'" *China Daily*, October 31, 2012. http://usa.chinadaily.com.cn/business/2012-10/31/content_15859665.htm.

Mahajan, Neelima. "3M Company, in China for China." *CKGSB Knowledge*, February 13, 2014. http://knowledge.ckgsb.edu.cn/2014/02/13/china/3m-company-china-china/.

Mankotia, Anandita Singh. "Bharti Airtel Recasts Unprofitable Africa Operations." *Economic Times*, January 30, 2014. http://articles.economictimes.indiatimes.com/2014-01-30/news/46828270_1_african-operations-airtel-africa-christian-de-faria.

McGirt, Ellen. "How Nike's CEO Shook Up the Shoe Industry." *Fast Company*, September 2010. www.fastcompany.com/1676902/how-nikes-ceo-shook-shoe-industry.

"The Millennial Myth." Corporate Leadership Council (CLC) (2014).

Minter, Adam. "China's Runaway Steel Industry." *Bloomberg View*, September 2, 2014. www.bloombergview.com/articles/2014-09-02/china-s-runaway-steel-industry.

Mitra, Sounak. "Bharti Airtel's Overseas Operations Continue to Struggle." *Business Standard*, November 5, 2014. www.business-standard .com/article/companies/bangladesh-goes-africa-way-for-bharti-airtel-114110400936_1.html.

Mohr, Detlev, et al. "The Road to 2020 and Beyond: What's Driving the Global Automotive Industry?," McKinsey & Company, August 2013.

Morrison, Sarah. "Which Is the Fairest Firm of All?," *The Independent*, September 1, 2013. www.independent.co.uk/news/business/news/ which-is-the-fairest-firm-of-all-8793024.html.

Murphy, Colum. "China's Automobile Sales to Slow Further in 2015." *Wall Street Journal*, January 12, 2015. www.wsj.com/articles/ chinas-automobile-sales-slow-in-2014-1421046195.

Ng, Winnie, and Kate Vernon. "Adopting an Asian Lens to Talent Development." Hong Kong: Community Business, March 2012.

Olaoye, Dupe, and Adline Atili. "NLC Protests Sack of Airtel's 4000 Workers." *The Nation*, October 5, 2011. www.thenationonlineng.net/ 2011/index.php/mobile/business/21833-nlc-protests-sack-of-airtel% E2%80%99s-4000-workers.html.

Olive, David. "Auto Comebacks Without Borders." *Toronto Star*, January 16, 2015. www.thestar.com/business/2015/01/16/auto-comebacks-without-borders-olive.html#.

O'Neill, Jim. "Who Defines the Next Economic Giants?," *New York Times*, December 4, 2014. www.nytimes.com/2014/12/04/opinion/jim-oneill-who-defines-the-next-economic-giants.html?_r=0.

Olaoye-Osinkolu, Emele, and Adline Atili. "NLC Protests Sack of Airtel's 4000 Workers," *The Nation*, October 5, 2011, www.thenationonlineng .net/2011/index.php/mobile/business/21833-nlc-protests-sack-of-airtel %E2%80%99s-4000-workers.html.

Onu, Emele. "Airtel Nigeria Closes Call Centres After Ex-Workers Make Threats." *Bloomberg Business*, October 4, 2011. www.bloomberg .com/news/articles/2011-10-04/airtel-nigeria-closes-call-centres-after-ex-workers-make-threats.

Palepu, Krishna, and Tanya Bijlani. "Bharti Airtel in Africa." Case Study, Harvard Business School (April 10, 2012).

Passel, Jeffrey, and D'Vera Cohn. "U.S. Population Projections: 2005–2050." Pew Research Center, February 11, 2008. www.pewhispanic.org/2008/ 02/11/us-population-projections-2005-2050/.

Patna, Bihar, "Wasting Time." *The Economist*, May 11, 2013. www .economist.com/news/briefing/21577373-india-will-soon-have-fifth-worlds-working-age-population-it-urgently-needs-provide.

"Perspectives on Merger Integration." McKinsey & Company, June 2010.

Prashar, Sanjeev, B. Adeshwar Raja, V. S. Parasaran, and Vijay Kumar Venna. "Apple iPad in India: Was There a Way Out?" Case Study, Richard Ivey School of Business Foundation (2012).

Quah, Danny. "The Global Economy's Shifting Centre of Gravity." *Global Policy* 2, Issue 1 (January 2011): 3–9.

Quaile, Irene. "Polar Ice Sheets Melting Faster than Ever." *Deutsche Welle*, April 2, 2013. www.dw.de/polar-ice-sheets-melting-faster-than-ever/a-16432199.

Quandzie, Ekow. "Airtel Denies Media Reports on Dismissals, Salary Reductions," *Ghana Business News*, October 4, 2011. www.ghana businessnews.com/2011/10/04/airtel-denies-media-reports-on-dis missal-salary-reduction/.

Ramaswamy, Kannan. "Renault-Nissan: The Challenge of Sustaining Strategic Change." Case Study, Thunderbird School of Global Management (January 5, 2009).

Rand Corporation. "Foreign-Educated Health Workers Play Vital Role in the U.S. Health System." *ScienceDaily*, November 4, 2013. www .sciencedaily.com/releases/2013/11/131104162708.htm.

"Samsung Tops Indian Tablet Market Share, Followed by Micromax, iBall." Trak.in, November 28, 2014. http://trak.in/tags/business/2014/ 11/28/indian-tablet-market-share-growth/.

Schiavenza, Matt. "A Surprising Map of the World's Population Shows Just How Big China's Population Is." *The Atlantic*, August 14, 2013. www.theatlantic.com/china/archive/2013/08/a-surprising-map-of-the-world-shows-just-how-big-chinas-population-is/278691/.

Schifrin, Debra, Glenn Carroll, and David Brady. "Nike: Sustainability and Labor Practices 1998–2013." Case Study, Stanford Graduate School of Business (2013).

Shonhardt, Sara. "7-Eleven Finds a Niche by Adapting to Indonesian Ways." *New York Times*, May 28, 2012. www.nytimes.com/2012/05/ 29/business/global/29iht-stores29.html?pagewanted=1&_r=0.

Sim, Shuan. "Is U.S. Ready for Hydrogen Cars? After Toyota Frees Hydrogen Cell Patents, Market Could Be Slow to Act." *International Business Times*, January 6, 2015. www.ibtimes.com/us-ready-hydrogen-cars-after-toyota-frees-hydrogen-cell-patents-market-could-be-slow-1775082.

Sussmuth-Dyckerhoff, Claudia, Jin Wang, and Josephine Chen. "Women Matter: An Asian Perspective." McKinsey & Company, June 2012.

"Too Many Car Factories in China?," *Bloomberg Business*, February 12, 2015. www.bloomberg.com/news/articles/2015-02-12/china-s-car-fac tory-binge-risks-hurting-automakers-margins.

Turk, Gregory. "3M Sees China's Sales Growth Triple Global Pace, CEO Says." *Bloomberg Business*, March 17, 2014. www.bloomberg.com/ news/articles/2014-03-18/3m-sees-china-s-sales-growth-triple-global-pace-ceo-says-1-.

VanSickle, Abbie. "Not Just Your Grandma's Car: Buicks Shine in Chinese Luxury Market." *Seattle Globalist*, May 19, 2014. www .seattleglobalist.com/2014/05/19/not-just-your-grandmas-car-buicks-shine-in-chinese-luxury-market/25116#sthash.2aABan82.dpuf.

"World Energy Outlook 2014. International Energy Agency, 2014. https://www.iea.org/publications/freepublications/publication/WEO_ 2014_ES_English_WEB.pdf.

"The World in 2050: Will the Shift in Global Economic Power Continue?," PricewaterhouseCoopers, 2015. www.pwc.com/gx/en/ issues/the-economy/assets/world-in-2050-february-2015.pdf.

Yoshino, Michael, and Perry Fagan. "The Renault-Nissan Alliance." Case Study, Harvard Business School (May 9, 2003).

"Youth in Developing Countries: A Generation Looking for Work." European Development Days, November 18, 2013. http://eudevdays .eu/news-views/youth-developing-countries-generation-looking-work#. VYGkUPlViko.

WEBSITES

3M Company Website. http://solutions.3m.com/wps/portal/3M/en_US/ 3MCompany/Information/AboutUs/WhoWeAre/.

Carlowicz, Michael. "Global Temperatures." *NASA Earth Observatory*. http://earthobservatory.nasa.gov/Features/WorldOfChange/decad altemp.php.

The Economist. "An Indian Summary." www.economist.com/content/ indian-summary.

"The Extinction Crisis." *Center for Biological Diversity*. www.biological diversity.org/programs/biodiversity/elements_of_biodiversity/extinc tion_crisis/.

Ghosn, Carlos. "Carlos Ghosn of Nissan/Renault: Look Ahead, Don't Stand Still." YouTube video. 55:26. Posted by Stanford Graduate School of Business, February 4, 2010. www.youtube.com/watch? v=yChtop17sd8.

Gilbert, Jay Coen. "In Their Own Words: Jay Coen Gilbert, 2011 Finalist." YouTube video. 6:05. Posted by *John McNulty Prize*, May 17, 2012. www.youtube.com/watch?v=2-msUrbFvQ0&noredirect=1.

Infosys Foundation. www.infosys.com/infosys-foundation/initiatives/karna taka-flood-relief.asp.

Ito, Joi. "Joi Ito Discusses the Changing Meaning of Leadership with Errol Morris." YouTube video. 2:22. Posted by IBM THINK, September 21, 2011. www.youtube.com/watch?v=ukNFAEbXkoE.

Plous, S. "UnderstandingPrejudice.org: Implicit Association Test." Social Psychology Network, January 2002, https://implicit.harvard.edu/ implicit/.

"Sustainability at Wipro." Wipro, Ltd. (2015). www.wipro.org/resource/ WiproSustainabilityBrochure.pdf#/16/.

Transparency International Website. 2015. www.transparency.org/.

"Triple Bottom Line." *The Economist* (Online extra, November 17, 2009). www.economist.com/node/14301663.

United Nations, Department of Economic and Social Affairs. *World Population Prospects: 2012 Revision* (June 2013). http://esa.un.org/ unpd/wpp/index.htm.

USGS Cement Statistics 1900–2012; USGS, Mineral Industry of China 1990–2013. Quoted in Bill Gates. *gatesnotes*, June 25, 2014. www .gatesnotes.com/About-Bill-Gates/Concrete-in-China.

"U.S. Luxury Car Market Share in 2014, by Brand." *The Statistics Portal*. www.statista.com/statistics/287620/luxury-vehicles-united-states- premium-vehicle-market-share/.

"What Are B Corps?," B Lab. www.bcorporation.net/what-are-b-corps.

World Bank. "India Overview." www.worldbank.org/en/country/india/ overview.

Every day we have the chance to work with the finest colleagues in the world. Our mission—to enable individuals, teams, and organizations to work effectively boundaries—is a worthy cause that is far bigger than all of us. We appreciate the dedication, camaraderie, and insight that each of our colleagues contributes on a daily basis.

It is also a pleasure and a privilege to support global leaders who are doing good work in their own respective professions, and from whom we are constantly learning. We have served many clients for a decade or more, and it has been inspiring to see their enterprises evolve, with people from around the world stepping into roles of greater responsibility. The growth of these new leaders—including the obstacles they have faced and the ways they have found to over-come them—has pointed the way for this project.

There are many people we would like to single out for their support to this project. Within Aperian Global, these include Laurette Bennhold-Samaan, Sarah Cincotta, Ted Dale, David Everhart, Carrie Henry, Lisa Kieffer, Celeste Kruse, Joe Loree, Michelle Mascarenhas, Adwoa Osei, Amanda Paulson, Ethan Prizant, Simone-Eva Redrupp, Dave Reilly, Darcy Roehling, Jesse Rowell, Keiko Sakurai, Nicole Stephenson, and Michael Van Vleet. Special thanks to Ruth Sasaki for her contributions to the Global Teams chapter and to Bill Doherty for his careful analysis of our GlobeSmart Profile[SM] data.

Among our clients and peers in the field, we would like to express appreciation to Dino Anderson, Linda Arsenault, Rajiv Ball, Janet Bennett, Rita Bennett, Kathy Biermann, Eva Boesze, Brad Bungum, Kathie Burch, Patrick Carmichael, Betty Chung, Jack Condon, Yolanda Conyers, Tracy Ann Curtis, Marjorie Derven, Andreea Diaconescu, Patty Drury, Paul Engleson, Tom Fadrhonc, Peter Franklin, Gerry Fry, John Fu, Barb Gamm, Pankaj Ghemawat, Erin Gore, Tom Grant, Guillermo Gutierrez, Gale Halsey, Mike Hayes, Shelli Hendricks, John Hine, Whitney Hischier, Terry Hogan, Elisa Johnson, Hiroshi Kagawa, Tomoko Koarai, Brian Kropp, Pascalis Kruijsifix, Sanjiv Kumar, Rolland Kwok, Glyn Lawrence, Patrick Lee, Ray Leki, Pamela Leri, George Liang, Daryl Mahon, Gregg Meder, Eliska Meyers, Linda Miller, Shelley Morrison, Kyoung-Ah Nam, Yi Min, Joyce Osland, Sofia Osterberg, Sudeep Pandey, Jason Patent, Roger Pearman, Tom Pedersen, Gina Qiao, Kamali Rajesh, Ferran Raurich, George Renwick, Susan Ridge, Arlene Roane, Jeff Rosenthal, Dave Schoch, Bob Schoultz, Sue Shinomiya, Bill Saverance, Shrimathi Shivashankar, Jim Sieleman, Brian Szepkouski, Kazuo and Mika Tagawa, Mikhail Talanov, Stijn Uitterhaegen, Jan Van Acoleyen,

Gayatri Varma, Caroline Visconti, Brian Walker, Charlie Wang, Darlene Weghorst, Steve Weitz, Antje Wessel, Steve Wheeler, Kathy Wood, Bob Wright, Phil Wyckstandt, Ma Xinghai, Wayne Xue, Anita Zanchettin, Audrey Zavodsky, The Conference Board, The Corporate Leadership Council, and the Society for International Education for their interest in our work and/or contributions to this project.

There is a growing cadre of perceptive and innovative scholars doing research on various aspects of globalization. They, too, have helped to shape, confirm, and extend our thinking. We have tried to cite them in the text where their contributions have been relevant. Please also see a list of recommended case studies in Appendix C— these are excellent materials for generating spirited discussions among current or future leaders. We have listed a number of these authors in the bibliography as well.

Thanks to Jesse Wiley for a conversation over coffee in San Francisco that set this project in motion, and to Richard Narramore at John Wiley & Sons for seeing its potential and for his patient, good-humored advice on writing a book that appeals to a broad audience as well as to specialists. Christine Moore at Wiley has been a very helpful and accurate editor with astonishingly quick turnaround time, and Dawn Kilgore has handled our formatting ideas with tactful grace and attention to detail.

There are many others whose names deserve mention. We hope they will consider this book itself to be part of our way of saying thanks to them.

In this field we have the daily challenge of trying to practice what we preach. We face many of the same challenges as our clients: a growing global workforce, virtual meetings, long travel days, time zone differences, and the pressure to deliver high-quality results. Some days we do better than others, and at times we are reminded of our shortcomings. But these reminders, too, are a privilege and an inspiration to open our hearts and minds and get back to work. There is a saying in Japanese, "Fall down seven times and get up eight," and we've definitely exceeded the count for both. We apologize for any errors or omissions in the text.

A number of the anecdotes in this text are fictionalized, composite versions of actual events. We have also changed names, industries, and locations wherever necessary to protect client confidentiality. In each instance we have attempted to remain true to the original examples and to draw out the general lessons that are important to readers. There are many common issues that are a mirror for all of us, and if we have done our job well, these anecdotes will resonate with people in a variety of companies and countries around the world. We have done our best throughout the book to reflect the changing global realities that we see and feel every day.

Page references followed by *fig* indicate an illustrated figure; *t* indicate a table; *s* indicate a sidebar.